Joan
Deddo
10-2014

Expert Advice From The Home Depot®

Plumbing
1-2-3®

Meredith® BOOKS

Plumbing 1-2-3®
Writer: Steve Cory
Copy Chief: Terri Fredrickson
Publishing Operations Manager: Karen Schirm
Senior Editor, Asset and Information Manager: Phillip Morgan
Edit and Design Coordinator: Mary Lee Gavin
Editorial and Design Assistant: Renee E. McAtee
Book Production Managers: Pam Kvitne, Marjorie J. Schenkelberg,
    Rick von Holdt, Mark Weaver
Contributing Proofreaders: Cheri Madison, Joel Marvin, Vicki Sidey
Indexer: Don Glassman

**Additional Editorial and Design contributions from
    Abramowitz Creative Studios**
Publishing Director/Designer: Tim Abramowitz
Graphic Designer: Joel Wires
Photography: Image Studios
    Account Executive: Lisa Egan
    Photographers: Bill Rein, John von Dorn
    Assistants: Rob Resnick, Scott Verber
    Technical Advisor: Rick Nadke
Additional Photography: Doug Hetherington
Illustration: Jim Swanson, Performance Marketing

Meredith® **Books**
Executive Director, Editorial: Gregory H. Kayko
Executive Director, Design: Matt Strelecki
Managing Editor: Amy Tincher-Durik
Executive Editor/Group Manager: Benjamin W. Allen
Senior Associate Design Director: Tom Wegner
Marketing Product Manager: Isaac Petersen

Publisher and Editor in Chief: James D. Blume
Editorial Director: Linda Raglan Cunningham
Executive Director, New Business Development: Todd M. Davis
Director, Sales-Home Depot: Robb Morris
Executive Director, Sales: Ken Zagor
Director, Operations: George A. Susral
Director, Production: Douglas M. Johnston
Director, Marketing: Amy Nichols
Business Director: Jim Leonard

Vice President and General Manager: Douglas J. Guendel

Meredith Publishing Group
President: Jack Griffin
Senior Vice President: Bob Mate

Meredith Corporation
Chairman and Chief Executive Officer: William T. Kerr
President and Chief Operating Officer: Stephen M. Lacy

In Memoriam: E.T. Meredith III (1933-2003)

The Home Depot®
Marketing Manager: Tom Sattler
© Copyright 2005 by Homer TLC, Inc. Second Edition—2.
All rights reserved. Printed in the United States of America.
Library of Congress Control Number: 2005921289
ISBN: 978-0-696-22247-4
The Home Depot® and **1-2-3**® are registered trademarks of Homer
TLC, Inc.

Distributed by Meredith Corporation.
Meredith Corporation is not affiliated with The Home Depot®.

Note to the Reader: Due to differing conditions, tools, and individual skills,
Meredith Corporation and The Home Depot® assume no responsibility for
any damages, injuries suffered, or losses incurred as a result of following
the information published in this book. Before beginning any project,
review the instructions carefully, and if any doubts or questions remain,
consult local experts or authorities. Because codes and regulations vary
greatly, you always should check with authorities to ensure that your
project complies with all applicable local codes and regulations. Always
read and observe all of the safety precautions provided by any tool or
equipment manufacturer, and follow all accepted safety procedures.

We are dedicated to providing accurate and helpful do-it-yourself
information. We welcome your comments about improving this book and
ideas for other books we might offer to home improvement enthusiasts.
Contact us by any of these methods:
Leave a voice message at: 800/678-2093
Write to: Meredith Books, Home Depot Books
    1716 Locust St.
    Des Moines, IA 50309-3023
Send e-mail to: hi123@mdp.com.

How to use this book

Professional plumbers and store associates from The Home Depot stores across the country created Plumbing 1-2-3 to give homeowners a comprehensive and easy-to-follow guide to the most common home plumbing tasks. Their expertise and years of experience help any homeowner tackle every plumbing project, from basic repair and maintenance to installation of major appliances and new systems. Clear instructions and step-by-step photography make every project accessible and easy to understand.

The first eight chapters cover plumbing repairs and replacements—projects that do not involve running new pipes, and that can probably be done without an inspection. Chapters 9 through 12 tackle more ambitious projects that involve new supply and/or drain lines, so you'll probably need to schedule inspections.

Chapter 1: Understanding Plumbing gets you started by presenting an overview of a typical residential plumbing systems. It also helps you inspect your own home's system, both to spot possible problems and to figure out where all the pipes go. You'll also learn how to pick projects within your skill range to help you gain confidence. We'll even show you the tools required for basic plumbing jobs. Refer to it when you're planning a project or when you want to know what something is for.

Chapter 2: Repair and Maintenance covers repairs for most sink faucets as well as tub and shower faucets. **Chapter 3: Faucets** shows how to replace sink or tub and shower faucets with a variety of new types.

Chapter 4: Dealing with Clogs gives you the information you need to clear stopped-up drain pipes—from a simple clogged sink to a balky main drain line.

Chapter 5: Toilets shows you how to keep that most important of fixtures operating efficiently, as well as how to install a new toilet. **Chapter 6: Appliances** covers water heaters, clothes washers, dryers, and sump pumps.

Chapter 7: Supply Pipes and Filters covers repairs and installations to supply pipes that can be done without cutting into pipes and running new pipes. **Chapter 8: Sinks** describes installing replacement sinks, garbage disposers, and dishwashers.

Chapter 9: The Supply System introduces you to the world of rough plumbing. Here you'll learn how to cut, join and run various types of supply pipes. In **Chapter 10: The Drain-Waste-Vent System** you'll learn how these (sometimes complicated) pipe systems are configured as well as how to install them.

Chapter 11: Tubs and Showers shows you the ins and outs of installing all the supply pipes and drains needed behind the walls so your tub or shower is properly connected. Finally, in **Chapter 12: Outdoor Systems**—you can take your plumbing expertise outside and learn how to design and install an underground irrigation system for your lawn and garden, as well as installing a hose bib to give you another spot to hook up a hose outside.

As you use this book, you'll learn what tools you need and how to plan a project. Best of all, you'll begin to see the big picture of remodeling projects after you tackle some of the more modest projects early in the book.

Even if local codes require a professional installation or if you want to hire a contractor, learning about the projects will give you an overview that will be useful when you're negotiating a contract or approving finished work.

Everyone knows the importance of working safely in the home, so be sure to read the **Safety Alerts** that are included with the projects. Pay close attention to **red type** and safety tips marked as safety alerts; they're there to protect the safety and health of you and your family.

And finally, the experts at The Home Depot in your area are great resources for advice on projects and problems. Take advantage of their experience and skills.

Plumbing 1-2-3®
Table of contents

TABLE OF CONTENTS

Understanding plumbing

Chapter 1 highlights

CLOSER LOOK

EVOLUTION

Early pipe was constructed of wood or earthenware. Lead became popular because of its durability. In fact, the Latin word "plumbus" means "lead." Lead was difficult to work with and proved to be a health hazard, so other materials were developed to carry water and waste, making installation easier and safer.

 rchaeologists speculate that the first plumbing system was probably installed on the isle of Crete around 4,000 years ago. It's a pretty safe bet that the first leak was noticed about the same time and that some ancient plumber made the first house call.

A modern homeowner would actually be familiar with the layout. Four separate drainage systems emptied waste into stone sewers. Terra-cotta pipe ran under the floors, providing hot and cold running water to fixtures and fountains. There's even evidence of the first working toilet—complete with a wooden seat and a small reservoir.

Technology and materials have definitely improved over the centuries, but the basics of getting water in and waste out of our homes—along with the associated problems—haven't changed (right down to finding the leaks and getting them fixed).

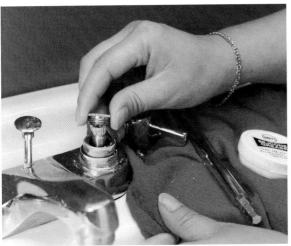

Your plumbing system brings luxuries which make daily life easier and better.

Plumbing isn't scary

In the old days veteran plumbers joked that plumbing was easy—all you had to know was that "water flowed downhill and payday was on Friday." Actually, plumbing in those days was much more complicated. Working with lead pipe and cast iron required experience, a level of skill, and an investment in time beyond what most do-it-yourselfers were interested in tackling.

Even with all the advances in materials and technology, the average homeowner may still think of plumbing as mysterious and difficult. (Everyone's afraid of flooding their home.) The truth is that most home plumbing projects are accessible to anyone who's interested in doing things themselves and saving money. **As long as you shut the water off— or are prepared to shut it off—plumbing projects will not be dangerous.**

Simplified installation

Manufacturers have simplified installations and provided detailed instructions along with technical support for their products. Home centers and hardware stores have knowledgeable staff who will answer questions and provide resources. Plumbing codes in general are becoming more standardized so materials are easier to find and installation procedures are more universal.

Better—and safer

Today's plumbing systems use materials that are longer lasting, safer, and more user-friendly. A few basic tools and a little patience while learning the ropes are all you need. Some plumbing jobs, like unclogging a drain line or fixing a leaking pipe or toilet, may not be exciting work, but look at it another way. Most plumbing materials are inexpensive in relation to other do-it-yourself jobs—it's the labor that drives up the final cost. The money you will save by knowing a few basic plumbing skills can stay in your pocket or be applied to higher-quality fixtures than you might otherwise have budgeted.

Where it comes from and where it goes

Plumbing seems mysterious, mostly because so much of it is hidden inside walls. However, it will likely take you no more than a couple of hours to gain a good basic understanding of your home's system. Read this page, study the illustration at right, and follow the instructions on pages 10–13 to learn how to shut off your water and perform a basic inspection of your home's plumbing system.

Household plumbing consists of a supply system, which brings water to the house and distributes it to various faucets and fixtures; a drain-waste system, which carries waste water away from the house; and a vent system, which carries away noxious gases and enables waste water to flow freely through drain pipes. In addition, you likely have gas lines, and you may have a septic system.

Supply system

Supply pipes are pretty straightforward. In most cases, a single supply pipe, usually an inch or larger in diameter (though sometimes ¾ inch in older homes) runs through a main shutoff valve or two (see page 10) and a water meter to the water heater, where it branches into cold and hot water pipes.

Hot and cold water pipes travel in pairs towards the various plumbing fixtures in the house. Vertical pipes are called "risers." Supply pipes in an older home are likely made of galvanized steel, which corrodes and gets blocked up with deposits in time. Most newer homes use copper pipe, which reliably supplies good water pressure. Some newer homes use rigid plastic pipe such as CPVC, or flexible or cross-linked polyethylene (PE or PEX) pipe, but these materials are approved only in some locales.

After entering the house, supply pipes usually narrow. The larger the pipe diameter, the better the water pressure. Ideally, pipes that run to various rooms will be ¾ inch, and only the pipes inside a room will be ½ inch. However, in many homes nearly all the pipes are ½ inch. This can be a problem, especially if the pipes are made of galvanized steel, which when it gets clogged with mineral deposits can limit water pressure.

At each fixture, there should be a stop valve—also called a fixture shutoff valve—for the hot and cold lines. From the stop valve, flexible supply tubes (sometimes called risers) usually lead to the faucet or toilet. A shower has a particular configuration of supply pipes (see pages 192–194).

Drain system

Drain pipes are more complicated, especially when you include the vent pipes (see opposite page). Drain pipes must be installed according to exacting specifications. Never install drain pipes without consulting your local building department and getting a permit.

Older homes often use cast-iron drain pipes. These typically last for many decades, but they sometimes rust or corrode in places. Newer homes use plastic pipe—either white PVC or black ABS. Plastic pipe is more reliable, and easier to install as well. In some cases, copper pipe is also used for some drains. In an older home, some of the smaller drain pipes—typically, the horizontal runs from a faucet to the main drain—are made of galvanized steel.

The main stack is usually a pipe 3 or 4 inches in diameter that runs straight down to the sewer line and up through the roof, where it serves as a vent. Many homes also have one or two secondary stacks, typically 2 or 3 inches in diameter; these usually provide drainage for a specific room—most often, the kitchen.

Branch drain pipes usually travel horizontally from a fixture to a stack. These pipes are often 1¼ to 2 inches in diameter—1½ inches in the case of a bathroom sink. Horizontal branch drain pipes must slope at a rate of at least ¼ inch per foot at all points. Plumbing codes specify the use of certain types of fittings to ensure smooth flow of drain water. In general, a fitting that makes a slow, sweeping turn is preferable to one that makes a sharp turn.

A good drain system has cleanouts located in places that are easy to access. These cleanouts allow access to the pipes so you can auger the pipes to clear away clogs.

Leading from a sink to a drain pipe in the wall, you will usually find a trap made of special materials that can be easily disassembled for cleaning and augering. Traps are usually P-shaped, so that a slug of water forms a seal at the bottom; this seal prevents gases from entering the room.

Vent system

For drain water to flow freely, there must be air behind or above the water. If water completely fills the diameter of a drain pipe and there is no source of air behind it, the water will gurgle and flow sluggishly. In some cases, water that fills a pipe can actually siphon, causing waste water to back up into a toilet or sink. In a home plumbing system, vent pipes supply the air that makes for smooth-flowing waste water.

Vent pipes also allow methane and other nasty gases to escape out the roof, rather than into a bathroom. Such gases are both unpleasant and dangerous, so it's important that the vent system works well.

The portion of a main or secondary stack that extends out the roof is called a main or secondary vent. Branch vents lead to these stacks. Plumbing codes are very specific about how and where these pipes should run and what size they should be. See pages 180–181 for various ways to run branch vent lines.

One important venting consideration is the diameter of the drain pipes. If a drain pipe is large enough, it will virtually never get filled with water at any point, and so virtually acts as its own vent.

Every plumbing fixture must be connected to a vent of some sort, and it must be connected in a way that meets local plumbing codes. In some cases, a special fitting called an air admittance valve (AAV) is allowed to augment or even take the place of a vent that runs through the roof.

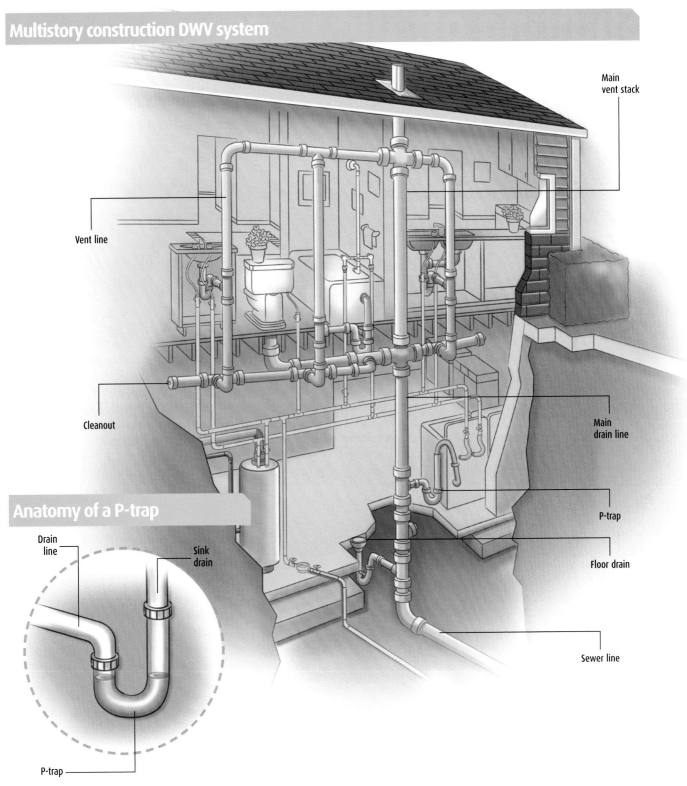

Main vent stack

Vent line

Cleanout

Main drain line

P-trap

Floor drain

Sewer line

Anatomy of a P-trap

Drain line

Sink drain

P-trap

P-traps are required by code wherever there is an open drain line that flows into the DWV system, such as from a sink, bathtub, or shower. It is constructed so that a water seal will form in the curve of the trap preventing backflow of air or gas from the sewer line while permitting free flow of liquids through the system.

Shutting off the water

Every homeowner should be prepared to quickly shut off the water, both to individual fixtures and to the entire house. In the event of a burst pipe or any other large leak, this knowledge can save you plenty. Also, most plumbing projects require that you shut off the water before beginning. Make sure that family members know how to shut off the water as well.

Shutoff methods vary from area to area. For instance, in some locales, it is common to have a main shutoff valve on the exterior wall; in other areas, shutoffs are located in an in-ground box just inside the house. This page shows some of the more common shutoff valves. If you are unsure how to shut off your water, contact your water company.

MAIN INDOOR SHUTOFF

Most homes have a shutoff valve inside the house that controls water to the entire house. Usually, it is located near the point where a large-diameter water pipe brings water into the house—perhaps in the basement or crawlspace. The valve may be near a water meter. Be sure you understand how the valve works. Some valves must be turned clockwise a number of revolutions; others shut water off when you turn them ¼ turn clockwise.

OUTDOOR SHUTOFF

In addition to the indoor main shutoff, there is usually a valve located outside the house. Often, it is between the house and the street. The valve may be located underground, in an enclosure that is sometimes called a Buffalo box. The cover may be hidden by foliage or even soil; you may need to have the utility company help you find it. Once the cover is removed, there may be a hand-turn valve, or there may be a valve that requires a special long-handled "key." If so, buy a key and keep it handy.

INTERMEDIATE SHUTOFFS

In utility areas, such as a basement, garage, or laundry room, you may also find valves that shut water off to one or several rooms in the house. These intermediate valves are typically found in pairs, to shut off both hot and cold lines. Close the valves and test to find which fixtures they control.

STOP VALVES

Also called fixture shutoff valves, these control water running to one fixture only. You'll find two—one for hot and one for cold—for each faucet, and one for a toilet. If a fixture does not have a stop valve, it's a good idea to install one. Many stop valves are poorly constructed, so handle with care. If a stop valve does not completely turn the water off, you may need to also close an intermediate or main valve.

IN-VALVE SHUTOFFS

To shut off water to a tub/shower valve, remove the faucet's cover and look to see if there are integral shutoffs like the ones shown. Turn the screws clockwise to shut the water off. If your shower does not have in-valve shutoffs, look for a removable access panel on the opposite side of the faucet (in an adjoining room). Remove the panel, and you may find shutoff valves.

Inspecting your system

I t's a good idea to have at least a general knowledge of where your pipes are and where they go. This will help you to find leaks in case of an emergency or to auger clogged pipes. It is also useful information when you decide to remodel or add a new fixture or two. And the ability to talk knowledgeably with a plumber may save you money; otherwise, you will have to pay him to find the pipes.

Architectural drawings can be very helpful. Be aware, however, that drawings do not always show the pipes and that plumbers often do not follow architect's instructions, so the drawings may not be accurate.

A pipe's size is indicated according to its inside diameter (i.d.); the outside diameter will be larger.

MODERN MAIN STACK
Start with the main stack, a vertical pipe 3 or 4 inches in diameter that runs all the way up through the roof. The stack will be visible in a basement or crawlspace. Often, the interior wall it runs through will be 6 inches thick or thicker (most walls are about 4½ inches thick), to allow for the stack and the pipes that connect to it. The stack may take a turn before exiting the roof. The plastic stack shown here is typical in a newer home. Note the cleanout plug, which allows you to auger the main sewer line (see pages 74–76).

OLDER MAIN STACK
An older home will likely have a cast-iron main stack, usually 4 inches in diameter. It is less likely to have turns.

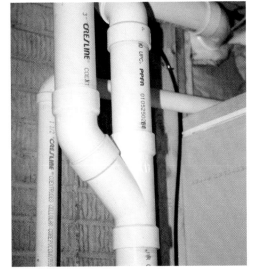

SECONDARY STACK
A secondary stack may be plastic in a newer home and either cast iron or galvanized steel in an older home. It may make a number of turns to go around obstacles.

CLEANOUTS
Locate all the cleanouts and make sure you can access them in case you need to auger. Main and secondary stacks should have cleanouts, either near the floor or 3–4 feet above the floor. You may also find cleanouts on the ends of some horizontal drain pipes.

WORK SMARTER

FOLLOW THE PIPES

Pipes are usually visible in a basement or a crawlspace. Shine a flashlight up, and you may see the direction the riser pipes travel. Take careful measurements and transfer them to the rooms upstairs to help locate pipes. To help find both supply and drain pipes in a wall, turn on the water and listen. It may help to use a stethoscope, but with an ear to the wall, you can usually hear running water.

You can also climb onto your roof and find the vent pipes, which are usually extensions of the main and secondary stacks. Run an auger or chain down a vent and wiggle it while a helper listens in a room below to locate the vent pipe's location.

Access panel

ACCESS PANELS

Bathtub and shower plumbing is usually hidden in a wall. In many cases, there will be a removable access panel that allows you to get at the pipes. Look in the adjacent room (or closet) on the opposite side of the shower faucet wall. The panel's cover may pop out when you pry it, or you may need to remove some screws first.

CATCH BASIN

Some older homes have a catch basin located outside, which traps the grease typically thrown down a kitchen sink. If the kitchen sink drains sluggishly, the catch basin may need to be cleaned out. If the home has been remodeled, a plumber may have bypassed the catch basin. Newer homes usually do not have catch basins.

PIPES AT THE WATER HEATER

The water heater is where the main supply pipe branches off into hot and cold pipes that run through the house. Often you can find clues to the overall supply system here.

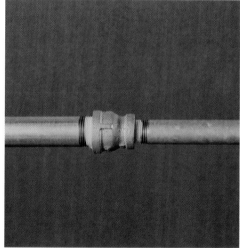

WHERE PIPES REDUCE IN SIZE

Find out where the supply pipes change in size, usually from ¾ to ½ inch, before supplying faucets and fixtures. If you have low water pressure in part of the house, it may be a good idea to replace some of the ½-inch pipe with ¾-inch pipe.

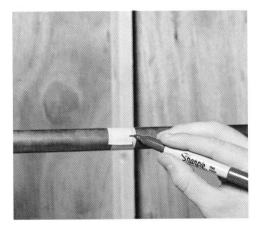

MEASURE A PIPE'S DIAMETER

To figure a pipe's size, wrap a piece of tape around the pipe and mark for the outside circumference. Then, use the chart at the right to calculate the inside diameter (i.d.).

Pipe sizes

PIPE MATERIAL	OUTSIDE CIRCUMFERENCE	INSIDE DIAMETER
COPPER		
	2"	½"
	2¾"	¾"
	3½"	1"
GALVANIZED OR BLACK STEEL		
	2"	⅜"
	2⅜"	½"
	3⅛"	¾"
	4"	1"
	4¾"	1¼"
	5½"	1½"
	7"	2"
PLASTIC		
	2¾"	½"
	3½"	¾"
	4¼"	1"
	5⅛"	1¼"
	6"	1½"
	7½"	2"
	10½"	3"
	14"	4"
CAST IRON		
	7"	2"
	10⅛"	3"
	13⅜"	4"

CLOSER LOOK

SUPPLY PIPE PROBLEMS

Galvanized steel pipe is strong, but after 50 years or so, it will develop rust at some joints, and mineral deposits will clog its interior, especially on horizontal pipes. These minerals will sometimes also clog faucet aerators and showerheads (see pages 24–25). And they may seriously decrease water pressure as well. When possible, replace old galvanized pipe with newer materials.

Copper and rigid plastic supply pipes will remain free of mineral deposits. However, they are easily damaged. If a nail or screw driven into a wall strikes, it will likely cause a puncture. Flexible copper and plastic supply lines are easy to run, but they can develop kinks when installed, and they are easily dented. As long as they are protected inside walls, these pipes will be reliable for a lifetime or more. However, take care to protect any exposed pipes.

GALVANIZED PIPE

Galvanized pipe is sometimes mistaken for lead pipe. A lead pipe has a similar dull gray color, but you can easily cut a nick in it using a screwdriver or pen knife; galvanized pipe is much harder. If you find a lead pipe, call in a plumber to see if it should be replaced; it may pose a health danger.

BALL VALVE

A newer ball valve, with a straight handle, will give reliable service for a very long time. It is a "full-bore" valve, meaning that when opened, water can flow through it just as well as through the pipe. To turn it off, turn the handle one quarter turn.

GATE VALVE

Older gate or globe valves have round handles. These valves have parts that can wear out in time, reducing their ability to fully shut off water and sometimes causing leaks below the handle. See page 140 for ways to repair these valves.

Qualifying yourself

Assess your basic skills accurately and honestly so you can pick projects that you can complete successfully and with confidence. Store associates at The Home Depot qualify customers for plumbing projects by asking some basic questions to get a sense of their abilities.

Qualifying quiz

- Do you mind getting your hands dirty? Some plumbing projects can get messy; that's just the nature of the job.
- How about doing physical labor? Some projects such as replacing a toilet can require a certain amount of heavy lifting. Enjoying the challenge of physical labor is an important attribute.
- Do you like working with tools? Most plumbing projects require some basic tools. If you don't know a screwdriver from a pair of pliers or a plunger from a snake, now's the time to learn. The best introduction to using a tool is to watch it in action. Pages 16–19 will give you basic information on the most common plumbing tools, and you'll find more tool details in the projects themselves.
- Are you a tinkerer? If you're good at taking things apart and putting them back together, you can learn plumbing skills.
- Are you willing to research projects and make a

Learning By Doing
The best way to develop your plumbing skills is to start with a simple project, such as replacing a faucet, then move on to more demanding projects as your skills develop.

plan? Doing your homework to develop an understanding of the process and scope of a project is essential. Learn the skills you'll need and explore all the safety issues before you start.
- Do you enjoy working on your house? If you don't enjoy maintaining and improving your home, you may not want to get involved in replacing a sink or fixing a leak.
- Do you know your limitations? It's OK to admit

that a particular project is a little beyond your current skill level. It's better to pay a professional to do a job you're not comfortable with rather than paying extra for one to fix your mistake.

OK, you're qualified
Once you've answered these questions and qualified yourself, you're ready to begin picking the right level of projects for you.

"REPAIRING A CARTRIDGE FAUCET,"
(SEE PAGE 28)

"TROUBLESHOOTING A LEAKING TOILET,"
(SEE PAGE 79)

"ADJUSTING A POP-UP DRAIN,"
(SEE PAGE 46)

Picking projects

You can't always pick your projects. Plumbing failures and leaks can happen at any time and have to be dealt with quickly and efficiently.

You do, however, have choices when you're remodeling or upgrading; you can pick projects within your skill level. You have the time to do your homework and make a good plan. Become familiar with the materials and equipment. Ask yourself: "Can I do this, and do I have the time?" If the answer is yes, get started!

Tools of the trade
Each project has a list of tools and materials you'll need to complete the job. Review the list for the project you select and make sure you understand how each tool is used. Ask the salespeople at your local home center how to safely and properly use the tool.

Know your plumbing system
A working knowledge of your plumbing system will help you understand why something isn't working properly. Look through pages 6–9 and 180 to learn how each system operates and to give you some troubleshooting tips. Make a map showing how the plumbing in your home is installed. Know where the water meter and the main shutoff valve are located. Find out where water comes into the house and where the drain pipes and traps go out.

Starter projects
Begin with easy projects. Most repair and maintenance jobs are fairly simple. Check through the house and see if repairs are needed. Does a faucet drip? Is the toilet acting up?

Or maybe it's time to finally address a slow-draining sink or dishwasher. You'll find repair and maintenance projects throughout this book.

Intermediate jobs
Getting comfortable with your plumbing skills? Consider tackling more complex projects, such as replacing a sink or toilet.

Advanced remodeling
Do you need to replace that tub or shower? Or maybe you'd like a shower stall downstairs? These projects require planning, and you'll need other skills besides plumbing. You'll need to pull a permit and deal with inspectors. Before you start, draw a detailed diagram. List the tools and materials you'll need for the job. Estimate the amount of time from start to finish and ask yourself if you can spare the time to do the job. Ask yourself not only if you have the plumbing skills required, but also if you have the electrical, tiling, painting, and carpentry skills needed. If the answers are all yes and you're comfortable with them, check out "Chapter 11, Tubs and Showers."

Working outdoors
Installing a below-ground irrigation system and placing a hose bib in a more convenient location are both outdoor plumbing projects. Installing an irrigation system requires solid planning, some advanced plumbing skills, a little electrical savvy, and the willingness to use a shovel.

Growing your skills

The key to growing your skills is learning to do things correctly from the start. Looking for shortcuts before you understand the basics can lead to very costly mistakes.

Plumbing is a process. It helps to know how something works before you try to fix it. Pick a project you're comfortable with, assemble all the tools and materials you're going to need, and review the entire process by reading all of the instructions before you start. Once everything is in place, all you have to do is follow the project through to completion step-by-step.

Your skills will grow in proportion to your willingness to do things right.

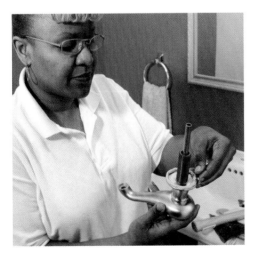

"INSTALLING A WIDESPREAD FAUCET,"
(SEE PAGE 55)

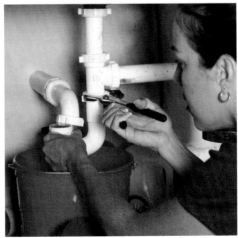

"UNCLOGGING DRAINS AND WASTE LINES,"
(SEE PAGE 74)

Plumbing tool kit

Here are some of the tools you'll use for the plumbing projects in this book. While many projects can be completed with a few common hand tools, some tasks require specialized items designed to make the job easier. As you expand your plumbing skills, you will also expand your tool kit.

If you do carpentry or electrical work around the house, you'll already have a lot of plumbing tools on hand. Purchase specialty items as you need them for projects. Consider renting tools that are very specialized or that you'll only need once or twice. Friends and neighbors are often good sources

for specialized items, but if you borrow tools, treat them carefully, clean them, and return them promptly.

Always use tools as they're intended to be used; an adjustable wrench is not a hammer. **Study the manuals and instructions that come with the tools so you can handle them safely and maintain them properly.**

Buy the best you can afford; good tools will last a lifetime and can be passed down through generations. The old adage remains true—take care of your tools, and they'll take care of you.

Tools arranged alphabetically, top to bottom, in columns left to right.

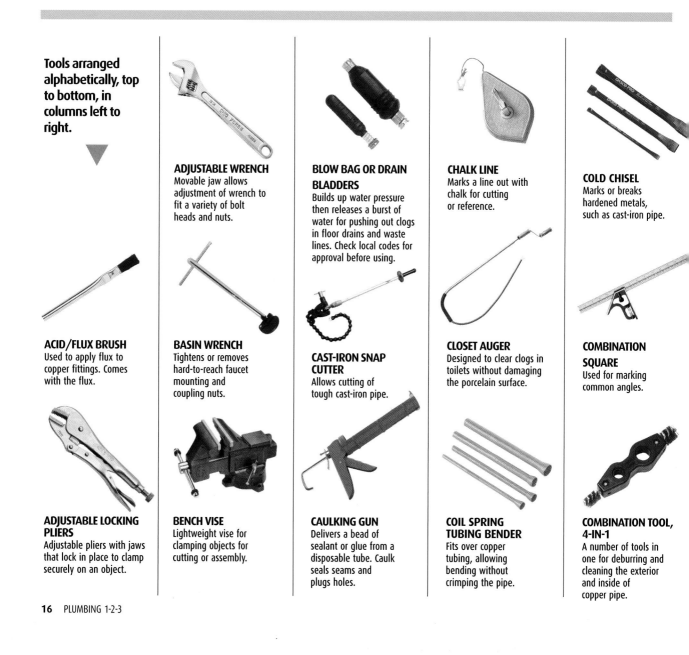

ADJUSTABLE WRENCH
Movable jaw allows adjustment of wrench to fit a variety of bolt heads and nuts.

ACID/FLUX BRUSH
Used to apply flux to copper fittings. Comes with the flux.

BASIN WRENCH
Tightens or removes hard-to-reach faucet mounting and coupling nuts.

ADJUSTABLE LOCKING PLIERS
Adjustable pliers with jaws that lock in place to clamp securely on an object.

BENCH VISE
Lightweight vise for clamping objects for cutting or assembly.

BLOW BAG OR DRAIN BLADDERS
Builds up water pressure then releases a burst of water for pushing out clogs in floor drains and waste lines. Check local codes for approval before using.

CAST-IRON SNAP CUTTER
Allows cutting of tough cast-iron pipe.

CAULKING GUN
Delivers a bead of sealant or glue from a disposable tube. Caulk seals seams and plugs holes.

CHALK LINE
Marks a line out with chalk for cutting or reference.

CLOSET AUGER
Designed to clear clogs in toilets without damaging the porcelain surface.

COIL SPRING TUBING BENDER
Fits over copper tubing, allowing bending without crimping the pipe.

COLD CHISEL
Marks or breaks hardened metals, such as cast-iron pipe.

COMBINATION SQUARE
Used for marking common angles.

COMBINATION TOOL, 4-IN-1
A number of tools in one for deburring and cleaning the exterior and inside of copper pipe.

COPPER FITTING BRUSH
Deburrs and cleans debris from the interior surface of copper pipe and fittings.

DRAIN SNAKE OR DRAIN AUGER
A slender tube with a handle on one end that clears blocked or slow-draining waste and drain lines.

FLANGED PLUNGER
Folds up into a cup during use, then discharges a forceful burst of water to clear clogs in sinks and toilets.

HAMMERS AND MALLET
Drive nails and are used for striking metallic objects.

INSPECTION MIRROR
A telescoping handle with an adjustable mirror at the end that allows seeing into tight locations.

COPPER TUBING DEBURRER
Deburrs and cleans debris from the exterior surface of copper pipe.

ELECTRIC ELEMENT SOCKET
Makes the job of removing the electrical element in a water heater easier.

FLARING TOOL
Fits over the end of copper pipe and flares out the end as the screw is tightened, so the end will seal properly with the gas line fitting.

HAND AUGER
A handheld device with a crank and a cylinder containing a coiled tube that is fed out by turning the crank to clear clogs.

KEYHOLE SAW
A handheld saw with a thin, replaceable blade for cutting in tight places.

CORDLESS REVERSIBLE ⅜-INCH DRILL
Makes it easier to drive screws and fasteners.

EMERY CLOTH
A very finely gritted sandpaperlike cloth used to remove burrs and clean debris from copper supply pipe.

FLASHLIGHT
A handheld light that directs light into hard-to-see places.

HANDLE PULLER
Removes stubborn handles without damaging them.

LEAD-FREE FLUX AND SOLDER
Flux cleans the surface of copper pipe; solder joins the pipe to the fitting with a tight seal.

CORDLESS REVERSIBLE SCREWDRIVER
Drives, as well as removes, screws and fasteners.

FILES—ROUND AND FLAT
Smooth metal, wood, or plastic files.

HACKSAW
Cuts metal, metal piping, and plastic piping.

HEX KEY OR ALLEN WRENCH SET
Tightens and loosens set screws.

LEVEL—CARPENTER'S
Determines vertical and horizontal level; used for determining slope of pipe runs.

DIAGONAL CUTTERS (LEFT- AND RIGHT-HANDED)
Prevents distortion of dryer pipe when cutting.

FLAME PROTECTION
A fireproof sheet of material to place between a propane torch flame and a flammable object such as wood while soldering.

HACKSAW—MINI
Cuts pipe and metal in hard-to-reach places.

HOLE SAW
A bit that fits on the end of a power or hand drill for cutting holes in wood.

LEVEL—LINE
A level that sits on a string to find slope for running pipe.

LEVEL— PLUMB BOB
Determines vertical leveling of an object.

LEVEL—TORPEDO
A small level that allows easy access to tight places. Often comes with a magnetic edge, which makes it a good choice for leveling metal appliances.

LONG-NOSED PLIERS
Grips wires and small objects while holding them in place in tight locations.

MITER BOX
Cuts pipe while holding it in place for square, even cuts.

NEEDLE-NOSE PLIERS
Grips small objects while holding them in place in tight locations.

PENETRATING OIL
Loosens "frozen" nuts, bolts, and threaded pipe by penetrating the threads.

PIPE JOINT COMPOUND
Ensures a perfect seal for threaded pipe.

PIPE WRENCH
Tightens, loosens, and clamps pipes and large fittings.

PLASTIC PIPE CEMENT
Solvent that cements plastic to plastic plumbing fittings. Available in all-purpose formulas.

PLASTIC PIPE PRIMER
Primer prepares PVC and CPVC plastic pipe for cement when connecting to a fitting.

PLASTIC TUBING CUTTER
Cuts plastic piping, providing a clean and square cut. Important when seating the pipe in a fitting.

PLUMBER'S PUTTY
Provides a watertight seal for fixtures. Make sure the type is compatible with materials and surfaces.

POWER CIRCULAR SAW
Use different blades to cut wood and plastic.

POWER REVERSIBLE ⅜-INCH DRILL
Used for driving screws and fasteners and drilling holes. No battery means unlimited use.

PROPANE TORCH
Supplies fuel from a cylinder and through a torch fitting to produce a flame for soldering copper pipe.

PRY BAR
A lever that allows lifting or separation of heavy objects.

PUTTY KNIFE
Used to apply to or scrape putty and caulk from surfaces.

RATCHET-TYPE PVC CUTTER
A tool for cutting plastic pipe that guarantees a square, smooth cut.

RATCHET WRENCH AND SOCKET SET
Easily tightens and removes bolts and nuts.

RECIPROCATING SAW
Cuts wood, metal, or plastic with the proper blade.

RETRACTABLE STEEL TAPE MEASURE
Measuring device. Purchase one that is at least 16 feet long.

RIGHT-ANGLE DRILL
Drills easily in hard-to-reach places.

SAFETY GOGGLES
Protect the eyes from flying particles or splashing fluids.

SCRATCH AWL
Marks metal by etching the surface.

SEAT DRESSING TOOL
A specialized tool that smooths and resurfaces nonremovable seats.

SEAT WRENCH
A specialty tool designed to reach into the faucet stem to remove or tighten removable seats.

SLOTTED AND PHILLIPS SCREWDRIVERS
Drive and remove screws by hand.

SPEED BITS
High-speed bits designed for drilling through metal, plastic, or wood.

STRAINER LOCKNUT WRENCH
A specialty wrench with a locking jaw used to remove the basket strainer on a sink drain.

TWEEZERS
Small hand pliers that grasp, remove, and hold small objects.

SELF-ADJUSTING PLIERS
Provides an instant, positive grip for removing or tightening pipe.

SMALL WIRE BRUSH
Cleans debris and mineral deposits from pipe and fittings.

SPIRAL SAW
A high-speed cutting tool with a drill-like blade for cutting holes in countertops, drywall, and other soft surfaces.

STRAP WRENCH
Allows a secure hold to remove or tighten pipe or fittings without marring them.

UTILITY KNIFE
Cuts and trims a variety of materials.

SHOWER STEM SOCKET
Deep-throated socket used to remove compression stems embedded in shower walls.

SNAKE FLASHLIGHT
A flexible flashlight that can be wrapped and positioned to direct light into hard-to-see places, freeing hands to work.

SPUD WRENCH
Specially designed tool to remove and tighten very large (2- to 4-inch) nuts by grabbing onto the lugs for increased leverage.

TEFLON TAPE
A ribbon of Teflon that wraps around threaded pipe, providing a secure seal.

VOLTAGE TESTER
Checks for voltage across an electrical circuit.

SILICONE GREASE
Lubricates faucet and valve assemblies.

SPADE BITS
Specifically designed for wood. Bits range from $\frac{1}{4}$ to $1\frac{1}{4}$ inches. Use when running pipe through studs or joists.

SQUARE— CARPENTER'S
Used to lay out right angles and check corners for "square" (90 degrees).

TOOTHBRUSH
Cleans screens of mineral deposits and debris.

WATER-PUMP PLIERS
A multipurpose gripping tool with ridged jaws for secure contact. Tape jaws to prevent damage to fragile fixtures.

SLIP PLIERS
The jaws adjust to two settings by slipping from a smaller setting to a larger one.

SPARK LIGHTER
A tool that produces a spark to light a propane torch for soldering copper pipe.

STEEL WOOL
Smooths and cleans metal surfaces. Graded by numerals with 000 being the finest.

TUBING CUTTER
Creates straight, smooth cuts in plastic or metal pipe.

Safety first

Know when to call a plumber!

Homeowners often like to take on new challenges, but when it comes to home repair, sometimes it's best to be cautious. Flooding your basement or having to tear down a finished project because you didn't do the installation properly can be an expensive lesson. Don't be afraid to call in a plumber when there's an emergency or if you're just not sure how to proceed with a project.

I f you use common sense and follow the instructions, you can do any plumbing project safely and with confidence. But there are safety issues to consider, such as pipes that carry potentially hazardous liquids and gases in and out of the house. It's essential to have a proper working environment.

Remember that safety is always your number one priority.

Plumbing and electricity
Water and electricity don't mix. Use proper precautions and follow all manufacturer's instructions when combining plumbing and electrical work.

Respecting natural gas
Gas is very safe, but sometimes there are leaks. If you suspect a gas leak, open windows and doors for ventilation. Don't touch electrical switches.

If the odor is faint and it's near a gas appliance, check the pilot light. If the pilot light is on and you're certain the gas is coming from the appliance, turn off its gas supply. If the smell persists, leave your home immediately. Call the gas supplier's emergency phone number from a neighbor's house.

Carbon monoxide
Carbon monoxide (CO) is odorless, colorless, and tasteless. Any fuel-burning appliance can be a source of CO. Vent properly. Follow codes and manufacturer's instructions. Install a CO detector in any room that has a gas-burning appliance and in living areas as well.

SAFETY ALERT
No matter how carefully a system was installed, eventually pipes will burst, a toilet or tub will overflow, a joint will break, or a drain line will crack. Remaining cool, calm, and collected in such emergencies is the key to minimizing damage and making cost-effective repairs.

Take a walk around your home and map out your plumbing system (see pages 8–13). Know where the main shutoff valve is and know how to shut it off. Map all individual shutoffs near appliances and fixtures and install new ones where they'd be useful. (See "Shutoff Valves," page 140.)

You should read Chapter 4, "Dealing with Clogs," before you are faced with an emergency. That way you won't have to read instructions to know what to do during the crisis.

Safety equipment
- **Wear eye protection.** Safety goggles are an absolute must whenever you're cutting, pounding, soldering, or working above your head. They protect against splashing liquids and airborne particles. Get used to wearing them when you're working.
- **Wear a respirator.** Airborne particles can damage your lungs. Use dust masks when cutting materials and respirators specified by manufacturers when you're working with any chemicals.
- **Wear gloves.** Sturdy gloves are essential for handling chemicals, sharp objects, or heavy, awkward loads. Special gloves are designed for different types of protection.
- **Wear good-quality work clothes.** Protect yourself from physical injury and the potentially high bacteria content of wastewater and debris by wearing heavy clothing—especially long sleeves and long pants. Launder clothing immediately after each use.
- **Clean your hands.** Always clean your hands with an antibacterial soap.
- **Use the right tool.** Use your tools for the job for which they were designed. A screwdriver isn't a cold chisel and an adjustable wrench isn't a hammer. Improper tool use can cause injuries and damage fixtures and equipment.
- **Respect ladders.** If you're working from a ladder, read and follow the precautions printed on the side. Never stand on the top or higher than the third step from the top. A helper should always be present to steady the ladder, and all four of the ladder's feet should be seated firmly on level ground.

Costs, codes, and contracts

Estimating job costs

The cost of a project is based on materials and labor. If you're doing the work yourself, you'll only be concerned with materials; but if you're hiring a plumber, you'll have to figure in his or her rate. Before you start, know what you want to do and list what you need to complete the project. Shop around and compare prices. Compare low-, middle-, and high-end fixtures. You may find that the cost difference between good and best isn't prohibitive.

Purchase products and materials from businesses that back what they sell with good service, and have a clear return policy if problems arise. They have a presence in the community and a reputation to maintain. Older hardware stores and secondhand shops are potential sources for antique fixtures. Consider places that sell discontinued items, but keep in mind it may be very difficult if not impossible to find replacement parts.

When estimating costs, add 10 to 15 percent to the total bill so you can cover unexpected expenses without blowing a hole in your budget.

Dealing with plumbing codes

Whenever you run new pipes to install new service (as opposed to replacing a fixture or appliance), you need to pull a permit and pass local codes. Plumbing codes—both local and national—are standards and guidelines intended to make sure plumbing installations are safe and will work properly. Together, they codify plumbing techniques and proper use of materials throughout the United States.

IMPORTANT NOTE: The projects in this book follow common national guidelines, but local codes are often stricter than national standards. Also be aware that codes can vary from location to location in both materials and installation methods for the same project. Check with your local building department for requirements and to schedule inspections.

Do your research before you start actual work to make sure you're meeting code. If the inspector doesn't approve your work, you'll have to do the work all over again and that gets expensive. When applying for permits, present precise drawings of your plans that are easy to read. Include a complete list of materials to be used in the project.

Installations need to be seen to be inspected. Don't put up the drywall or cover pipes until the inspector has signed off.

Hiring a plumbing contractor

Great word of mouth is the sign of a good contractor. Get at least three different quotes. The bids should include a list of materials or "specs" of everything that will be installed and a work schedule. Payments should be made in at least three phases: no more than half of the money up front, a payment during the course of the job, and a final payment after the job is completed to your satisfaction. Be aware that not all types of plumbers will handle all types of work. A contractor should be responsible for getting necessary permits, as well as scheduling and dealing with inspectors.

Make sure the contractor's license is valid in your area and that he or she has valid insurance to protect you from liability for the duration of the job. Ask for references and visit the contractor's finished sites, as well as some works in progress. Check with the Better Business Bureau if you have any concerns about a contractor's reliability.

Question everything. Ask the contractor to explain what he or she is doing and why. And finally, don't accept shoddy work.

Repair and maintenance

Chapter 2 highlights

 he repair and maintenance projects in this chapter will show you how to fix everything from sink and shower drains to repairing faucets. Whatever your skill level, you'll find projects you can handle. As you solve basic plumbing problems, you'll gain the experience and confidence to move on to bigger, more complicated jobs.

Repair or replace?

Professional plumbers usually hate faucet repair jobs, and sometimes refuse to perform them. That's because you often spend more time shopping for parts than actually doing the work. And in some cases, the faucet will continue to malfunction after a repair because another problem needs to be addressed. However, as a homeowner, your time is not as costly as a professional plumber's, so it may be worthwhile to attempt a repair.

Many repairs are easy to perform, inexpensive, and effective. However, if the repair parts are difficult to find, or if you are having difficulty figuring out what's wrong with your faucet—or if you don't like the way your current faucet looks—you may be better off replacing rather than repairing. Often, the most difficult part of a faucet repair is working in a cramped space underneath the sink; other than that, a replacement is usually pretty easy. See chapter 3 for instructions on various types of faucet installations.

Getting the parts

At a home center you will likely find replacement parts for faucets that are common in your area. If you don't find what you need, you may be able to special order it.

If the faucet has the manufacturer's name printed on it, you know which brand of repair part to look for. If not, take apart the faucet and bring as many parts as possible to your home center or plumbing supply source. For some repairs, such as replacing an O-ring or compression washer, you may be able to use general parts, such as are found in a little tub of washers and O-rings. Most repairs, however, require specific parts made for your model faucet.

The faucets shown in this chapter are representative of the major faucet types. However, there are hundreds of variations out there, so your faucet may not look just like the one in the photo. If you are at all uncertain about the parts you need, ask a salesperson to assist you. If the first salesperson doesn't seem knowledgeable, ask to talk to someone else.

Cleaning a faucet aerator, sink sprayer, and showerhead

PROJECT DETAILS

SKILLS: Connecting plumbing fittings
PROJECT: Cleaning a faucet aerator, sink sprayer, and showerhead

TIME TO COMPLETE

EXPERIENCED: 10 min.
HANDY: 20 min.
NOVICE: 30 min.

STUFF YOU'LL NEED

TOOLS: Water-pump pliers, small wire brush, toothbrush, paper clip, small bowl
MATERIALS: Masking tape, white vinegar solution or lime-dissolving solution

GOOD IDEA

KEEP THINGS TIDY
Get in the habit of setting out the parts of a fixture in the order that you removed them so you can easily put them back together. You'll have lots of little pieces that are easy to lose.

Hard water is rich in minerals that build up and eventually clog aerators, sink sprayers, and showerheads. Often, you can clean an aerator by removing it and running water backwards through it. If deposits have hardened, remove the parts and soak them in a solution of 1 part white vinegar and 1 part water or in lime-dissolving solution, then clean them with a small brush or paper clip. This will usually restore water flow. Or, install a new aerator—they're usually inexpensive. If your shower is clean but isn't running at the pressure you might like, it's usually because of a flow restrictor. To conserve water, flow restrictors are required by code and by law and cannot be removed from the showerhead.

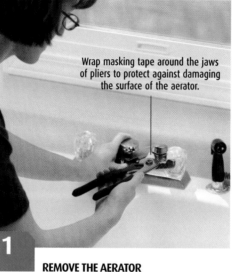

Wrap masking tape around the jaws of pliers to protect against damaging the surface of the aerator.

1

REMOVE THE AERATOR
Use a pair of water-pump pliers to unscrew the aerator from the faucet spout. Protect the surface of the aerator by wrapping the jaws of the pliers with masking tape. Be careful as you apply pressure to the pliers when removing the aerator. Too much pressure can crush the aerator cylinder.

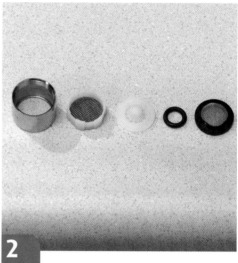

2

DISASSEMBLE THE AERATOR
Remove the internal parts of the aerator by pushing them out with your fingers. If the components are stuck, presoak the aerator in a vinegar solution. Use a pick or tweezers, but be careful not to damage any of the parts. Once they're removed, lay out the parts and inspect them for damage. Damaged components will have to be replaced. Soak reusable parts in a vinegar solution overnight to loosen mineral deposits.

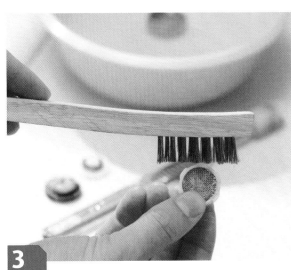

Showerhead

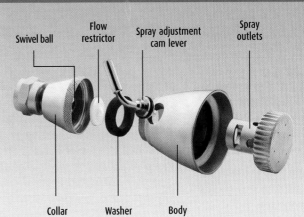

Swivel ball | Flow restrictor | Spray adjustment cam lever | Spray outlets

Collar | Washer | Body

3

CLEAN THE AERATOR PARTS

Remove the parts from the vinegar solution and wipe them dry with a rag. Use a small wire brush to remove mineral deposits. It may be necessary to soak the parts again if they are not clean. Inspect all parts for damage after cleaning. Purchase a replacement kit or a new aerator if parts are damaged or if you are unable to clean any of the parts. Reassemble the aerator and screw it back into the spout hand-tight. Turn on the water and check for leaks. Tighten if necessary.

CLEANING A SHOWERHEAD

Not all showerheads break down the same way, but what's shown above is a common example. Newer showerheads come with a water-conservation device called a flow restrictor that cannot be removed. Unscrew the swivel ball nut and remove the showerhead. Disassemble the internal parts. Soak overnight in white vinegar or a lime-dissolving solution. Use a small wire brush to clean mineral deposits. Use a paper clip to remove mineral deposits from holes in the disk. Inspect for damage and replace any damaged components. Reassemble the showerhead. Apply silicone grease to the shower arm threads and install the showerhead. Turn on the water and inspect for leaks.

Sink sprayer

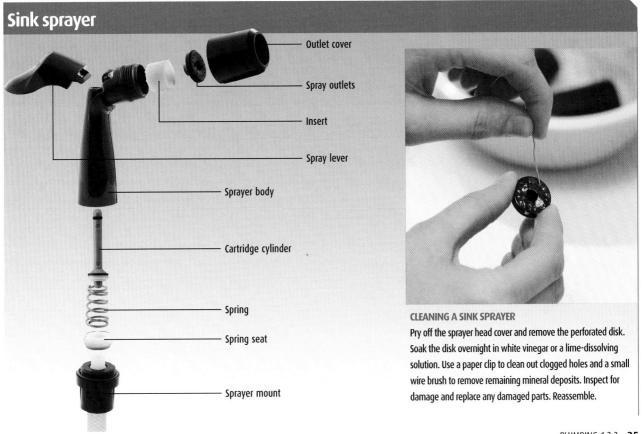

Outlet cover

Spray outlets

Insert

Spray lever

Sprayer body

Cartridge cylinder

Spring

Spring seat

Sprayer mount

CLEANING A SINK SPRAYER

Pry off the sprayer head cover and remove the perforated disk. Soak the disk overnight in white vinegar or a lime-dissolving solution. Use a paper clip to clean out clogged holes and a small wire brush to remove remaining mineral deposits. Inspect for damage and replace any damaged parts. Reassemble.

Repairing a rotary ball faucet

Rotary ball faucets (made by Delta and others) have a smooth plastic or metal ball which rotates in the socket of the faucet body when the faucet handle is moved. Grooves in the ball pass over or away from the water inlet valve seats that control the amount and mixture of hot and cold water that is supplied to the spout.

Leaks at the spout or the handle can be easily fixed by tightening the housing or adjusting the ring. If this doesn't work, buy a replacement kit. If you aren't sure of the faucet type, take the parts with you to the store.

A ball faucet is easily clogged. If water flow is restricted, disassemble and clean the grooves and inlets.

WORK SMARTER

DON'T TOSS THE OLD PARTS
Don't throw away any old parts until you're finished with the job; you may want them for reference.

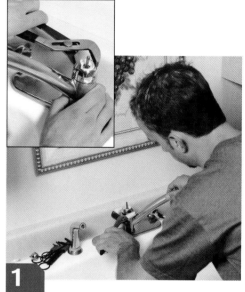

1

SHUT OFF THE WATER AND UNSCREW THE CAP
Use a pair of water-pump pliers to remove the cap. Wrap the jaws of the pliers with masking tape to prevent damage to the cap.

GOOD IDEA

FOLLOW THE DIRECTIONS
To work properly, the springs need to be installed per manufacturer's instructions.Put the springs on a piece of tape in the order you took them out so you know exactly how they go back into place.

2

REMOVE THE CAM
Lift off the cam housing, seal, and ball. Inspect each part for damage. Replace damaged parts. A metal ball will last longer than a plastic ball.

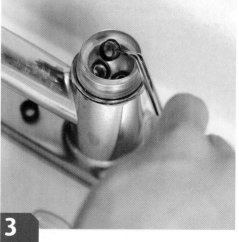

3

LIFT OUT THE SEATS
Use tweezers to remove the valve seats and springs. The springs are cone-shaped, with one end larger than the other. Note how the springs are installed before you lift them out—you must install the replacement springs in exactly the same order you remove them or the faucet won't work properly. Remove the spout by twisting and lifting at the same time.

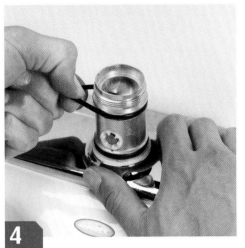

4 PEEL OFF (DON'T CUT) THE O-RING

Slip the O-ring from its groove and peel it from the housing. It's important to keep the ring whole so you can find an exact replacement at the store. Use the tip of a screwdriver to help release it if necessary. If you can't peel it off, pry it out with a screwdriver and cut the ring with a utility knife.

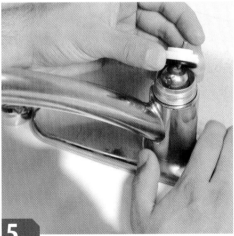

5 REASSEMBLE THE FAUCET

Take the old parts to your local home center to find the right replacement. Coat the new O-ring with silicone grease and seat it in the faucet housing groove. Push the spout over the O-ring and faucet housing. Install the new valve seals and springs. Make sure the seats and springs are installed correctly—they will only work correctly if installed properly, so read the installation instructions carefully. Place the cam ball in the housing. The tab on the cam fits into the notch in the body. Screw the cam housing onto the threads of the housing using the wrench that comes with the kit. Screw on the cap and install the handle. Turn the water on and check for leaks. Tighten the adjusting ring firmly to prevent leaks.

Rotary ball faucet

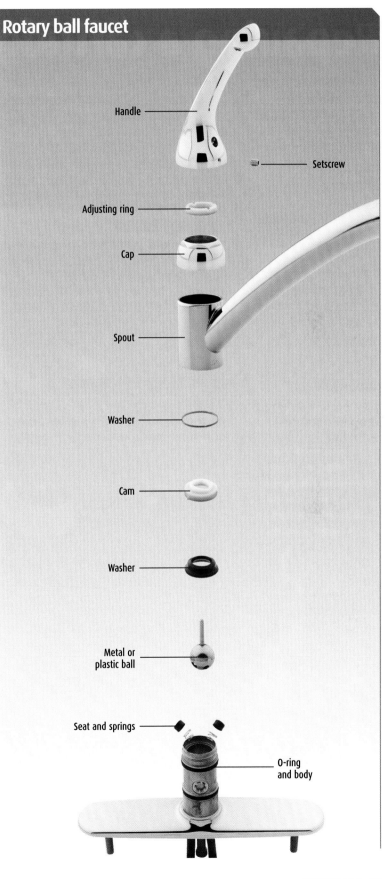

Handle

Setscrew

Adjusting ring

Cap

Spout

Washer

Cam

Washer

Metal or plastic ball

Seat and springs

O-ring and body

Repairing a cartridge faucet

PROJECT DETAILS

SKILLS: Connecting plumbing fittings
PROJECT: Repairing a cartridge faucet

TIME TO COMPLETE

EXPERIENCED: 20 min.
HANDY: 40 min.
NOVICE: 1+ hrs.

STUFF YOU'LL NEED

TOOLS: Screwdriver, water-pump pliers, needle-nose pliers, utility knife
MATERIALS: New cartridge, O-ring, silicone grease

CLOSER LOOK

THE CARTRIDGE JUNGLE
Just in case you thought it was easy, cartridges come in many shapes and sizes. Take the one you want to replace to the store so you can get an exact match and save yourself an extra trip.

Cartridge faucets (made by Moen and others) control the flow by channeling water through passageways inside the cartridge. Depending on how the faucet is rotated, the cartridge exposes an opening for incoming water and allows water to flow to the spout with the desired mix of hot and cold. To stop the flow, the cartridge is rotated so an opening does not face the water supply. O-rings seal the interior housing of the cartridge body. Leaks occur when an O-ring is worn.

The hardest part of replacing a cartridge faucet may be finding the correct replacement kit. Even though the operating principle is the same, faucet designs vary. (See "Closer Look," below.)

Cartridge faucet

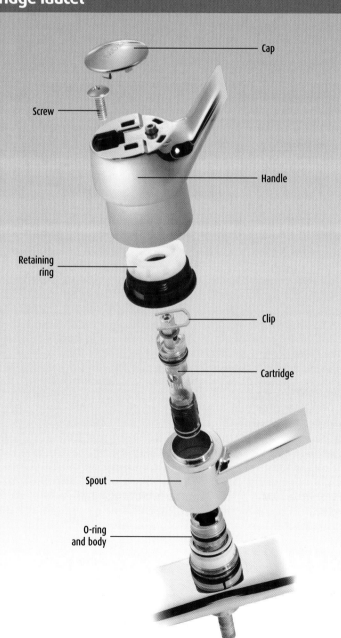

- Cap
- Screw
- Handle
- Retaining ring
- Clip
- Cartridge
- Spout
- O-ring and body

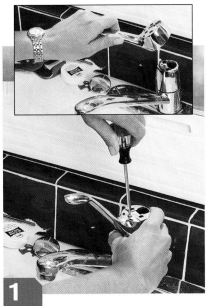

1

TURN OFF THE WATER SUPPLY AND REMOVE THE FAUCET HANDLE

Turn off the water at the shutoff valves or the main valve. Pry off the handle cap. Unscrew the faucet handle screw using a screwdriver. Lift the handle from the faucet assembly (see inset).

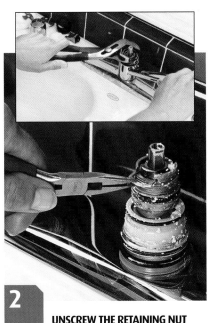

2

UNSCREW THE RETAINING NUT AND REMOVE THE RETAINING CLIP

Spin the faucet out of the way and use water-pump pliers to remove the plastic retaining nut. (See inset.) Pull out the retaining clip that is just beneath it with needle-nose pliers. Lift the faucet spout straight up from the faucet body and remove.

3

PEEL OFF (DON'T CUT) THE O-RING

Slip the O-ring from its groove and peel it from the housing. It's important to keep the ring whole so you can find an exact replacement at the store. Use the tip of a screwdriver to help release it if necessary. If you can't peel it off, pry it out with a screwdriver and cut the ring with a utility knife.

4

PULL OUT THE CARTRIDGE STEM

Grip the exposed end of the cartridge stem. Pull it straight up and out of the faucet body. Some brands of faucets may require a cartridge puller especially made for the job. Check the manufacturer's instructions. If that's the case, don't use pliers to remove the cartridge or you might damage or destroy it.

5

CLEAN AND REASSEMBLE THE FAUCET

Clean the faucet body to remove debris. Coat the new O-ring with silicone grease to lubricate it, then seat it into the faucet body O-ring groove. Insert the new stem cartridge. Replace the faucet spout and reassemble. Turn on the water. Check the hot and cold water to make sure they are not reversed. If reversed, disassemble the faucet and rotate the cartridge 180 degrees, then reassemble.

WORK SMARTER

LOOK BEFORE YOU LEAP!
There are many little pieces in a faucet, and they all need to be in exactly the right place for the faucet to work. It's easy to lose track of the assembly order and even easier to lose the parts themselves. Read the instructions carefully before you begin and arrange the parts on a flat surface as you remove them.

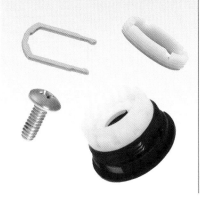

Repairing a ceramic disk faucet

PROJECT DETAILS

SKILLS: Assembling plumbing fittings
PROJECT: Repairing a ceramic disk faucet

TIME TO COMPLETE

EXPERIENCED: 20 min.
HANDY: 40 min.
NOVICE: 1 hr.

STUFF YOU'LL NEED

TOOLS: Screwdriver or hex key set
MATERIALS: Ceramic disk faucet replacement kit with seals, abrasive pad, silicone grease

GOOD IDEA

INSTALL SHUTOFF VALVES
No shutoff valves below the sink? Think about installing them now. See "Installing Stop Valves," pages 61–62.

D isk faucets (made by Price-Pfister and others) rely on replaceable neoprene seals to ensure a tight water seal. The seals are set in the bottom of the disk. If water drips from the spout or pools around the top of the faucet during use, replace the seals. If leaks persist, replace the entire disk.

To work on the faucet, first shut off the water supply. Turn on a faucet farther down the line to help drain water before you begin.

Most ceramic disk faucets come with a lifetime warranty for some of the parts. Check with the manufacturer for information on how to order.

Ceramic disk faucet

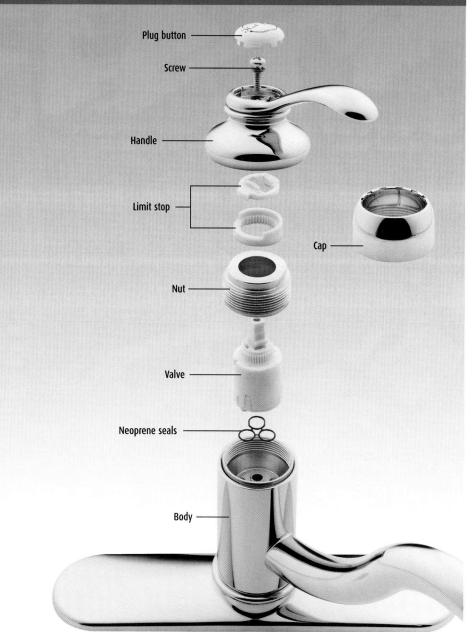

- Plug button
- Screw
- Handle
- Limit stop
- Cap
- Nut
- Valve
- Neoprene seals
- Body

1 **TURN OFF THE WATER AND REMOVE THE FAUCET HANDLE**
Use a hex key set or screwdriver to loosen the setscrew. Lift off the handle and dome housing.

2 **LIFT OUT THE DISK**
Unscrew the disk cartridge screws with a screwdriver. Lift the disk up and out. Inspect the disk for cracks—replace the disk if damaged.

3 **TAKE OUT THE SEALS**
Take the disk and seals to your local home center to find the right replacement parts. Some disks can be partly disassembled to expose rubber seals, which can be replaced.

4 **CLEAN SEAL SEATS**
Use an abrasive pad or toothbrush to clean the seal seats.

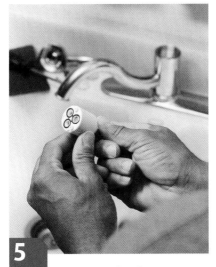

5 **INSTALL NEW SEALS**
Line up the disk seals with the faucet body and install the disk.

6 **ASSEMBLE THE FAUCET**
Install the cap and handle and tighten the setscrew. Remove air from the line before opening the supply valves fully. (See "Work Smarter," below.)

 **WORK SMARTER**

DON'T CRACK THAT CERAMIC DISK
Air rushing through a ceramic disk can crack it. First, open the faucet in the center position to balance the flow of water, then gradually open the shutoff valves to bleed out the air. Don't turn off the faucet until water flows freely and all the air is out.

Repairing a compression faucet

PROJECT DETAILS

SKILLS: Connecting plumbing fittings
PROJECT: Repairing a compression faucet

TIME TO COMPLETE

EXPERIENCED: 20 min.
HANDY: 40 min.
NOVICE: 1 hr.

STUFF YOU'LL NEED

TOOLS: Screwdriver, water-pump pliers, utility knife
MATERIALS: Universal washer kit, O-ring, silicone grease

Compression faucets (also called stem faucets) have been around for more than a century. Rubber washers are compressed into the valve seat to stop the flow of water. Damaged seats and worn washers cause compression-stem faucets to leak from the spout.

Compression faucets are designed with separate hot and cold water valves. This flexibility allows for many design sizes and shapes.

Repair kits with everything you'll need are available at home centers. Take the parts to your local home center so you can buy exact replacements. A small tub of all-purpose washers and O-rings may contain the parts you need.

Never reuse an old washer, no matter how good it looks!

OLD vs. NEW

CLAMPING STOCK
You may find packing string rather than an O-ring in some compression assemblies. If that's the case, you'll need to replace the packing string before you reassemble the faucet.

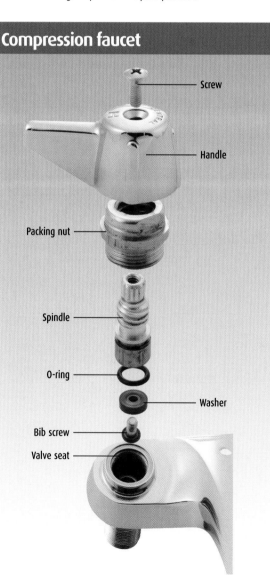

Compression faucet

- Screw
- Handle
- Packing nut
- Spindle
- O-ring
- Washer
- Bib screw
- Valve seat

1 **TURN OFF THE WATER AND UNSCREW THE STEM ASSEMBLY**
Pry off the handle cap. Remove the handle screw with a screwdriver. Lift it up and off the handle. To remove corroded handles, you may have to use a handle puller (see "Closer Look" on page 33). Unscrew the packing nut from the faucet body with water-pump pliers.

2

TAKE OFF THE WASHER

Use a screwdriver to remove the bib screw that holds the washer in place. Pry out the worn washer and discard it. The bib screw can deteriorate and should be replaced when a faucet is repaired. While the valve is out, examine the valve seat (see "Compression Faucet" on opposite page) by touch. If you feel any roughness, replace it (see "Replacing a Worn Valve Seat," page 34).

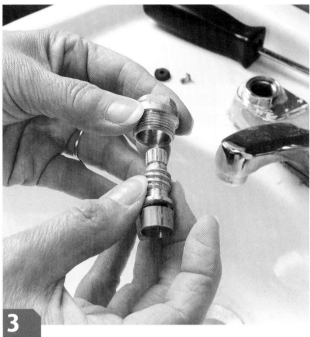

3

REMOVE THE STEM FROM THE RETAINING NUT

Inspect the threads for damage and replace the stem if necessary. You may need to special order a stem to match.

CLOSER LOOK

4

PEEL OFF (DON'T CUT) THE O-RING

Slip the O-ring from its groove and peel it from the housing. It's important to keep the ring whole so you can find an exact replacement at the store. Use the tip of a screwdriver to help release it if necessary. If you can't peel it off, pry it off with a screwdriver and cut the ring with a utility knife.

REMOVING A STUBBORN HANDLE

Not able to budge that old handle? A handy tool to remove corroded handles is a handle puller. Clamp the side extensions of the handle puller beneath the handle. Thread the puller into the faucet stem. Continue to tighten the puller until the handle is free.

Replacing a worn valve seat

PROJECT DETAILS

SKILLS: Connecting plumbing fittings
PROJECT: Replacing a worn compression valve seat

TIME TO COMPLETE

EXPERIENCED: 20 min.
HANDY: 40 min.
NOVICE: 1 hr.

STUFF YOU'LL NEED

TOOLS: Screwdriver, water-pump pliers, seat wrench, seat cutter
MATERIALS: Valve seat, silicone grease

REAL WORLD

FLUSH OUT THE FAUCET BODY
Resurfacing a valve seat is an easy job, but be mindful of the amount of debris that is ground off and possibly left inside the faucet body. There may be enough debris inside the faucet to ruin the washer that was just replaced. Flush the system before reassembling the faucet. Cover the hole with a rag and turn on the water gently to remove any debris or other gunk. This will result in a longer-lasting repair.

Only compression valves have valve seats. The seat is screwed into the faucet body. When repairing a compression valve, check to see if the valve seats need to be resurfaced. Poke your finger down into the faucet body to feel if the valve seat is rough. A rough seat will quickly damage a new washer. You should either replace or resurface the valve seat at the same time you are replacing the faucet washer.

1 TURN OFF THE WATER SUPPLY AND DISASSEMBLE THE FAUCET VALVE

Lower the sink stopper and cover it with a cloth so loose parts won't fall into the drain. Pry off the handle cap. Remove the handle with a screwdriver.

GOOD IDEA

WHILE YOU'RE AT IT...
If you're replacing one valve seat, you might as well do the other. And since you've already got the assembly apart, replace the washers, bib screws, and O-rings on the valves.

2 REMOVE THE VALVE

Loosen the compression valve with water-pump pliers and remove the valve. Keep any washers or O-rings with the valve and set it aside.

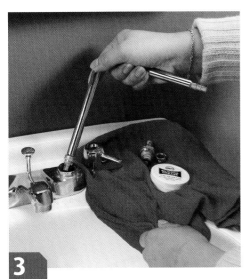

3

BACK OUT THE SEAT

Use a seat wrench to remove the valve seat. Select an end that will fit snugly into the seat. Insert the end of the wrench into the seat and tap the top to seat it firmly. The valve seat may be stuck, so the first turn should be quick and firm to release it without stripping the threads. Once it's loose, turn the wrench counterclockwise and remove it. Take the old seat to your local home center to be sure you replace it with the correct part.

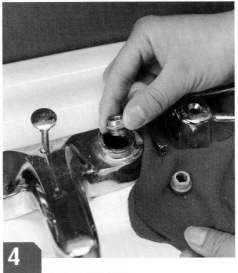

4

REPLACE THE SEAT

Install the new seat into the faucet. Insert the end of the seat wrench into the seat and set the seat in place. Screw the valve into place and tighten firmly. Assemble the compression valve, faucet handle, and handle cap. Turn on the water supply and check for leaks.

CLOSER LOOK

RESURFACING A WORN VALVE SEAT

Unable to remove the valve seat? You don't have to replace it. Worn valve seats can be resurfaced using a seat dressing tool (also called a seat grinder or seat cutter) that can be bought at a home center or hardware store. Follow the instructions that come with the specific tool you purchase. Generally, you should select a seat dressing tool that will fit snugly inside the retaining nut. Slide the valve retaining nut on the shaft of the seat dressing tool. Attach the locknut and cutter head to the shaft of the tool. Carefully screw the retaining nut into the faucet body. To resurface the seat, lightly press down on the handle while turning it clockwise two to three complete turns. This should be enough to resurface the seat. Remove the tool and inspect the seat by feeling it to make sure it's smooth. If smooth, reassemble the faucet.

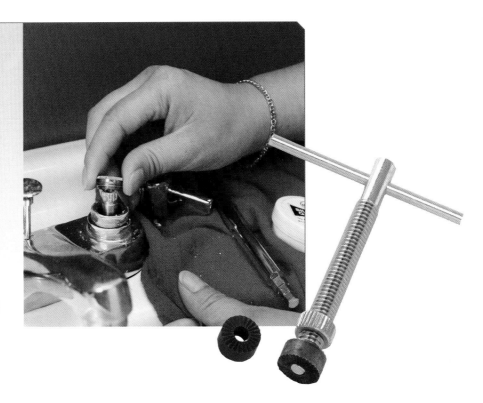

Repairing a cartridge tub and shower faucet

PROJECT DETAILS

SKILLS: Connecting plumbing fittings
PROJECT: Repairing a single-handle tub and shower faucet

TIME TO COMPLETE

EXPERIENCED: 30 min.
HANDY: 45+ min.
NOVICE: 1+ hr.

STUFF YOU'LL NEED

TOOLS: Screwdriver, strap wrench or taped water-pump pliers, adjustable wrench, small wire brush, plastic putty knife
MATERIALS: O-ring, silicone grease, replacement cartridge kit, silicone caulk

GOOD IDEA

DEBRIS IN SUPPLY LINE IS A BAD THING

It's a law of plumbing that dirt and gunk will find their way into any opening. Debris in your pipes can damage fixtures and cause blockages. Before you install a new faucet or fixture, turn on the water for a second to flush out the line. (You can cover the opening with your hand or a rag so you don't spray the room.)

It's also a good idea to flush the toilet or turn on an outside hose bib. This will also bleed the rest of the system of dirt and air.

Single-handle faucets for tubs can be of disk, cartridge, or rotary ball design. Whatever the style, one handle controls both the water flow and the temperature. To repair other types of single-handle tub and shower faucets, see pages 38–39. A diverter in the spout directs the flow of water to the spout or showerhead. The diverter gate seldom requires repair. When it does need repair, it's usually because the lever is not working properly—either it won't stay up or it's broken. Don't fix it; replace the spout. (See "Replacing a Tub Spout," page 45.)

In some cases, it's easier to replace the entire cartridge than it is to repair it, and cartridges often come with lifetime warranties. Check with your home center or the manufacturer.

Know the locations of the main shutoff valve or the supply valves for each fixture in your home.

1

TURN OFF THE HOT AND COLD WATER SUPPLY VALVES OR THE MAIN SHUTOFF AND REMOVE THE HANDLE
Pry off the handle cap. Remove the screw holding the handle in place. If there are screws holding the escutcheon cap in place, remove them as well.

2

SLIDE OFF THE ESCUTCHEON CAP
If the edge is sealed with caulking, pry off the escutcheon using a plastic putty knife. Clean the old caulking off the cap with the putty knife and set aside.

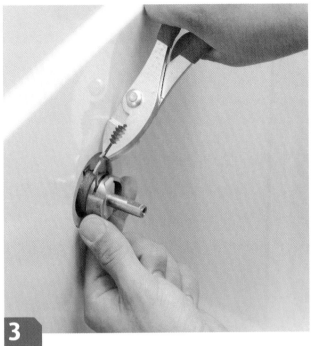

WORK SMARTER

SAVE THE TUBS!

PREVENT LOSING PARTS!

Don't assume that a screw or a small part can't slip through a screen or drain opening, or that a pair of water-pump pliers won't chip the surface of your tub. Work smarter by:

■ Protecting your tub from cracking or chipping by covering the surface with a piece of carpet, a blanket, or a towel.

■ Covering or blocking the drain opening with a rag or a piece of duct tape.

■ Closing any plunger-style drains and covering them with a screen.

3 REMOVE THE RETAINING CLIP

You can't get the cartridge out without first removing the retaining clip. Remove the sleeve, grip the clip end with a pair of pliers, and pull it out.

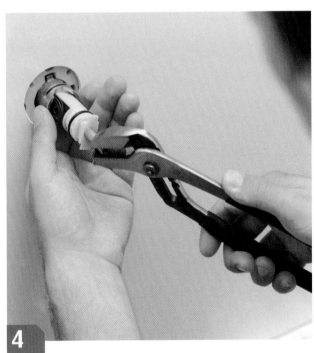

4 PULL THE CARTRIDGE STRAIGHT OUT

Grab the end of the faucet cartridge with a pair of pliers. Pull it straight out of the housing. If the cartridge gets stuck, apply white vinegar with a small brush to dissolve lime. Take the cartridge with you to your local home center so you can purchase an exact replacement, if needed.

5 REPLACE THE O-RING

Slide off the old O-ring. Coat the new O-ring with silicone grease. Install it on the cartridge. Reassemble and test the faucet. The hot feed should be on the left; if it isn't, you've reversed the cartridge. Disassemble the faucet and rotate the cartridge 180 degrees. Don't forget to recaulk the escutcheon plate.

Repairing a disk-type tub and shower faucet

PROJECT DETAILS

SKILLS: Connecting plumbing fittings
PROJECT: Repairing a disk-type tub and shower faucet

TIME TO COMPLETE

EXPERIENCED: 30 min.
HANDY: 45 min.
NOVICE: 1.5 hrs.

STUFF YOU'LL NEED

TOOLS: Screwdriver, taped water-pump pliers, adjustable wrench
MATERIALS: Repair kit for your model of faucet, silicone grease

This single-handle tub and shower faucet typically has a cylinder that holds two disks that contain a number of rubber seals.

If water flow is restricted, turn off the water, disassemble the faucet, then turn the water back on briefly to flush the system of debris. Also clean out any small particles you see in the disks. If the faucet leaks, replace the rubber seals and O-rings or replace the entire cylinder.

If leaks continue after replacing the parts, the entire cylinder will need to be replaced.

1

REMOVE THE CYLINDER

Shut off the water. Open the faucet and allow the water to drain out. Remove the handle and the escutcheon. To remove the cylinder that contains the disk, remove three screws and pull the cylinder out.

2

REPLACE O-RINGS

If you will not replace the entire cylinder, carefully pry out the O-rings. Take care not to nick the plastic housing.

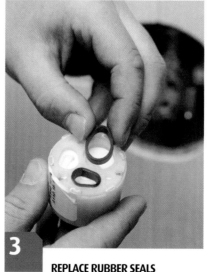

3

REPLACE RUBBER SEALS

Also remove any rubber seals. Clean the openings by running them under water and brushing with a toothbrush. Replace the seals with exact duplicates.

4

APPLY SILICONE GREASE

Rub a bit of silicone grease onto the rubber parts and reassemble the faucet. If leaks continue, replace the entire cylinder.

Repairing a ball tub and shower faucet

2

REPAIR AND MAINTENANCE

PROJECT DETAILS

SKILLS: Assembling plumbing fittings

PROJECT: Repairing a ball tub and shower faucet

TIME TO COMPLETE

EXPERIENCED: 20 min.

HANDY: 40 min.

NOVICE: 1 hr.

STUFF YOU'LL NEED

TOOLS: Screwdriver, water-pump pliers, adjustable wrench

MATERIALS: Repair kit for your model of faucet, silicone grease

L ike its sink counterpart (see pages 26–27), a tub and shower ball faucet contains a ball that has grooves through which water passes. Water flow is controlled by rubber seats, which are pressed against the ball with small springs.

Restricted water flow can often be solved by disassembling the faucet and flushing out the openings. If the faucet leaks, first try tightening the adjusting ring; your faucet may come with a special tool for this. If that does not solve the problem, you may need to replace rubber seats, springs, or the ball itself.

1

SHUT OFF THE WATER AND DISASSEMBLE

After shutting off the water, allow water to run until it stops. Unscrew and remove the handle and the escutcheon. You will first need to pry off a retaining clip and/or unscrew a retaining ring. Then pull out the cylinder.

2

FLUSH THE FAUCET

Slowly turn the water on and let it flow for a few seconds to flush out any debris. If you see lots of debris and the cylinder looks sound, reassemble and see if that solved the problem. If not, move on to the next step.

3

REPLACE THE RUBBER PARTS

Pry off all rubber parts and replace them with new parts that match exactly. Also replace the springs (a weak spring leads to imperfect seals). Rub a bit of silicone grease on the rubber parts.

4

REINSTALL AND ADJUST

Slip the cylinder back into place and reattach the retaining clip and/or the adjusting ring. Hand-tighten the adjusting ring and turn on the water to test. If the faucet leaks, tighten the ring further.

Repairing a two-handle cartridge tub and shower faucet

PROJECT DETAILS

SKILLS: Connecting plumbing fittings
PROJECT: Repairing a two-handle cartridge tub and shower faucet

TIME TO COMPLETE

EXPERIENCED: 20 min.
HANDY: 40 min.
NOVICE: 1 hr.

STUFF YOU'LL NEED

TOOLS: Screwdriver, plastic putty knife, shower stem socket kit, pliers, utility knife, flashlight, allen wrench (for set screws)
MATERIALS: O-ring, cartridge replacement kit, silicone grease, white vinegar or lime-dissolving solution

A two-handle tub and shower faucet has separate handles to control the water flow and the mixture of hot and cold water. One handle controls the flow of hot water, and the other controls the flow of cold water. The faucet can have either a compression or cartridge valve.

To divert the water flow from the spout to the showerhead, lift the lever for the diverter gate located on the spout. If the diverter gate doesn't work, replace the spout. (See "Replacing a Tub Spout," page 45.)

Replacing one cartridge? Replace them both; you'll save time and effort.

1
TURN OFF THE WATER SUPPLY AND REMOVE THE HANDLE
Pry off the handle cap. Use a screwdriver to remove the handle.

Know the locations of the main shutoff valve or the supply valves for each fixture in your home.

2
PRY OFF THE ESCUTCHEON
If there is caulking around the escutcheon, use a plastic putty knife to remove the caulk. Slide the escutcheon off the stem.

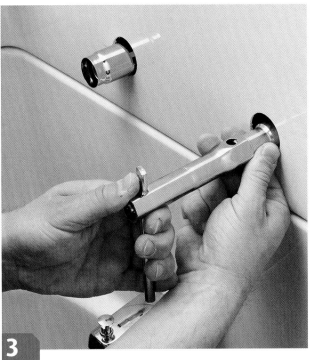

3
UNSCREW THE RETAINING NUT
Use a shower stem socket (available at home improvement centers and hardware stores) to remove the retaining nut.

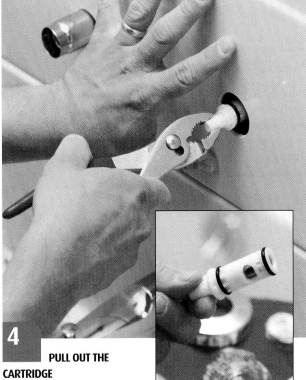

4
PULL OUT THE CARTRIDGE
Once the retaining nut is removed, grasp the end of the cartridge with a pair of pliers. Pull it straight out.

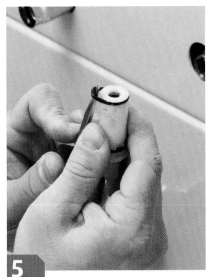

5
PEEL OFF (DON'T CUT) THE O-RING
Slip the O-ring from its groove and peel it from the housing. It's important to keep the ring whole so you can find an exact replacement at the store. Use the tip of a screwdriver to help release it if necessary. If you can't peel it off, pry it off with a screwdriver and cut the ring with a utility knife.

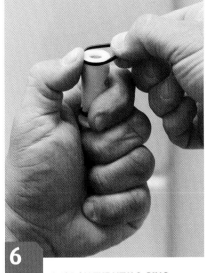

6
SLIDE ON THE NEW O-RING
Apply silicone grease to the new O-ring. Slide it over the cartridge, seating it into the O-ring groove.

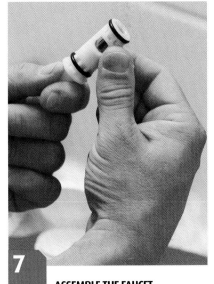

7
ASSEMBLE THE FAUCET
Turn on the water supply and test for leaks.

Repairing a three-handle tub and shower faucet

PROJECT DETAILS

SKILLS: Connecting plumbing fittings
PROJECT: Repairing a three-handle tub and shower faucet

TIME TO COMPLETE

EXPERIENCED: 50 min.
HANDY: 1.5 hrs.
NOVICE: 2 hrs.

STUFF YOU'LL NEED

TOOLS: Screwdriver, stem socket set, utility knife, water-pump pliers
MATERIALS: Compression replacement kit, silicone grease, white vinegar solution, toothbrush

A third or middle handle diverts the flow of the water from the spout to the showerhead. The diverter valve can be either a compression or cartridge type. Compression valves can be easily repaired. Cartridge valves that are worn or damaged will have to be replaced.

Separate handles control the water flow and the mixture of hot and cold water. As with the two-handle tub and shower faucet, the valves in the faucet can have either compression stems (as shown here) or cartridge valves. If you have cartridge valves, see pages 36–37 and 40–41.

Here we show repairing a diverter. If the faucet leaks, repair the stems in the same way. If washers wear out quickly, replace the seats as well (see pages 34–35).

The hot side is often the first to go so when pros do the job, they will repair or replace the hot, cold, and diverter while they have everything apart. You should too.

CLOSER LOOK

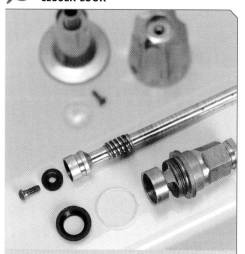

DIVERTERS USUALLY HAVE COMPRESSION FITTINGS
Parts for a compression diverter include the handle cap, handle, escutcheon, stem, bonnet nut, washers, and screws.

1 REMOVE THE HANDLE AND ESCUTCHEON CAP
Place a blanket in the tub to protect it from dropped tools. Shut off the water supply. Pry the cap off the diverter handle. Remove the screw with a screwdriver and slide off the handle. The escutcheon may just slide off, or you may have to unscrew it to remove it. If using water-pump pliers or a strap wrench to remove the escutcheon, wrap the jaws of the pliers with masking tape.

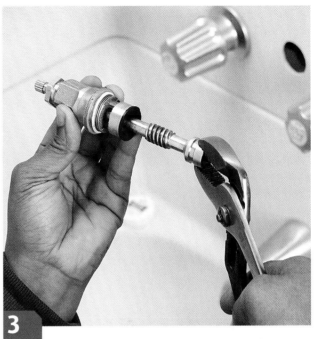

2

DISCONNECT THE BONNET NUT

Use a shower stem socket set to remove the bonnet nut and stem.

Know the locations of the main shutoff valve or the supply valves for each fixture in your home.

3

UNSCREW THE STEM FROM THE BONNET NUT

Hold the bonnet nut with one hand. Use your other hand to remove the stem from the bonnet nut with water-pump pliers. Inspect the threads of the stem for damage. If there is evidence of damaged threads, replace the stem. Check the valve seat with a flashlight to make sure it's OK. It may need resurfacing or replacement. (See "Replacing a Worn Valve Seat," pages 34–35.)

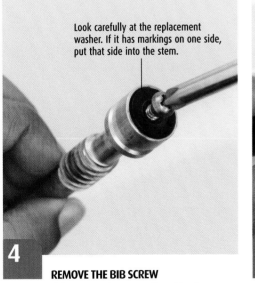

Look carefully at the replacement washer. If it has markings on one side, put that side into the stem.

4

REMOVE THE BIB SCREW

Clean mineral deposits on the stem with a white vinegar solution or buy a solution to dissolve mineral deposits at your local home center. A toothbrush easily removes deposits.

5

REPLACE THE OLD WASHER

Seat the new washer in the stem. Apply silicone grease to the washer so it seats properly. Replace the bib screw with a new one. Reassemble the faucet. Turn on the water supply and check for leaks and drips.

WORK SMARTER

TILE CAN BE TRICKY!
If your shower is finished in tile— especially in an older home— replacing faucets can be a little more difficult. That's because the controls may be set way back in the wall, so they are more difficult to reach. You may have to knock out enough tile to get the access you need to do the job. Replacing those tiles can become part of the project.

Tub and shower facelifts

PROJECT DETAILS

SKILLS: Assembling and disassembling plumbing parts
PROJECT: Replacing handles, escutcheons, and a drain cover

TIME TO COMPLETE

EXPERIENCED: 20 min.
HANDY: 40 min.
NOVICE: 1 hr.

STUFF YOU'LL NEED

TOOLS: Screwdriver, water-pump pliers, adjustable wrench
MATERIALS: Replacement parts (perhaps in a kit) for your shower, Teflon tape

G ot a dingy-looking shower? You can spruce it up without delving into the plumbing. First, consider retiling or adding an enclosure (see pages 201–211). You can also make the plumbing look brand-new by installing new finish parts, including handles, escutcheons, overflow flange, and drain flange. Buy parts that are made to fit your model of tub and shower faucet. In many cases, they come in an inexpensive kit.

You can also replace the showerhead. Just unscrew it, wrap the threads of the shower arm (the chrome pipe that comes out of the wall) with Teflon tape, and screw on another showerhead. To replace a spout, see the next page.

Seat · Stem · Escutcheon · Stop tube · Handle · Handle cap

HANDLE AND STEM PARTS

If you have an older two- or three-handle shower faucet, you can likely find a kit that includes not only an escutcheon and handle, but a stem and seat as well. Installing all these parts will give you a shower that both looks and feels brand new. To install a new stem and seat, see pages 36–42.

STEM EXTENDER

If the stem doesn't protrude far enough from the wall, the handle will not fit. (This often happens when a shower wall is tiled over, for instance.) Purchase a stem extender, which can be cut to the length you need. Or, you may be able to purchase a shallower type of handle.

FACE KIT

You can also buy face kits for various types of single-handle shower faucets. Some kits can fit faucets from several manufacturers.

TUB DRAIN KIT

Overflow covers and drain covers are usually easy to replace. However, sometimes the drain arms move a little when you take the old covers off, so be sure you can get at the plumbing from an access cover in an adjoining room (or closet) in case you need to have a helper hold the drain body still while you screw on the overflow or drain cover. Wrap the threads of the drain cover with Teflon tape before installing it.

Replacing a tub spout

PROJECT DETAILS

SKILLS: Simple mechanical skills
PROJECT: Replacing a tub spout

TIME TO COMPLETE

EXPERIENCED: 20 min.
HANDY: 40 min.
NOVICE: 1 hr.

STUFF YOU'LL NEED

TOOLS: Large screwdriver, water-pump pliers, hex (allen) wrench
MATERIALS: New spout, perhaps adapter parts, Teflon tape

Most modern spouts have diverters, but if the shower has a three-handle faucet, there will be no diverter. If the diverter has trouble staying up, or if you don't like the looks of your spout, replace it. A spout may be connected in one of three ways: via a setscrew underneath the spout to an unthreaded pipe; to a threaded pipe that protrudes 6 inches or so from the wall; or to a threaded pipe that barely protrudes from the wall.

If the diverter on your spout has trouble staying up or you don't like the way your spout looks, replace it.

REMOVING A SPOUT HELD BY A SETSCREW
Look under the spout to see if it is attached with a hex (allen) setscrew. If so, find a hex wrench that fits tightly. Loosen the setscrew and pull the spout out.

REMOVING A SCREWED-ON SPOUT
To unscrew a spout that is not held by a setscrew, use a large pair of water-pump pliers, or insert a large screwdriver (or a hammer handle, if it fits) and unscrew.

INSTALL A NEW SPOUT
Once the spout is off, measure the distance the pipe protrudes from the wall and buy another spout to fit. If the spout will be screwed onto a pipe, wrap Teflon tape around the pipe's threads. Screw on the spout by hand, then use a pair of taped water-pump pliers. Take care not to overtighten, or you may crack wall tiles. If the spout attaches with a setscrew, slip the spout in place and tighten the setscrew.

RETROFIT PARTS
If you have trouble finding a spout to fit an old setup, it may help to unscrew the pipe coming out from the wall and replace it with a shorter or longer length of threaded pipe. Or, purchase a spout with retrofit parts like those shown, which allow you to attach the spout to most any kind of pipe.

Adjusting a pop-up drain

PROJECT DETAILS

SKILLS: Using needle-nose pliers and connecting fittings
PROJECT: Adjusting a pop-up drain

TIME TO COMPLETE

EXPERIENCED: 20 min.
HANDY: 40 min.
NOVICE: 1 hr.

STUFF YOU'LL NEED

TOOLS: Needle-nose pliers, water-pump pliers, small wire brush
MATERIALS: Vinegar

Pop-up drain assembly

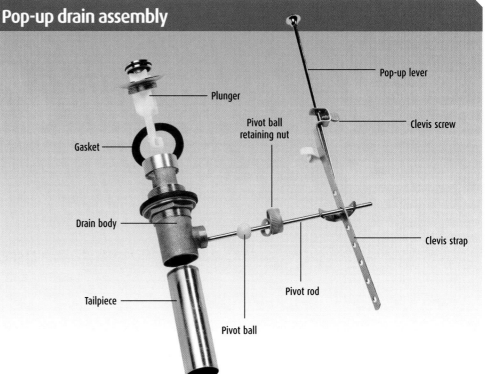

Plunger
Pop-up lever
Gasket
Pivot ball retaining nut
Clevis screw
Drain body
Clevis strap
Pivot rod
Tailpiece
Pivot ball

F our common problems occur with pop-up drains: The stopper won't lift out with the control, it won't remain in the closed or open position, the stopper doesn't hold water, or water leaks from the pivot ball. All are easy to fix:

■ **Stopper won't stay open or closed.** Tighten the pivot ball nut with water-pump pliers until the stopper maintains either an open or a closed position.

■ **Water leaks from pivot.** Unscrew the pivot ball retaining nut with water-pump pliers. Remove the pivot rod, ball, and gasket. Replace the gasket and reassemble.
■ **Stopper won't lift out.** (Below left)
■ **Stopper won't hold water.** (Below right)

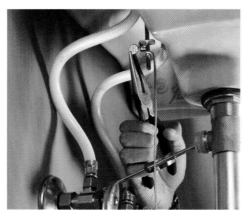

ADJUST THE STOPPER WITH NEEDLE-NOSE PLIERS
To adjust a stopper that won't lift, loosen the clevis screw and pull the strap down an inch or two. Tighten the setscrew and test. You may need to readjust.

REMOVE THE PIVOT BALL RETAINING NUT
If the stopper won't hold water, pull out the rod and lift out the stopper. Clean the rubber seal by soaking it in vinegar and scrubbing with a small wire brush. Insert the stopper. Engage the pivot rod and replace the nut.

Faucets

Chapter 3 highlights

Today's sink faucets are easy to install. Connections are simple, as long as you have the right parts. You will likely find that the biggest challenges are removing the old sink and working in a tight space. So remove all obstructions, place tools where they will be easy to reach (or have a helper ready to hand you tools), and make the work space as comfortable and well-lit as possible.

In addition to several types of faucets, this chapter also shows how to install a kitchen sink strainer, new stop valves, and a hand-held shower unit.

Faucet options

3

FAUCETS

When you purchase a faucet, you get exactly what you pay for, so get the best you can afford. Purchase products and materials from businesses that back what they sell with good service and have a clear return policy in case problems arise. They have a presence in the community and a reputation to maintain. Older hardware stores and secondhand shops are potential sources of antique fixtures. Consider places that sell discontinued items, but keep in mind that it may be very difficult, if not impossible, to find replacement parts. Check sales and comparison shop; high- and medium-level fixtures can often be found at low prices.

So many styles, but...

There are so many styles, finishes, and features to choose from that finding a match for your decorating tastes and functional needs is easy. Finishes vary. Chrome is popular because it is durable and easy to clean. New techniques in metallurgy have created brass finishes that are durable and easy to clean. Satin-nickel has gained in popularity because of its warm, soft color.

The faucet still has to fit the sink

Regardless of how much you may love the style of a faucet, it still needs to fit your sink. Measure the distance between the tailpieces to determine the correct faucet size. Bathroom faucets are 4 to 12 inches apart on center. The spacing will vary for kitchen sinks by the number of holes in the sink. Three- and four-hole sinks are the most common. Some sinks offer only one hole for a single-control faucet and as many as five for accessories, such as a hot-water dispenser, water filter, or soap dispenser.

Popular faucet styles

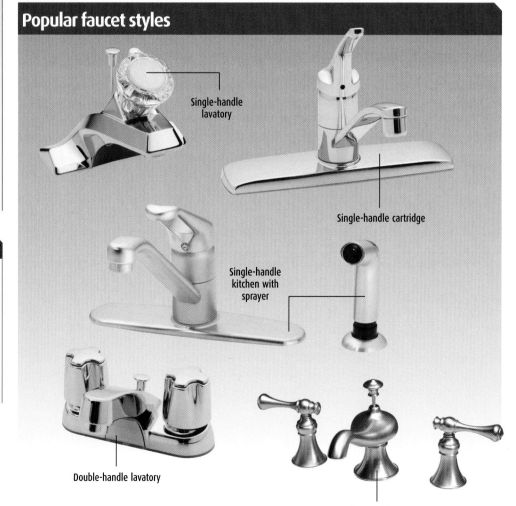

Single-handle lavatory

Single-handle cartridge

Single-handle kitchen with sprayer

Double-handle lavatory

Widespread lavatory

Faucet mounting options

In most cases a kitchen faucet will fit a kitchen sink, and a bathroom faucet will fit a bathroom sink. However, pay attention to the details to minimize repeat visits to your home center for parts. The new faucet may have inlets of a different width or length from the old faucet, which may mean you will need to buy new supply tubes. See page 50 for supply tube options. When you install a bathroom faucet, you will likely also replace the drain body and pop-up assembly, which typically come with the faucet.

TWO-HANDLE KITCHEN FAUCET

This is often the least expensive option for a kitchen faucet. There are separate inlets for the hot and cold lines. A disadvantage of this faucet type is that you cannot install the supply tubes prior to installing the faucet (when it is easiest). You must first tighten a mounting nut at each inlet, then screw on the supply tubes while working from below.

SINGLE-HANDLE "ONE-TOUCH" KITCHEN FAUCET

Most single-handle faucets allow you to install the supply tubes before mounting the faucet. There may be a mounting nut at both of the side holes, or the unit may mount via a large washer and nut at the center hole only.

BATHROOM FAUCET WITH POP-UP ASSEMBLY

A bathroom faucet nearly always has a pop-up assembly, which looks complicated but should take less than half an hour to install. Sometimes called a lav faucet, for lavatory, look to purchase one with a metal ball, which will last longer than a plastic ball.

Supply tubes

The connection between a stop valve and a faucet or toilet is nearly always made using a flexible supply tube, sometimes called a supply riser. A flexible supply tube is much easier to install and easier to dismantle than hard pipes.

You have a choice of materials. In older installations, these tubes are made of copper tubing that is usually chrome-plated. Copper tubing takes patience and a little skill to bend, and it must be cut to length (see below). If the end has a bulbous shape, connect to the valve or the faucet inlet using a nut only. If there is no bulbous end, you will also need to slip on a special copper or plastic ring called a ferrule. Plastic supply tubes install in the same way, but are easier to bend and cut.

Newer installations often use tubes that are more flexible and simple to connect. Braided plastic and braided stainless-steel supply tubes have integral nuts, so you just screw the nut onto the valve or faucet inlet. Braided stainless steel costs more but looks best; and in some locales, braided plastic is not allowed by code.

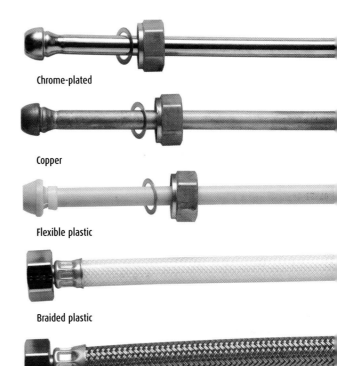

Chrome-plated

Copper

Flexible plastic

Braided plastic

Braided stainless steel

 **CLOSER LOOK**

GETTING THE SIZES RIGHT
It is best to buy supply tubes that are longer than you think you need, because they usually have to make a bend or two. Make sure the nuts on one end will fit the faucet inlets (typically ½ inch) or toilet inlet (typically ⅜ inch), and that the other nut will fit the stop valve—which may be either ½ or ⅜ inch.

INSTALLING SOLID TUBING
Many people like the look of solid tubing. Installing it will take a bit more time and patience than installing a braided tube. Install onto the sink or toilet inlet first. Bend the tubing very gently; if you kink it, you will have to discard it and start with a new tube. It helps to use a coil spring tubing bender (see page 16). Cut using a tubing cutter; a hacksaw will likely squash the tubing out of round, and it will not work. Slide on the nut, then the ferrule. Insert the tubing into the stop valve, slip the ferrule down, and tighten the nut.

Replacing a kitchen faucet and sprayer

WORK SMARTER

USE THE RIGHT PIPE SEALANT

When you're using a pipe or thread sealant like silicone, pipe compound, Teflon tape, or plumber's putty, read the label to make sure it's compatible with the materials in the sink or fixtures. Plumber's putty, for instance, will dissolve plastic parts and rubber fittings and discolor cultured marble sinks.

Living with a faucet that drips or constantly leaks is bad for the environment, your pocketbook; and, on top of that, it's annoying. Wear and tear or a kitchen remodel can prompt a faucet replacement. Anyone can replace a faucet and sink sprayer. The difficult part of the job often is removing the old fixtures. Corrosion can stiffen connections, and working under a sink isn't exactly convenient.

Choose the new fixtures

Kitchen faucet-sprayer systems come in many types and styles. Just make sure you select one that will fit your sink. Measure the distance between the centers of the sink openings, then measure the diameters of the openings.

Prepare the work area

Here's how to get ready to go to work:

- Purchase all the fixtures and gather all the tools you'll need for the job. Lay them out near the installation so you don't have to keep looking for what you need instead of staying on the job.
- Clear all the detergents, rags, and kitchen gear from the cabinet. Get under the sink with a flashlight and inspect the job site.
- Turn off the hot and cold water supply lines at the shutoff valves beneath the sink. If there are no shutoff valves, you'll need to turn off the main water supply. Install stop valves as part of this project (see pages 61–62).
- Place a bucket, pan, or rags below the work area. Even with the water off, there will be some water in the lines.
- Make the job site comfortable—or at least, less uncomfortable. Position heavy towels so the cabinet will not dig into your back as you work.

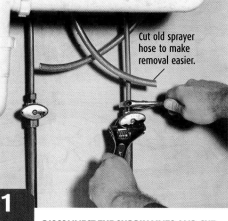

Cut old sprayer hose to make removal easier.

1

DISCONNECT THE SUPPLY LINES AND CUT THE SPRAYER HOSE

Turn off the water. Disconnect the hot and cold supply lines using two adjustable wrenches. If you're replacing the sprayer hose, save a little time by cutting it with a utility knife, so that you only have to disconnect it from the faucet body.

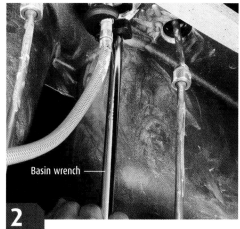

Basin wrench

2

REMOVE THE RETAINING NUTS WITH A BASIN WRENCH

Getting to the tailpiece nuts can be tricky. A basin wrench will take a little practice, but it allows easier access. Lift out the faucet body and clean up old putty from the sink. If the old sprayer flange base is OK, leave it alone. If you're replacing it, run a bead of silicone caulk around the base and seat it in its hole in the sink. Thread the new sprayer and hose into the sink.

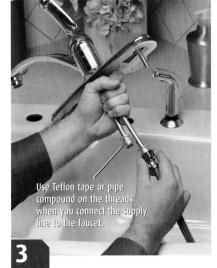

Use Teflon tape or pipe compound on the threads when you connect the supply line to the faucet.

3 ATTACH THE SUPPLY LINES TO THE FAUCET BODY

It's much easier to work above the sink than below it, so plumbers will attach anything they can before they install the faucet. Label the hot and cold supply lines so you won't have to guess which is which when you're hooking them up underneath the sink. If manufacturer's instructions recommend it, put a bead of plumber's putty on the faucet base before you thread the supply lines into the hole.

4 SEAT THE FAUCET BODY ON THE SINK

Press the faucet body into the plumber's putty to seat it. Square the faucet on the sink before you go underneath to attach it. Have a helper check the faucet for straightness while you work.

TOOL SAVVY

WHY BASIN WRENCHES ARE COOL

After a few bruised knuckles, you'll learn why a basin wrench is the right tool for working with those pesky tailpiece nuts. Unlike an ordinary adjustable wrench, there's an extension that allows you to reach up into tight places. The head swivels to tighten or loosen nuts, and the jaws are self-ratcheting, so they will automatically tighten around the nuts. The right tool makes all the difference and helps avoid cuts and bruises. Basin wrenches with extensions for more flexibility and reach are also on the market.

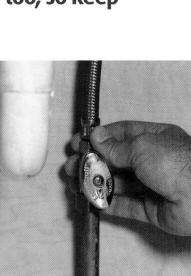

Feeling for leaks often isn't enough; you must look for them, too, so keep a flashlight handy.

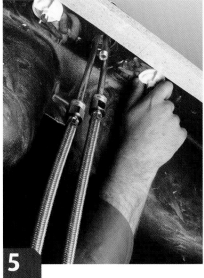

5 ATTACH THE FAUCET TO THE SINK AND CONNECT THE SPRAYER HOSE

Use the hardware that came with your faucet to attach the faucet to the bottom of the sink.

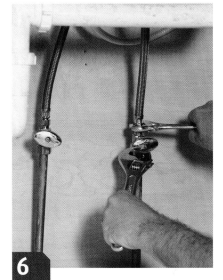

6 ATTACH THE HOT AND COLD SUPPLY LINES

Use two adjustable wrenches to attach the hot and cold supply lines to the correct compression fittings. Connect the sprayer hose to its nipple. Make sure you don't tangle the sprayer hose in the supply lines, or it won't extend to its entire length.

7 TURN ON THE WATER AND CHECK FOR LEAKS

Turn on the water and test the system for leaks by visually examining and feeling all the connections. Clean up any excess putty around the base of the faucet.

Installing a center-set faucet

PROJECT DETAILS

SKILLS: Connecting plumbing fittings
PROJECT: Installing a center-set faucet

TIME TO COMPLETE

EXPERIENCED: 20 min.
HANDY: 40 min.
NOVICE: 1 hr.

STUFF YOU'LL NEED

TOOLS: Putty knife, adjustable wrenches, basin wrench
MATERIALS: Center-set faucet, gaskets, plumber's putty or silicone caulk

Manufacturers are supplying center-set faucets in styles and colors to meet even the most discriminating decorating tastes and needs. Many finish types are available. The old standby of chrome is popular because of its durability and ease of maintenance. Porcelain finishes have gained popularity. Polished brass and satin-nickel are also available.

Before you choose a center-set faucet, measure the distance between the tailpieces of the one you are replacing. Faucets are 4 inches on center up to 12 inches on center. Purchase one that will fit the opening in your sink.

3

FAUCETS

Take your time when selecting a new faucet. And don't compromise quality. A new installation will provide years of service.

WORK SMARTER

OUT WITH THE OLD IS THE HARDEST PART
As opposed to other home improvement jobs, such as installing cabinets or hanging doors, the hardest part of almost any plumbing job is usually removing the old stuff. Corrosion and inaccessibility can make taking out an old faucet a real pain-in-the-neck. Give yourself extra time to remove old fixtures—it will save on frustration and bruised knuckles.

1 **SEAL AROUND THE LAVATORY OPENINGS WITH PLUMBER'S PUTTY OR SILICONE CAULK**
Apply a bead of plumber's putty or silicone caulk around the faucet openings.

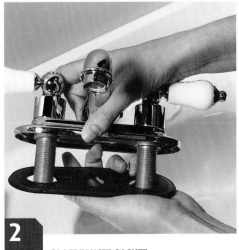

2 **PLACE FAUCET GASKET**
Slide the gasket over the tailpieces so that it is between the sink and the base of the faucet.

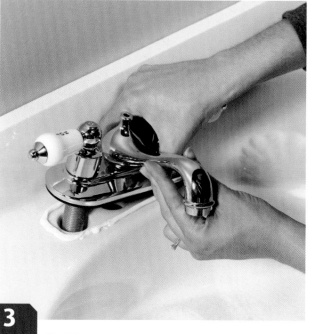

3

SET THE FAUCET

The valves should fit into the hole spacing in the sink. If they don't, you purchased the wrong set, and you'll need to return it.

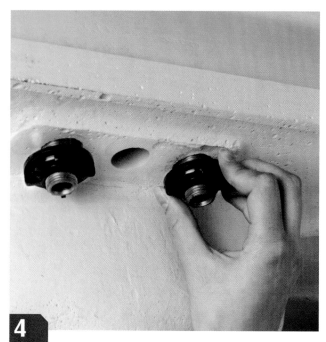

4

HAND-TIGHTEN THE BASIN NUTS

Thread each, alternating from one nut to the other to draw the faucet body evenly over the gasket. Don't tighten all the way.

Don't use plumber's putty on cultured marble or other composite sinks. Putty will discolor the sink. Use silicone caulk instead.

5

CENTER THE FAUCET BODY

Measure or visually center the faucet body on the lavatory.

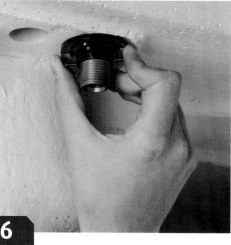

6

HAND-TIGHTEN THE BASIN NUTS UNTIL THEY'RE SNUG

Install the pop-up drain. (See "Installing a Pop-Up Drain," page 57.) Connect the water supply lines, turn on the water, and test for leaks.

 **REAL WORLD**

INSTALL FAUCETS AND DRAIN FITTINGS BEFORE YOU SET THE SINK

Depending on the size of the space, installing a sink can sometimes be a tight fit. To avoid any unwanted grief, install the faucets and as much of the water and drain piping as possible prior to setting the sink into the counter.

Installing a widespread faucet

PROJECT DETAILS

SKILLS: Connecting plumbing fittings
PROJECT: Installing a widespread faucet

TIME TO COMPLETE

EXPERIENCED: 20 min.
HANDY: 40 min.
NOVICE: 1 hr.

STUFF YOU'LL NEED

TOOLS: Plastic putty knife, adjustable wrenches, basin wrench
MATERIALS: Widespread faucet, gaskets, pipe compound or Teflon tape, plumber's putty

Some widespread faucets fit only sinks with holes that are a prescribed distance apart. Others, like the one shown here, can be installed with most any hole spacing.

Seize the moment

Don't wait until your old faucet fails to replace it. If you're ready for a change, that's reason enough to tackle this project. The good news is that installing a new faucet isn't a difficult job.

After you've installed the faucet, install the pop-up drain. See "Installing a Pop-up Drain" on page 57.

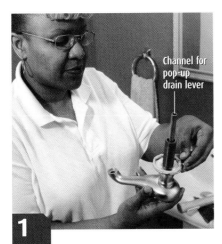

Channel for pop-up drain lever

1 SEAL THE SPOUT BASE

Form plumber's putty into a rope and place it on the base of the spout. Press the putty against the base. Set the spout into place.

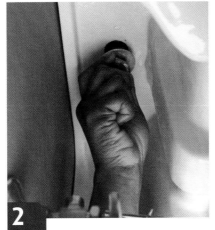

2 HAND-TIGHTEN THE BASIN NUT

Tighten the nut just enough to hold it in place. Don't overtighten, because you will need to center the spout on the sink in step 4.

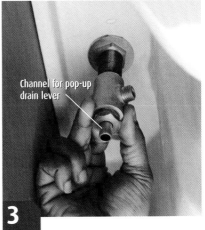

Channel for pop-up drain lever

3 THREAD THE TEE ON THE SPOUT

Center the tee so the outlets are approximately parallel to the back wall and line up with the faucets on either side. See step 7.

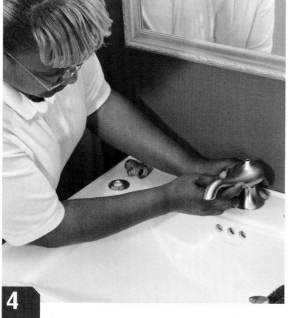

4 CENTER THE SPOUT

Once it's centered, tighten the spout from beneath the sink using a basin wrench.

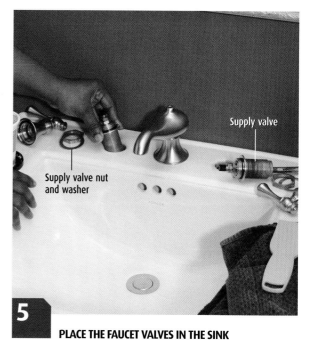

Supply valve

Supply valve nut and washer

5 PLACE THE FAUCET VALVES IN THE SINK

Slide the washer over the threads from beneath the sink. Tighten the valve nut until snug.

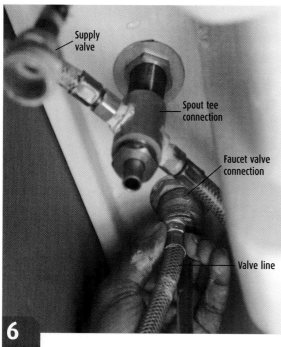

Supply valve

Spout tee connection

Faucet valve connection

Valve line

6 CONNECT THE FAUCET VALVE LINES TO THE FAUCET VALVE

Apply pipe compound or Teflon tape to the threads of the valve line, connect to the faucet valve, and hand-tighten. Apply pipe compound or Teflon tape to the other end of the valve line and hand-tighten onto the spout tee.

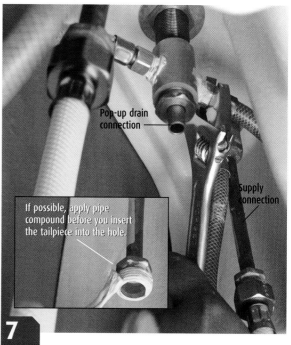

Pop-up drain connection

Supply connection

If possible, apply pipe compound before you insert the tailpiece into the hole.

7 FINISH THE ASSEMBLY AND TIGHTEN THE CONNECTIONS

Apply pipe compound or Teflon tape to the threads of the water supply tailpieces (see inset) and connect the hot and cold water supplies to the hot and cold supply valves. When the entire assembly is complete, go back and tighten all the connections with an adjustable wrench. The last step is to connect the faucet handles to the valves. Apply a bead of plumber's putty to the faucet handle base, attach the handle, center it, and tighten the faucet nut below the sink with a basin wrench. Turn on the system and check for leaks.

3

FAUCETS

Installing a pop-up drain

PROJECT DETAILS

SKILLS: Connecting plumbing fittings
PROJECT: Installing a pop-up drain

TIME TO COMPLETE

EXPERIENCED: 20 min.
HANDY: 40 min.
NOVICE: 1 hr.

STUFF YOU'LL NEED

TOOLS: Water-pump pliers, plastic putty knife
MATERIALS: Pop-up drain kit, plumber's putty, Teflon tape, silicone caulk, rag, 2×4 support

1 APPLY PLUMBER'S PUTTY
If the sink is not supported with a cabinet, use a 2×4 to support it while you're working. Cover the bottom of the flange with a rope of putty.

2 THREAD THE LOCKNUT ONTO THE DRAIN BODY
Add the friction washer and beveled gasket.

Unless your faucet can accept a pop-up drain, you will have to replace the fixture to get the convenience of a pop-up stopper.

3 INSTALL THE DRAIN BODY
Push the drain body up through the lavatory hole from underneath. Place a rope of putty under the drain flange, insert it into the hole from above, and screw it onto the drain body.

4 TIGHTEN THE LOCKNUT
Hold the drain body still while you tighten the locknut, first by hand and then with water-pump pliers.

3

FAUCETS

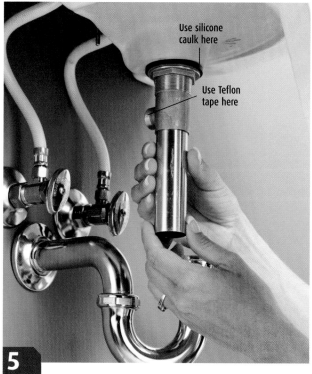

Use silicone caulk here

Use Teflon tape here

5

TURN THE DRAIN BODY TO THE REAR

This will line it up with the pop-up linkage. Apply silicone caulk at the drain and Teflon tape at the extension piece to seal the drain tube. Inside the sink, remove any excess putty with a plastic putty knife.

6

INSTALL THE DRAIN PLUNGER

Slide the plunger into the drain opening.

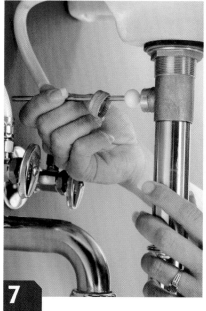

7

INSERT THE BALL INTO THE OPENING

The ball should fit snugly into the opening in the drain tailpiece.

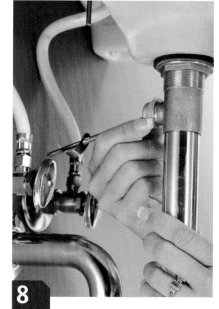

8

THREAD THE BALL NUT HAND-TIGHT

Slide the ball nut over the arm and screw it onto the threads of the drain tailpiece.

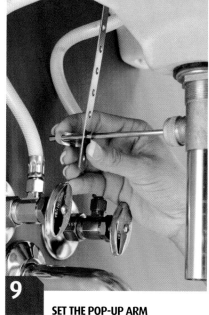

9

SET THE POP-UP ARM

Slide the arm through the nearest hole in the lever strap and fasten it with a clip. Connect the P-trap (see pages 149–150). Test the pop-up drain. Adjust the arm, if necessary (see page 46).

Repairing or replacing a sink strainer

The sink strainer assembly connects the sink to the drain line. To fix a leak, you'll need to take it all apart. Remove and clean the sink strainer basket, then replace any worn washers and gaskets. If the seal where the strainer basket meets the lip of the drain line was not properly installed, it may leak.

Repairing does not mean replacing every part. If you don't mind reusing old parts, don't replace them. The sink drain body may be usable even though it may not shine like a new one; reuse it or any of the metal parts. The drain locknut can be reused because it is hidden below the sink. The only parts you should not reuse are washers and gaskets; they may not provide a proper seal. Besides, they are the least expensive parts to replace.

1

GIVE YOURSELF ROOM TO WORK
Inspect the area below the sink and remove any obstacles.

Sink strainer assembly

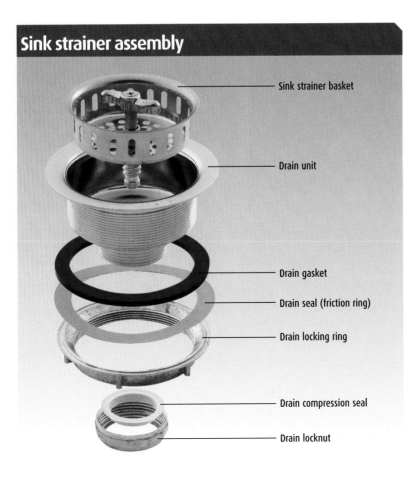

- Sink strainer basket
- Drain unit
- Drain gasket
- Drain seal (friction ring)
- Drain locking ring
- Drain compression seal
- Drain locknut

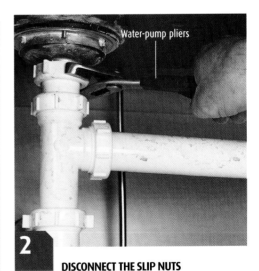

Water-pump pliers

2

DISCONNECT THE SLIP NUTS
Use water-pump pliers to loosen the slip nuts and slide them out of the way. Remove the tailpiece.

WORK SMARTER

DIFFICULT NUT TO CRACK
You may find the locking nut is very difficult to loosen. If all else fails, cut a groove in the nut at about a 30-degree angle with a mini hacksaw. Insert a screwdriver into the groove and twist or tap with a hammer until the nut breaks off.

GOOD IDEA

CAREFUL WHEN TIGHTENING
Even experienced plumbers sometimes break plastic fittings. That final turn with the pliers may seem like a good idea, but it can result in a cracked fitting and a trip to the home center. Tighten all fittings hand-tight, then a quarter-turn at a time with the pliers until the leaking stops.

Basket strainer wrench

3

UNSCREW THE LOCKING NUT
Use a basket strainer wrench to remove the sink strainer assembly locknut. If the locknut will not budge, tap on the lug with a hammer and screwdriver to loosen it.

4

SCRAPE OFF THE OLD PUTTY WITH A PLASTIC PUTTY KNIFE
If you reuse the old strainer, remove any old putty under the flange. Do not reuse old gaskets and washers. Replace them with new ones.

Plumber's putty

5

COAT THE FLANGE
Apply a bead of plumber's putty to the underside of the drain flange. Insert the drain unit into the sink. Insert the handles of pliers into the drain flange and have a helper hold it still while you assemble the strainer from below.

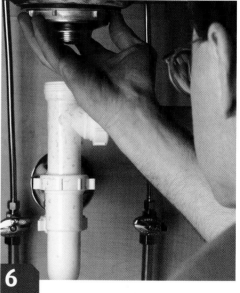

6

REASSEMBLE THE STRAINER
Install a new rubber gasket and friction ring. Hand-tighten the new locknut. Connect the tailpiece to the assembly body with slip nuts. Test with running water. Tighten the nuts if you see any leaks.

FAUCETS

3

Installing shutoff valves

PROJECT DETAILS

SKILLS: Connecting plumbing fittings
PROJECT: Installing valve stops and shutoffs

TIME TO COMPLETE

EXPERIENCED: 20 min.
HANDY: 40 min.
NOVICE: 1 hr.

STUFF YOU'LL NEED

TOOLS: Mini hacksaw or tubing cutter, two adjustable wrenches, emery cloth
MATERIALS: Compression valve, compression fittings

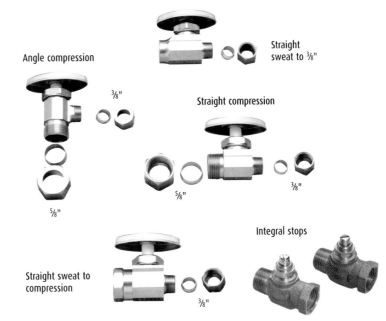

Angle compression

Straight sweat to ⅜"

Straight compression

Straight sweat to compression

Integral stops

⅜"

⅝"

⅝"

⅜"

⅜"

To buy the right size fittings, you need to know the size of the pipe. See "Rigid Supply Pipes," page 164.

ixture shutoff valves, also called stop valves, are fitted in several different ways: by soldering, threading, or compression. Compression fittings come in a variety of combinations that will give you options for connecting supply lines. They will also give you control of the water supply near your fixtures, so you don't have to go to the basement every time you need to make a repair. Compression fittings are easy to install and don't require pipe dope or compound—a compression ring makes the fitting watertight—as long as they are properly installed.

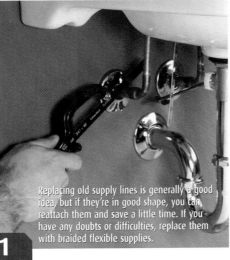

Replacing old supply lines is generally a good idea, but if they're in good shape, you can reattach them and save a little time. If you have any doubts or difficulties, replace them with braided flexible supplies.

1

CUT THE SUPPLY PIPE

Turn off the main water supply valve. Open the faucets to drain the line. A tubing cutter makes a truer cut, but you can also use a mini hacksaw if the cutter won't fit. Leave enough room between the escutcheon plate and the cut to allow installation of the fitting. Cut slowly and gently. If it's out of round, the copper won't accept the compression fitting and will leak.

2

SLIDE THE COMPRESSION NUT OVER THE SUPPLY PIPE

Deburr the pipe with emery cloth (see inset). Slide the nut as far back on the pipe as possible to give yourself room to work.

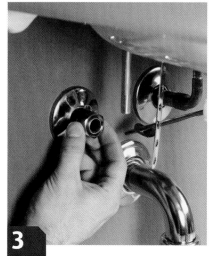

3

PLACE THE COMPRESSION RING OVER THE END OF THE SUPPLY PIPE
The ring, also called a ferrule, should completely cover the end of the supply pipe.

GOOD IDEA

SEAL THE JOINTS
If the supply pipe is galvanized steel, it will be threaded. In that case, you can install a regular threaded stop valve using Teflon tape or pipe compound to seal the joints.

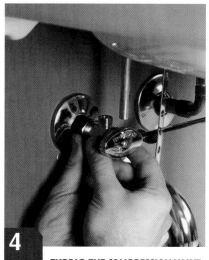

4

THREAD THE COMPRESSION VALVE INTO THE COMPRESSION NUT
The valve should slide squarely and snugly over the ring. Thread the compression valve onto the nut and hand-tighten. If the nut doesn't turn easily, add a tiny drop of oil to the threads. **Don't use pipe compound; the fitting doesn't require it, and it can actually make the fitting leak.**

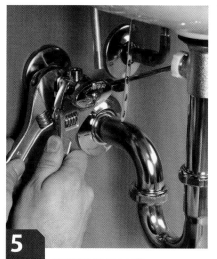

5

TIGHTEN (BUT DON'T OVERTIGHTEN) THE COMPRESSION VALVE TO THE NUT
Finish tightening the nut using one wrench to hold back the valve and keep it square and another one to turn the nut. Connect the other side in the same manner.

Just because you don't recognize a fitting or pipe doesn't mean you can't find out what it is and work with it.

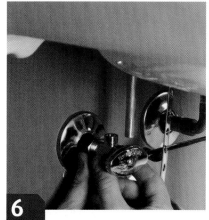

6

ATTACH THE SUPPLY LINES TO THE VALVE
See page 50 for supply tube options. If you are reattaching the old lines to the new valve, follow the same procedure you used to install the valve. If you are replacing the old supplies with new braided flexible lines, you will have to remove the old supplies from the faucets before you proceed.

7

TURN ON THE MAIN WATER SUPPLY VALVE
Turn on the main and open the supply valves. (See step 1.) Let the water flow through the faucet to clear air in the line, and test the fittings for leaks by feeling the fittings and examining them with a flashlight. Tighten as necessary until the joints are sealed.

OLD vs. NEW

REAL-WORLD SITUATIONS
In a new installation, you call the shots—everything fits easily because it's made to order. That isn't always the case when you're replacing parts or adding to an existing system. And, for reasons of aesthetics or design, you may choose to keep some of the original parts.

You may find that the supply pipe coming from the wall is copper, galvanized, CPVC, or PEX, all of which require different fittings.

In some cases, you may not have enough room for the new supply stops after you've cut away the old elbow. If the supply pipe is too short to take the fitting, you might need to knock away some wall to solder an extension on the supply pipe, or replace the supply line entirely.

Installing a hand-held shower unit

PROJECT DETAILS

SKILLS: Assembling parts and drilling holes
PROJECT: Installing a hand-held shower unit with spout

TIME TO COMPLETE

EXPERIENCED: 30 min.
HANDY: 45 min.
NOVICE: 1.5 hrs.

STUFF YOU'LL NEED

TOOLS: Drill, screwdriver, water-pump pliers, pipe wrench, hammer
MATERIALS: Hand-held shower unit with spout and mounting screws, Teflon tape

I f your tub has a spout but no shower, purchase a hand-held shower kit, which may be called a flex-line unit. If you have a shower but want to add the convenience of a hand-held unit (it works great for shampooing a child's hair), install the flexible unit shown at bottom right. If you install a unit like this on a clawfoot tub, or if the walls are not protected with tiles or other waterproof material, take steps to protect the walls with a shower curtain or new wall treatment.

Be sure that your walls are properly protected before installing a hand-held shower unit.

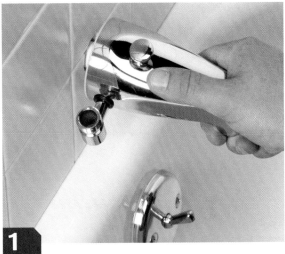

1 SCREW ON A DIVERTER SPOUT

See page 45 for instructions on removing and installing a new spout. You may need to remove the pipe coming from the wall and replace it with a shorter pipe. If you do so, wrap the pipe end with Teflon tape and screw it on tight using pliers and a pipe wrench. Wrap the other pipe threads with Teflon tape and screw on the spout.

2 DRILL HOLES FOR THE MOUNTING BRACKET

Hold the shower bracket where you want it to go and mark for the screw locations. Drill holes for the plastic anchors. If you are drilling through ceramic tile, first nick the surface with a hammer and nail, then drill using a masonry or tile bit.

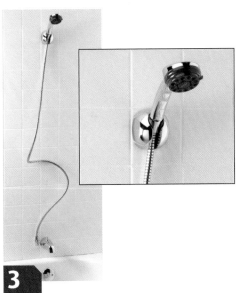

3 ATTACH THE BRACKET AND THE SHOWER LINE

Tap plastic anchors into the holes and attach the mounting bracket with the screws provided. Snap on the bracket cover. Screw the flex line to the top of the spout and to the showerhead and set the showerhead in the bracket.

BUYER'S GUIDE

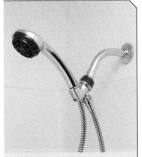

HAND-HELD UNIT FOR AN EXISTING SHOWER

To replace an existing showerhead with a hand-held flexible showerhead, remove the old showerhead. Wrap the shower arm with Teflon tape and twist on the plastic shower bracket. Tighten with water-pump pliers, but don't over-tighten. Connect the showerhead's flex line to the outlet on the plastic bracket.

Dealing with clogs

Stopped or slow-moving drains are seldom the result of collapsed or defective pipes. Blockage caused by the accumulation of solid waste in the lines, such as small objects, hair, or clumps of soap and grease, is usually the culprit.

Isolating the problem

If one fixture seems to be draining slowly or not at all, first check to see if other fixtures are having the same problem. If only one fixture is affected, the drain line to the fixture is likely the problem. If two or more fixtures are affected, the clog may be in the branch line, the main line, or the vent stack. If more than one fixture is affected and they are all on the second level of the house, the blockage may be high in the main line or in a vent stack. Isolating the affected area will help you decide how to clean out the line.

Drain lines are fragile

Drain lines are more fragile than you might expect, especially because of all the fixtures attached to them. Be careful when using chemicals and augering—some chemicals can weaken the walls of the drain lines, and augers can shatter porcelain fixtures. Try using a plunger first. If that doesn't work, move on to snakes and augers, but work carefully and slowly.

Household drain-cleaning tools

CLOG REMOVERS

There is a tool solution for almost every clogged drain you'll encounter, including A Common household plunger, B Pressure plunger, C Closet auger for toilets (won't damage porcelain), D Hand snake, E Power drill auger attachment, and F Hand spinner.

Use the right auger for the right job. It's easy to damage pipes or scratch fixtures.

📖 WORK SMARTER

PREVENTION IS GOOD

The only fixture or appliance that is designed to handle solid waste is the toilet. Use preventive measures to avoid clogs and try to keep solid matter out of drain lines.

1 Don't put dental floss, sanitary napkins, or paper towels down the toilet.

2 Hair and food clogs can be very difficult to clear. Clean tubs and sinks regularly.

3 Don't make the mistake of pouring grease down the drain unless you have a grease trap.

4 Disposers grind food into a paste that can collect in the drain line and eventually form a clog. Keep oily or dense matter out of the disposer and flush the lines thoroughly with cold water after each use.

5 A capful of bleach in the drain lines once a week will help keep them odor free.

🚫 SAFETY ALERT

Safety First. Waste lines are sources of biohazards and other potential health risks. Avoid contact with any solids or fluids from drain, waste, or vent lines.

■ Always tell a plumber if you've used a chemical drain cleaner in lines that will be worked on.

■ Wear safety goggles to protect your eyes from splashes.

■ Wear rubber gloves, a long-sleeve shirt, and heavy pants to prevent contact with skin.

■ Clean tools and launder clothes immediately after use.

■ Wash hands and exposed skin with antibacterial soap.

■ If you want to tackle the big clogs, rent a power auger from your local rental store. Read the instructions that come with the unit carefully and get a lesson from the salespeople before you attack the drain.

■ If you have a severe clog in a main or service line, you might want to consider hiring a pro to clear it out.

Unclogging a lavatory sink drain

Most clogs in lavatories are caused by hair getting caught in the pop-up mechanism. Often just removing the stopper will reveal the source of the problem. If you can't lift out the stopper, pull the pivot rod back. The pivot rod is located under the sink. It connects the pop-up stopper to the operating lever on top of the sink. Removing the rod and the stopper makes plunging easier.

Using a plunger

- Fill the sink with about 4 inches of water. Stuff a rag in the overflow so you don't lose water pressure while plunging.
- Vigorously plunge the drain. When water drains freely, the blockage is dislodged. If the water drains slowly, the blockage is still in place. Add more water and plunge again.

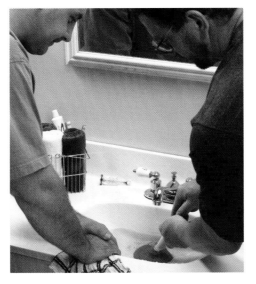

PLUNGE FIRST
Plungers are the safest and most economical tools for getting rid of clogs. They won't damage the fixture or the drain, and they're cheap.

Using a sink auger

- Place a bucket under the trap. Use water-pump pliers to remove the slip nuts connecting the trap.
- Remove the trap (see page 73), then drain any water in the line into the bucket.
- Insert the end of the auger into the drain and turn the crank to advance the auger toward the blockage. Pull out or dislodge the blockage.
- Reconnect the trap.

Still clogged?

Unable to dislodge or remove the blockage with the sink auger? It's time to call a plumber.

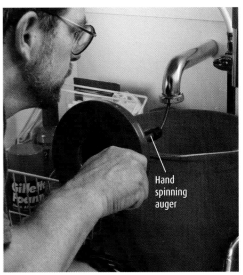

Hand spinning auger

SINK-AUGER STUBBORN CLOGS
Stubborn blockages may require using a sink or hand auger to pull out or dislodge the blockage.

Unclogging a sink with a disposer

PROJECT DETAILS

SKILLS: Connecting plumbing fixtures, using a plunger and sink auger
PROJECT: Unclogging a sink with a disposer

TIME TO COMPLETE

EXPERIENCED: 20 min.
HANDY: 40 min.
NOVICE: 1 hr.

STUFF YOU'LL NEED

TOOLS: Flange plunger, bucket, water-pump pliers, sink auger
MATERIALS: Rag

The steps for unclogging a kitchen sink basin that has a disposer are the same as unclogging anything else; the only issues are whether the sink has a single or double basin and whether or not there is a dishwasher hooked up to the system. You'll need to find some means of clamping the hose so you don't back flush waste into the dishwasher. Try clamping the hose from the dishwasher to the disposer with adjustable locking pliers or removing the hose and plugging the inlet to the disposer.

Single-basin sinks

Fill the sink so there is 4 inches of standing water in the basin. Using a plunger with a fold-out lip, plunge forcefully up and down a dozen times. If the blockage does not dislodge, run the disposer and then plunge vigorously again.

Clogs that are more stubborn will need to be augered. Place a bucket under the sink drain trap. Disconnect the trap slip nuts with water-pump pliers. Remove the trap. Loosen the setscrew on the auger and push about 6 inches of the cable into the drain—too much cable will kink. Tighten the setscrew and turn the crank clockwise while pushing with medium pressure. A sudden lack of resistance will mean that you have pushed past the blockage. You will need to either pull out the blockage by turning the crank counterclockwise or push it through, then flush out the drain. If the drain does not run freely, repeat the steps.

Double-basin sinks

Fill both basins with 4 inches of water. Have a helper hold a rag or a closed strainer over the opening of the disposer drain. Use a plunger to vigorously plunge the drain in the other sink. A dozen times should be enough for most clogs. If the drain is still clogged, switch positions with your helper and plunge the drain in the disposer basin.

You may have to use a sink auger to clear stubborn clogs. Augering a blockage in a double-basin sink is done the same way as for a single-basin sink.

HELPING HANDS
Double-basin kitchen sinks require an extra set of hands to clear the drain. Have someone block one drain with a rag while you plunge the other. That way, you can attack the clog with more force than if you try to plunge one drain while blocking the other by yourself.

4

DEALING WITH CLOGS

Unclogging jammed disposers

DEALING WITH CLOGS

4

PROJECT DETAILS

SKILLS: Connecting plumbing fittings and using a plunger or sink auger
PROJECT: Unclogging a jammed disposer

TIME TO COMPLETE

EXPERIENCED: 15 min.
HANDY: 30 min.
NOVICE: 45 min.

STUFF YOU'LL NEED

TOOLS: Flashlight, ¼-inch allen wrench, adjustable wrench
MATERIALS: None

GOOD IDEA

LEMON-FRESH SCENTED DISPOSER
To keep a garbage disposer smelling fresh and clean, grind up some lemon peels followed by a few ice cubes.

Turn off the power to the jammed disposer and unplug it. Look inside the opening with a flashlight to see what is jamming it. Remove the waste and restore power. If it's still jammed, try the following:

■ Check the bottom of the unit; find the reset button and press it. Turn on the power. The disposer should run freely. If the disposer is still stuck, turn the power off.

■ Insert a broom handle into the drain opening and try to free the impellers.

■ Next, insert a ¼-inch allen wrench into the hex socket on the bottom. The socket is connected to the impellers that crunch up the waste. Using the hex key, turn the impellers in both directions to free them up.

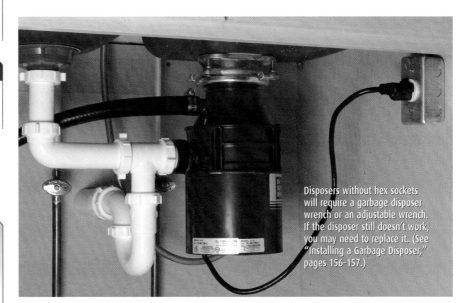

Disposers without hex sockets will require a garbage disposer wrench or an adjustable wrench. If the disposer still doesn't work, you may need to replace it. (See "Installing a Garbage Disposer," pages 156–157.)

SAFETY ALERT

WORK SAFELY
Before reaching into a disposer, disconnect the power. Unplug the unit from the outlet. If there is no outlet, turn off the circuit breaker. Never stick your hand into an operating disposer.

WORK SMARTER

SOLID DISPOSER INFORMATION

■ Make sure your sink is strong enough to support the unit. A disposer will shake and rattle in a thin, stainless-steel sink.

■ Garbage disposers use a lot of water, which can cause problems with septic systems. If you're willing to clean the tank more frequently, you shouldn't have any problems.

■ Stringy vegetables, such as artichoke pieces and corn husks, can become wrapped around the water seal and shorten its life.

■ There are two types of units on the market—continuous feed, which operates without having to close the unit's lid; and batch feed, which requires the lid in place to operate. Continuous feed is the most commonly used and most often recommended for the home kitchen.

■ Models with a self-reversing feature jam less often.

Unclogging a bathtub pop-up drain

A slow-draining bathtub can be a quick-fix project. Bathtub drains are usually clogged by soap scum and hair that collects in the trap. Stuff a rag into the overflow and fill the tub with 4 inches of water, if it doesn't already have standing water in it. While plunging, the vacuum created by the standing water helps to dislodge the blockage.

Place a flange plunger over the drain and plunge vigorously at least a dozen times. If the blockage is not dislodged, continue plunging vigorously until the line drains freely.

More serious clogs may have to be flushed or augered. Flushing the drain with a blow bag can be messy, especially if you don't have a good seal. The best way to clear more difficult blockages is to use a hand auger. The following steps describe how to use a hand auger to clean out the drain.

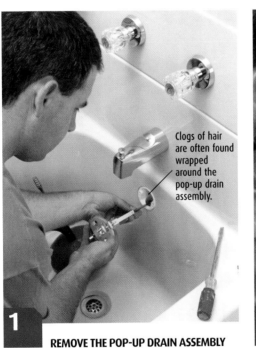

Clogs of hair are often found wrapped around the pop-up drain assembly.

1

REMOVE THE POP-UP DRAIN ASSEMBLY

Flip the drain lever up and pull out the drain plunger. Remove the screws from the overflow cover plate with a screwdriver, then lift out the linkage.

2

AUGER THE DRAIN

Insert the end of the hand auger into the overflow drain. Turn the handle clockwise, feeding out the cable until you meet resistance. Slowly withdraw the auger to dislodge or remove the blockage. Repeat until the tub drains normally. Insert the drain linkage back into the overflow. Install the cover. Flip the lever up and insert the stopper. **Don't use a power-driven auger in a bathtub drain; the assembly is too fragile and can be damaged easily.**

Removing bathroom drain assemblies

THREE POSSIBLE DRAIN ASSEMBLIES

A plunger assembly does not raise and lower a stopper. Instead, the plunger, which is a brass plug, slides up and down inside the tube to shut off or open the flow of water. The plunger is hollow, so overflow water can flow through it. Nowadays this plunger type is the most common because it is reliable and less prone to clogging. A linked rocker arm assembly has its stopper attached to a two-part rocker arm, which is in turn attached to a wire with a coil on the end. When the trip lever is raised, the stopper is pushed up. A solid rocker arm assembly works the same way, but there is a single spring-like rocker arm attached to the stopper, and a striker rather than a coil pushes down on the rocker arm.

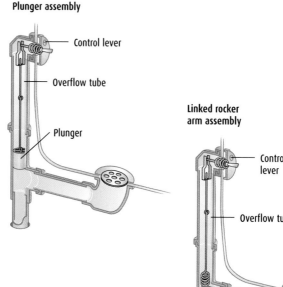

Plunger assembly
- Control lever
- Overflow tube
- Plunger

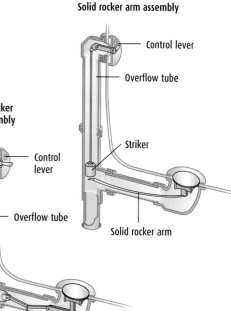

Solid rocker arm assembly
- Control lever
- Overflow tube
- Striker
- Solid rocker arm

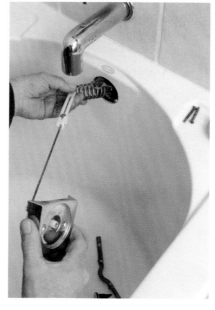

Linked rocker arm assembly
- Control lever
- Overflow tube
- Linked rocker arm

REMOVE THE STOPPER AND ROCKER ARM

To pull out the lower portion of a pop-up drain assembly, simply pry it up and pull out—carefully and slowly. You will likely find some gunk and hair at the joints. If you have a plunger-type assembly (see above), there will be nothing to pull out.

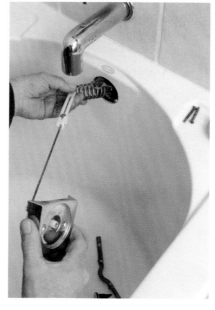

PULL OUT AN OVERFLOW ASSEMBLY

The upper portion of a drain assembly is similarly easy to pull out. Take care not to bend the wires, and clean away any debris that clings to the parts.

AUGERING THROUGH A DRUM TRAP

An older bathroom may have a drum trap, which is designed to collect debris from the tub. You may see a chrome cover on the floor near the tub, or, as shown, the trap may be in an unfinished basement below. Occasionally the drum trap may become clogged. Removing the trap cover gives you access for augering either the pipe between the trap and the tub or the pipe that leads away from the trap.

Unclogging a shower drain

PROJECT DETAILS

SKILLS: Removing plumbing fittings, using a plunger and a hand auger
PROJECT: Unclogging a shower drain

TIME TO COMPLETE

EXPERIENCED: 15 min.
HANDY: 20 min.
NOVICE: 30 min.

STUFF YOU'LL NEED

TOOLS: Flange plunger, screwdriver, hand auger
MATERIALS: None

Shower stalls work hard, especially the ones in utility areas. We use them to wash the dog, and we stick plants in the shower to wash the leaves and freshen them up. A shower is the perfect place to scrub down miniblind window treatments. When the weather is too cold to hose things down outside, we use the shower stall to clean dirty boots. It's no wonder that the drain will occasionally clog.

Plunge the shower drain vigorously with a flange plunger to unclog it. For stubborn clogs, use a hand or power-driven auger. Try both before calling a plumber or a drain cleaning service to unclog the drain.

Don't be surprised if your plumber isn't interested in going after a tough clog. He may suggest a drain cleaning service to handle the job instead. Plumbers have specialties too.

With all of the different kinds of dirt and grime that a shower drain has to deal with, it is no wonder that it will sometimes clog. Be prepared with a hand or power-driven auger.

1 USE A PLUNGER

Remove the screws from the shower strainer. Lift off the shower strainer. Fill the shower pan to a depth of 1 inch. Plunge forcefully about a dozen times. Remove the plunger and see if the water drains freely. If not, repeat.

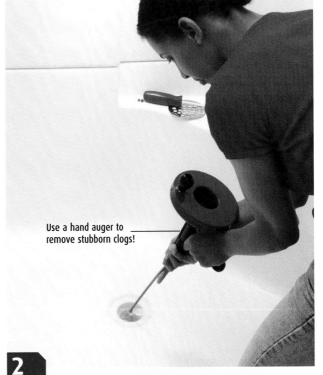

Use a hand auger to remove stubborn clogs!

2 HAND AUGER OR POWER AUGER THE DRAIN

Tougher clogs need a tougher approach. Feed a hand auger into the drain until there is resistance. Turn the auger handle in a clockwise direction and slowly withdraw the auger. Repeat until the shower drains normally. If the blockage refuses to clear, call a plumber or a drain service.

Unclogging a toilet

4

DEALING WITH CLOGS

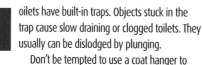

PROJECT DETAILS

SKILLS: Using a plunger and a closet auger

PROJECT: Unclogging a toilet

TIME TO COMPLETE

EXPERIENCED: 15 min.
HANDY: 30 min.
NOVICE: 45 min.

STUFF YOU'LL NEED

TOOLS: Flange plunger, closet auger, bucket
MATERIALS: Rags

WORK SMARTER

HOW TO TAME A CLOG
This recipe for a clog buster really works. Add 3 tablespoons of dishwashing soap to the bowl. The soap will lubricate the interior of the drain and help to loosen the clog when you plunge. Wait a few minutes for the soap to do its work, then plunge vigorously.

Toilets have built-in traps. Objects stuck in the trap cause slow draining or clogged toilets. They usually can be dislodged by plunging.

Don't be tempted to use a coat hanger to unclog a toilet. You will scratch the bowl. If the bowl is scratched, try removing the black marks with a heavy-duty powder-type cleanser with bleach.

Never use chemical drain cleaners in a toilet because the cleaner will stay in the bottom of the bowl and will probably not get to the clog leaving you with a chemical stew in the bottom of the toilet.

If there is no water in the bowl, pour some water into it. Water helps seal the plunger flange, creating a vacuum and allowing you to apply pressure to dislodge the blockage.

A Plunge forcefully about a dozen times. Remove the plunger to allow the toilet to drain. If it doesn't drain, or drains slowly, repeat plunging.

It's auger time

You may need an auger to remove stubborn objects, such as small toys. Never use a hand auger on a toilet. The force of the auger when turning the crank may shatter the porcelain bowl. A closet auger is designed specifically to be used on toilets. The closet auger has a long handle with a crank. A bend in the handle covered with a protective sleeve prevents scratching of the porcelain.

B Turn the crank clockwise and push. The auger can shove the blockage forward into the drain system. If the auger catches on the object, continue turning the crank as you pull out the cable until you can retrieve the object.

Remove the toilet

When plunging or augering doesn't work, your only option will be to remove the toilet (see "Removing an Old Toilet," page 91) and try to fish out the object from the other end.

COMMON HOUSEHOLD PLUNGER

CLOSET AUGER

Replacing a sink trap

4

DEALING WITH CLOGS

PROJECT DETAILS

SKILLS: Disconnecting and installing pipe fittings

PROJECT: Replacing a sink drain trap

TIME TO COMPLETE

EXPERIENCED: 10 min.

HANDY: 20 min.

NOVICE: 30 min.

STUFF YOU'LL NEED

TOOLS: Water-pump pliers, bucket

MATERIALS: Replacement sink trap, washers

SAFETY ALERT

DANGER IN THE DRAIN

If a chemical drain cleaner was used to try to clear the trap, you need to take some extra precautions when you open it up. Wear rubber gloves, a long-sleeved shirt, and safety glasses to prevent injury.

Sink traps may require periodic cleaning to dislodge clogs that prove too stubborn for plunging or removing with a plumber's snake. Replacement is the easiest and most direct way to solve this problem. Disconnect the trap with water-pump pliers, clean out the debris, and reinstall the trap.

Preparing for the job

A newer sink drain trap probably won't fail and need replacement because traps are constructed with more durable materials and are highly resistant to corrosion. Older sink drain traps may need replacing. You should replace yours if it is rusted or has developed leaks around the fittings.

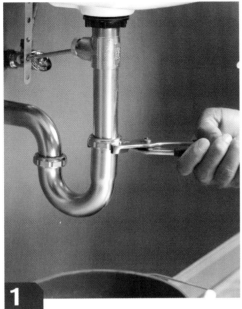

1 **REMOVE THE SLIP NUTS**

Place a bucket under the drain trap to catch debris and any wastewater remaining in the trap. If there is a clean-out plug, remove it and drain wastewater into the bucket. If there isn't, loosen both slip nuts with water-pump pliers and slide them out of the way.

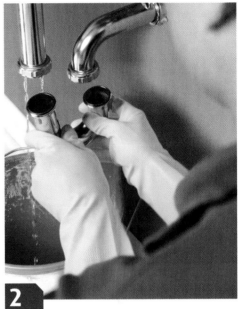

2 **REMOVE THE TRAP**

Pull down on the trap to dislodge it and remove the washers. Dump out any debris remaining in the trap or drain line. Take the trap and washers to your local home center so you can find the same size replacement parts. Slide on the new washers. Fit the new trap in place and tighten the slip nuts.

CLOSER LOOK

REPLACING THE WASHERS

Whenever you take apart a trap, it's a good idea to buy new rubber and plastic washers—they wear out in time and are likely to get damaged when you dismantle the trap. Buy washers to match the old ones. The most common washer is a rubber ring. There are also plastic rings that are beveled on one side; be sure to install them with the bevel facing the right way. Where the trap's tailpiece meets the sink's strainer, you will likely need a special plastic washer that has a lip. When replacing the trap parts, you often need to slip on the nut first, then the washer, then attach the next piece.

Unclogging drains and waste lines

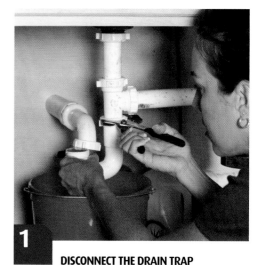

PROJECT DETAILS

SKILLS: Connecting plumbing fittings and using a hand auger
PROJECT: Unclogging drain traps, waste lines, and vent stacks

TIME TO COMPLETE

EXPERIENCED: 20 min.
HANDY: 45 min.
NOVICE: 1 hr.

STUFF YOU'LL NEED

TOOLS: Water-pump pliers, bucket, hand auger
MATERIALS: Rags for cleanup

DEALING WITH CLOGS

4

Small objects, such as toys, can be difficult to remove from a drain line. No matter how cleverly you try to snag them, they seem to defy removal. The only recourse may be to push the blockage further down the drain line system to a cleanout or to flush the line with water when the blockage has been jarred loose.

Remove the drain trap under the sink and use a hand auger to try to snag the blockage. If you can't pull it out, try pushing it into a larger waste line. Then, open up a line cleanout in the larger waste line and try snagging it with the hand auger.

If you don't have accessible cleanouts in your home, push the blockage out through the roof stack vent. Be careful when climbing onto the roof and don't try it in bad weather.

Pushing an object farther down the system can cause a clog where it's difficult to auger. You might have to call a plumber or drain cleaning specialist to clear out the main drain line to the house.

You can clear a drain through the elbow with a hand spinner but for a stubborn clog, remove the elbow and go straight into the drain line.

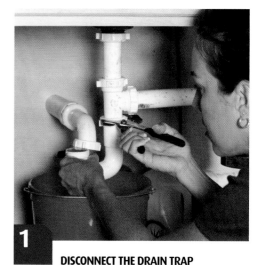

1 DISCONNECT THE DRAIN TRAP
Place a bucket under the drain trap to catch wastewater. Loosen and slide back the slip nut couplings with water-pump pliers. Remove the trap. Clean out any debris stuck in the trap. Look for cracks in the pipe or sediment buildup in the trap; either means you'll have to replace it (see "Replacing a Sink Trap," page 73).

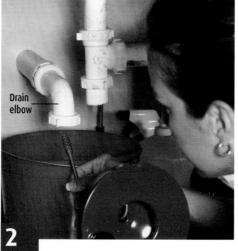

Drain elbow

2 INSERT THE AUGER
Feed 6 inches of the hand auger cable into the drain pipe by turning the auger handle clockwise—a greater length may crimp the cable. Extend the auger until you find resistance. Give yourself a little more room to work by removing the drain elbow.

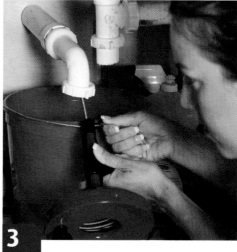

3 TIGHTEN THE AUGER LOCKNUT
Tighten the locknut on the side of the auger. Maintain the 6 inches of exposed cable. Rotate the handle clockwise and continue to push. Repeat until the auger will no longer advance. If you are able to snag the blockage, rotate the auger handle clockwise and pull the cable out slowly. If nothing is snagged, replace the trap and try augering the main drain line.

WORK SMARTER

BANG THE DRAIN, SLOWLY!

If you are having trouble locating the exact position of a clog in the main drain line, here's a tip to speed up the search. The street side of the drain line to the point of the clog will be empty and the house side will be full of waste and water. Tap along the pipe from the street side with a broomstick or a piece of scrap lumber. (Don't use a hammer or piece of metal.) A ringing or hollow sound means a clear pipe. When you hear a thud, you've found the clog. Open up the nearest cleanout and put the auger to work!

You can learn from the pros at a local rental center.

MAYBE IT'S TIME FOR A HEAVY-DUTY SOLUTION

If you have heavy blockage in a main stack or drain, you will need to rent a commercial auger to remove the blockage. This might be the time to bring in a pro; but if you want to do it yourself, get some lessons from the rental people, take every precaution, and work carefully. Sometimes the best approach is to attack main-line blockage from the roof, running the auger down through the vent. Take plenty of precautions when working on the roof.

CLOSER LOOK

CLEARING A DRAIN THROUGH A CLEANOUT

Wearing protective clothing, gloves, and eye protection, place a bucket under the cleanout. Carefully remove the end cap. Use water-pump pliers to loosen the end and slowly remove it by hand. Be careful! Wastewater trapped in the line will be under pressure, so it may gush or spray out of the end. Insert the hand or power auger cable through the opening, leaving 6 inches of cable exposed. Advance until you meet resistance. Tighten the locknut. Rotate the handle clockwise and continue pushing. Try snagging the blockage and slowly pulling it out. If you are unable to clear the drain, try augering through the roof vent.

REAL WORLD

DON'T FORGET ACCESS PANELS

A common remodeling mistake includes repairing or installing a wall without taking into consideration a system behind the wall may be affected. For example, a new wall built over a plumbing cleanout could cause serious problems when it comes time to repair a clogged drain. If there is no access panel, a hole would need to be cut into the wall. Know the placement of the plumbing system and the accessibility to the cleanouts when building or remodeling—access panels should be built to all cleanouts.

Using a hand-held power auger

Plumbers often use professional-quality power augers that are permanently attached to a motor shaped like an electric drill. You probably don't want to pay for an expensive item like that, but you can buy a crank auger with a shaft that fits onto a power drill. This tool will clear clogs much faster than a hand-crank model. Instead of a setscrew that you must loosen and retighten every time you play out more cable, a tool like this has a trigger that you pull to release the cable, then release to grab the cable.

GOOD IDEA

ACCESSING AN OLD CLEANOUT

The cleanout plug in a newer, plastic drain pipe will be fairly easy to unscrew and reattach. An old cast-iron cleanout is another matter, especially if it hasn't been used in a decade or two. Have a bucket handy and spread plenty of rags on the floor, because wastewater could come pouring out when you remove the plug. Squirt penetrating oil around the plug, wait a few minutes, then unscrew using a pipe wrench. If it doesn't budge, try adding a "cheater bar"—a length of 1¼-inch galvanized pipe—to the end of the pipe wrench to lengthen its handle and give you more turning power. Or, place the tip of a cold chisel on the edge of the plug and tap counterclockwise with a hammer. To ensure a good seal and make it easier to remove the plug the next time, replace the plug with a plastic plug of the same size or install a rubber plug, as shown.

4

DEALING WITH CLOGS

Toilets

Chapter 5 highlights

There are at least two reasons to replace your toilet. The decision can be a practical one, based on wear and tear in the form of cracks, chips, and leaks that can't be repaired. Stains will eventually develop that won't go away, no matter how hard you clean.

Second reason, you may also want to replace a toilet as part of a general bathroom remodeling or to get a model in a color that fits with updated bathroom decor. Toilets are available with round or oval bowls and in one- or two-piece models. Corner toilets are popular in some parts of the country.

You aren't limited to replacing a toilet with one of the same shape or style either. Elongated rounds and regular rounds will usually fit in the same drain hole.

What about the environment?

There's an environmental issue as well. Older toilets use 3½ to 5 gallons of water per flush. To meet federal regulations, new models must use 1.6 gallons or less. The earliest low-flow toilets often clogged and required more than one flush, but current water-conserving toilets virtually eliminate these problems. You can also install a gravity flush or pressure-assisted flush toilet. Pressure-assisted toilets are more expensive and noisier but are also more efficient. Gravity flush toilets are less expensive, but they may occasionally require extra flushes.

Installation isn't hard

Installing a toilet isn't as hard as it may seem. While it may be a little heavy and awkward as an object, the mechanics of operation are about as basic as it gets. If your drain is in good shape and you're up to a little lifting, installing a toilet is an easy afternoon's work.

WORK SMARTER

CONNECTING OLD DRAINS TO NEW TOILETS

Before buying a new toilet, make sure the location of its drain valve is in the same place as the "rough-in" dimensions of the drain on the bathroom floor.

In newer bathrooms, the center of the floor outlet is 12 inches from the wall. Most new toilets are designed to fit these specifications. If you live in a house built before the mid-1940s, the outlet may be 10 or 14 inches from the wall. You can get some toilets with a 10- or 14-inch rough-in, but not in all models, styles, and colors.

If you have your heart set on a toilet with a 12-inch rough-in, but your rough-in is 10 or 14 inches, it can be fixed. It's a big job, but you can cut the drain line and install what's called an offset flange, then connect the new toilet's drain to the floor outlet.

Offset flange

CLOSER LOOK

GOT SOME TOUGH NUTS TO CRACK?

Nuts and bolts on toilet bowls can become so corroded that an adjustable wrench won't budge them, or the wrench will round the corners of the nut, making removal next to impossible. You may expand your vocabulary, but you won't budge the nut without applying some special techniques.

1 Before you attack the nut in the first place, assume it may be seized and squirt on penetrating oil. Let the oil soak in thoroughly before you try removing the nut.

2 Try a mini-hacksaw. Protect the base of the toilet with masking tape and cut the nut at a slight angle (about 30 degrees) until you have a deep groove. Insert a screwdriver into the groove and twist to break the nut.

3 As a last resort (or first resort if you have one in your toolbox), you can use a nut splitter, which is a tool often found in the automotive section of your hardware store. The splitter fits over the nut. You hold it in position with an adjustable wrench and tighten it with a socket wrench that closes the jaws of the nut splitter against the nut and cuts it in half.

National Kitchen and Bath Association (NKBA) Guidelines for Bathroom Accessibility and Safety

■ **Handles:** Entrance doors, drawers, and faucets should have lever- or D-shaped handles. They're easier to operate than knobs, especially for people with arthritis.

■ **Grab bars:** People with limited mobility need grab bars next to the toilet, behind it, and in the tub and shower stall. Although the NKBA recommends lengths, locations, and installation methods, the user is always the best judge of what will—and won't—work.

■ **Buy bars with a nonslip texture.** Bars available at most medical supply outlets and home centers are usually limited to white and stainless steel. Some searching through catalogs of the retailer or on the internet may be required to find a variety of colors.

■ **Avoid installing towel bars,** which aren't as firmly anchored, at the same level as grab bars. In a fall, a towel bar could easily be mistaken for a grab bar. Better yet, don't use towel bars at all. Install extra grab bars to hold towels.

■ **Windows:** For wheelchair users, don't install double-hung or sliding windows in a barrier-free bath. Casements are easier to operate. Put windows 24 to 30 inches above the floor so wheelchair users can open and close them easily.

■ **Tubs:** To make a barrier-free bathtub, have enough clear space in front so a wheelchair can roll up to it. Include grab bars and a seat in the tub.

Troubleshooting a leaking toilet

Before you begin working on the toilet, put on a pair of rubber gloves and clean the base thoroughly with a disinfectant. It will make the job a little more pleasant!

Fix a leaking toilet immediately. A leak that is not repaired may become more than an annoyance. It can develop into structural damage not only to the floor, but also to the ceiling below the toilet. Both may require hiring a contractor for a repair which can be extensive and expensive.

Troubleshooting

Troubleshooting a toilet to locate a leak is easy. There are no tools required, just food coloring (red is recommended) and paper towels. The food coloring makes the leak easily visible, so you can see what repairs are needed.

Anatomy of a toilet

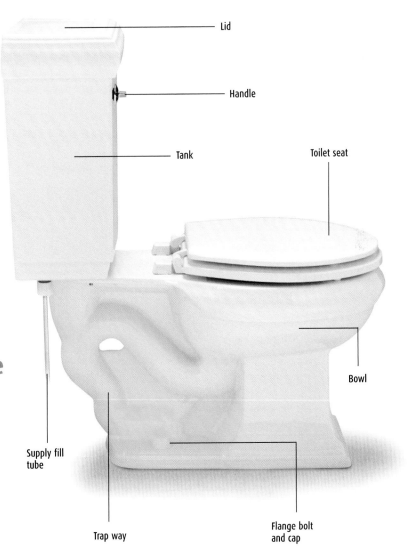

Lid

Handle

Tank

Toilet seat

Bowl

Supply fill tube

Trap way

Flange bolt and cap

1

CLEAN THE OUTSIDE OF THE TOILET

Flush the toilet. Thoroughly dry all exterior surfaces. This will help you spot a leak easily.

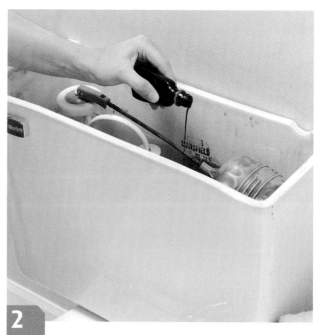

2

ADD RED FOOD COLORING

Pour about a teaspoon of red food coloring into the water in the tank and a teaspoon into the bowl. Wait an hour.

3

CHECK FOR LEAKS

Wipe a dry paper towel around the base and under the tank. Red coloring on the towel shows there's a leak. If the leak is around the base, you will need to replace the wax ring (see pages 92–93). Leaks under the tank could be either a leaking fill valve, bolt gasket, or spud washer (see pages 87–88).

WORK SMARTER

CLAMPING STOCK

If your paper towel turns red around the base of the toilet, you'll probably need to replace the wax ring. Red beneath the tank may mean the gasket between the bowl and tank needs to be replaced. A damp paper towel that shows no red is a sign that the tank is sweating and you may need to insulate the tank (see page 89).

Toilet valve assemblies

oilet tank and bowl configurations have changed little over the years, but the valves that fill the tank and drain out when you flush have undergone a number of transformations. Here are the valves you are most likely to encounter. If yours does not look like any of these, bring the parts to a plumbing expert at a home improvement center. He or she can likely recommend ways to replace the parts or install a new valve.

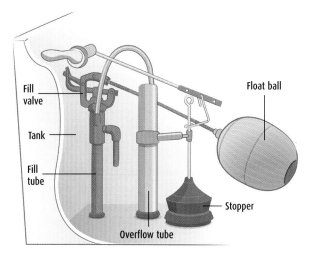

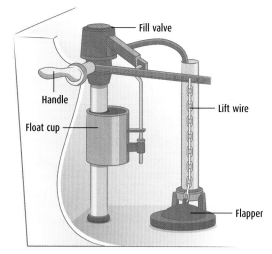

OLD BALLCOCK VALVE

This is a common arrangement in many older toilets. A brass ballcock valve is attached via a rod to a float ball. When the ball lowers, the valve opens and lets in water; and when the ball rises high enough, the water shuts off. When the tank's handle is flipped, a stopper, attached to a lift rod, is raised to allow water to flow down through the flush valve. In many models, the rod and stopper are replaced with a flapper that is attached to a chain. The parts of an old valve like this can be purchased and installed, but often people prefer to install a newer valve instead.

FLOAT CUP WITH FLAPPER

In this arrangement, a float cup rather than a float ball rises and falls with the water level to turn the valve off and on.

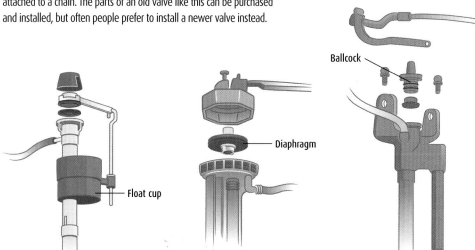

💡 GOOD IDEA

THERMAL EXPANSION
If you have thermal expansion issues in your home, perhaps the easiest way to deal with the problem is to install a special ballcock valve in your toilet that provides expansion relief. See page 129 for more information.

INSIDE THREE TYPES OF FILL VALVES

Whichever type of valve you have, it can be disassembled to reveal rubber or plastic parts that need to be replaced when they wear out.

Adjusting the tank handle and water level

PROJECT DETAILS

SKILLS: Very basic mechanical and plumbing skills
PROJECT: Adjusting the tank handle and water level

TIME TO COMPLETE

EXPERIENCED: 10 min.
HANDY: 20 min.
NOVICE: 30 min.

STUFF YOU'LL NEED

TOOLS: Adjustable wrench, screwdriver
MATERIALS: Bucket, sponge

GOOD IDEA

Float arm adjustment screw

ADJUST THE FLOAT ARM
Before you resort to more complicated measures, try adjusting the float arm first. Turn the screw on top to lift or lower the float.

T he sound of water bubbling from a fountain may be relaxing. But, if it's coming from your toilet, it's just adding to the water bill. If the water is running over and into the overflow valve, lower the water level. If the flapper or ball is not seating fully, adjust the chain or lift wire. If these measures don't solve the problem of water run-on, you may need to replace a flapper (see page 85) or replace the fill valve (page 83).

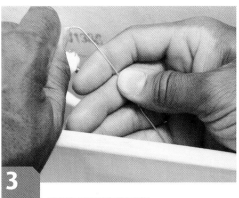

1 ADJUST THE TANK HANDLE
If the handle has too much play or binds, use an adjustable wrench to tighten the nut inside the toilet. Unlike other nuts and bolts, the threads on a tank handle are left-handed, so you'll tighten clockwise.

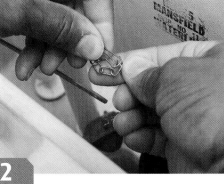

2 SHORTEN THE CHAIN
This will help if you have to hold the handle down to flush all the water from the toilet tank.

3 BEND THE UPPER WIRE
If the tank doesn't have a chain, it has a wire you can bend.

4 BEND THE FLOAT ARM
To adjust the water level in the tank, bend it up for a higher water level or down to lower the water level.

5 SLIDE THE FLOAT CYLINDER
Squeeze the float clip to release the float cylinder, which can be raised or lowered to adjust the water level in float-style toilets.

Replacing a toilet fill valve

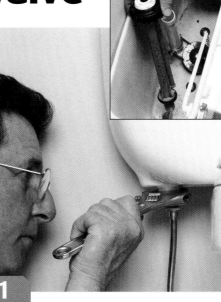

PROJECT DETAILS

SKILLS: Connecting and disconnecting fittings
PROJECT: Replacing a toilet fill valve

TIME TO COMPLETE

EXPERIENCED: 20 min.
HANDY: 40 min.
NOVICE: 1 hr.

STUFF YOU'LL NEED

TOOLS: Adjustable wrench
MATERIALS: Fill valve, fill gasket

Old toilet fill valves can develop leaks. If water continues to run after you have made the adjustments on page 82, you may need to remove and replace the fill valve. You may also have to replace the supply line, so the new valve will fit.

Know the locations of the main shutoff valve or the supply valves for each fixture in your home.

SHUT OFF THE WATER AND DRAIN THE TANK

Drain the tank by shutting off the water and then flushing the toilet. Use a sponge to remove any remaining water. Disconnect the fill valve nut and remove the old fill valve (see inset).

BUYER'S GUIDE

**THREE VALVE TYPES—
ONE WAY TO REPLACE**

There are three basic types of fill valves: the plunger valve, the diaphragm, and the float cup. You replace all three the same way. It may not be necessary to replace the fill valve with the exact same type that you remove, but it may be easier for you because the installation process is the opposite of the removal sequence.

Toilet fill valve components

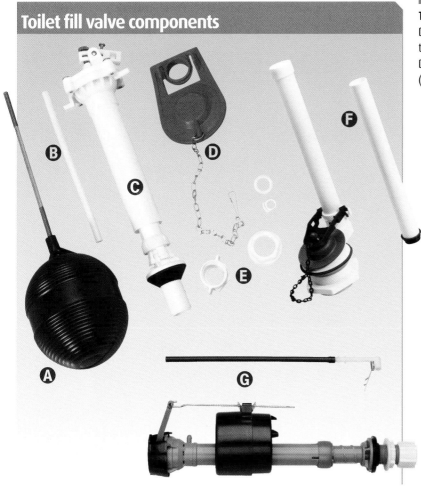

◀ **FILL VALVE COMPONENT NAMES**

A **Float with float arm**
B **Refill tube**
C **Fill valve assembly**
D **Flapper**
E **Plastic washers and nuts**
F **Overflow tubes**
G **Fluid master valve assembly**

5

TOILETS

2

ADJUST THE HEIGHT OF THE VALVE
Adjust the height so the marking on the top of the valve is at least 1 inch above the overflow tube.

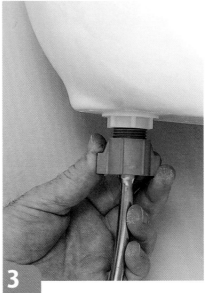

3

POSITION THE VALVE IN THE TANK
Push down on the valve shank and tighten the locknut one-half turn beyond hand-tight. Connect the supply.

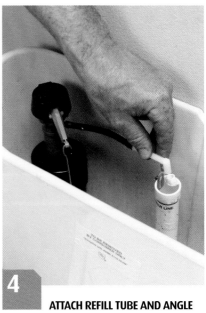

4

ATTACH REFILL TUBE AND ANGLE ADAPTER TO THE OVERFLOW
Trim the tube, if necessary, so there aren't any kinks.

5

FLUSH THE SYSTEM
Remove the top valve. Hold a cup over the uncapped valve and turn on the water supply to flush the system of rust and debris. Turn off the water.

6

REPLACE THE TOP VALVE
Replace the top valve by engaging the lugs and rotating one-eighth turn clockwise. Make sure it's firmly locked into position.

7

ADJUST THE WATER LEVEL
Turn the water supply back on, allow the tank to fill and adjust the water level by squeezing the adjustment clip and moving the float cup up or down.

Replacing a flapper

PROJECT DETAILS

SKILLS: Replacing the flapper and adjusting the chain
PROJECT: Replacing a toilet flapper

TIME TO COMPLETE

EXPERIENCED: 5 min.
HANDY: 10 min.
NOVICE: 15 min.

STUFF YOU'LL NEED

TOOLS: None
MATERIALS: Bucket, sponge, scrub pad, flapper or tank ball that fits your toilet

WORK SMARTER

FLAPPER TIPS

Have about a half inch of slack in the chain that connects the flush lever to the flapper.

Most replacements have side tabs or a ring that slides over the overflow tube, so they can work with any system.

Make sure the flapper can move up and down freely.

 f you have hard water, you will probably need to change the toilet flapper occasionally. Minerals in hard water build up around the base of the flapper and the opening of the toilet. The sediment will eventually destroy the flapper, causing the toilet to leak. No tools are needed for this project.

 **REAL WORLD**

DON'T USE TANK TABLETS

Tank tablets contain chlorine that can eat away at rubber and cause flappers and washers to require replacement often. It's advisable to not use tank tablets.

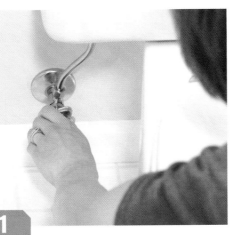

1

TURN OFF THE WATER SUPPLY SHUTOFF VALVE

If there isn't a shutoff valve, turn off the water at the main valve; this is also a good time to install a shutoff valve for future use. (See pages 61–62.)

2

FLUSH THE TOILET

Dry the inside walls and base of the tank with a sponge. Have a bucket handy to wring out the sponge.

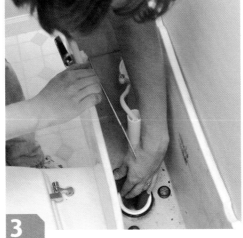

3

REMOVE THE OLD FLAPPER

Pull the flapper from the pivot arm. For ball-style toilets, grip a loop of lift wire and unscrew the old tank ball. Clean the surface area of the opening with a scrub pad to remove the sediment.

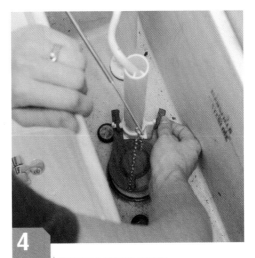

4

INSTALL A NEW FLAPPER

Buy a new flapper that matches the old one. Line up the flap or ball with the valve seat by straightening the lift wire or adjusting the guide arm. This will provide a sufficient seat and keep the tank from leaking.

Dealing with weak flushes

I f water runs continuously even though the valve is in the off position, or if you see water leaking out of a valve, you likely need to perform a little surgery. Shut the water off, flush the toilet, and disassemble your valve. Work systematically so you can keep track of all the little parts and where they go. Take the parts to a home improvement center and look for exact replacements. If you are at all unsure about which parts to get, ask a knowledgeable salesperson.

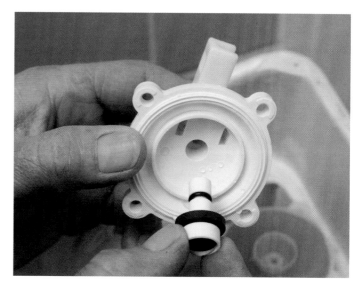

DIAPHRAGM BALLCOCK
This is also called a piston-type ballcock valve. Remove the top screws and lift up the bonnet. Inside you will find a plunger with two or more rubber rings and a large rubber diaphragm. Replace all the rubber parts or install a new ballcock assembly.

OLDER BRASS BALLCOCK
Remove the nuts and pull the plunger out. There will likely be an O-ring or packing near the top, and a plunger washer at the bottom, which may be held in place with a screw. Remove the rubber parts and clean the plunger with a toothbrush. Turn the water on briefly to flush out any sediment. Replace the O-ring and the washer and reassemble.

FLOATLESS BALLCOCK
A unit like this, also called an actuator assembly, uses a pressure-sensing device rather than a float to determine when to shut off the water. There may be an adjustment screw that raises water level when you turn it clockwise. Inside you will find a rubber seal; if it is damaged, replace it or the entire valve.

OVERFLOW AND FLAPPER UNIT
If water continues to seep into the bowl and you cannot find a new flapper that seals the flush hole, the solution may be a unit like this, which installs over the flush hole and has its own flapper. You will need to drain and dry the tank, so that the unit will seal tightly at the bottom.

Repairing a leaking tank

PROJECT DETAILS

SKILLS: Removing and connecting fittings
PROJECT: Repairing a leaking toilet tank

TIME TO COMPLETE

EXPERIENCED: 45 min.
HANDY: 1.5 hrs.
NOVICE: 2 hrs.

STUFF YOU'LL NEED

TOOLS: Two adjustable wrenches, screwdriver, helper, spud wrench, small wire brush
MATERIALS: Flush valve gasket, fill valve, gaskets, spud washer, plumber's putty, white vinegar

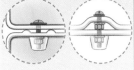

WORK SMARTER

DON'T OVERTIGHTEN

Overtightening the bolts that connect the tank to the toilet base can crack the base, the tank, or both. Tighten gently until snug and alternate from side to side so they seat evenly.

If water keeps running even after you've tried adjusting the water level (page 82) and replacing the flapper (page 85), you may need to repair a leaky tank. Water may be leaking into the toilet bowl or leaking out of the tank. Once you've figured out which is occurring, you are close to solving the problem.

Three common leaks

There are three common areas of the toilet that might need repair. The fill valve may be leaking, there may be a leak around a tank bolt, or the spud washer may have developed a leak. Here's how to fix them.

Don't worry about touching the water in the tank. Unlike the water in the bowl, it's clean.

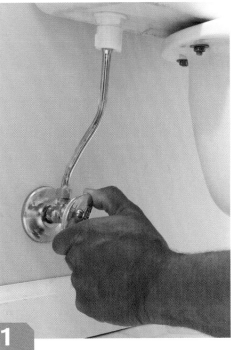

1

DRAIN AND CLEAN ALL SURFACES

Turn off the water supply valve. Flush the toilet. Disconnect the supply line from the tank and sponge the inside of the tank until it's dry.

2

DISCONNECT THE FILL VALVE

Use two adjustable wrenches to remove the fill valve. Remove the old fill gasket. Take the gasket with you to the home center, so you'll be sure to get the right size part. If you're not replacing other parts, install the new fill valve and gasket. Turn on the supply line and check for leaks. If necessary, tighten a quarter turn. Otherwise, proceed to step 3.

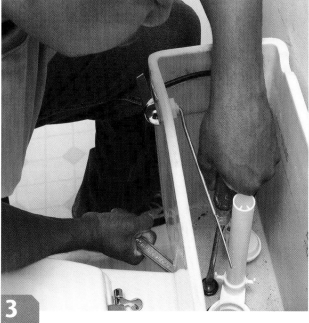

3 UNSCREW THE TANK BOLT

A screwdriver and adjustable wrench will remove most tank bolts. Remove the tank bolt, nut, and gasket. Clean the bolt and nut with white vinegar and a small wire brush. If you aren't replacing the spud washer, reinstall bolts and nuts with new gaskets. Alternate the tightening of the nuts to evenly draw the tank tight. If you are replacing the spud washer, continue to step 4.

4 LIFT THE TANK

Lift the tank straight up and off the toilet base to remove it. Make sure you have a helper; toilet tanks are usually in an awkward place and are heavier than they appear to be. Set the tank upside down on the floor. It's best to set it on an old towel or rug because there may be some water left in the tank.

5 REPLACE THE SPUD WASHER

Take the spud washer to your local home center to find the right replacement. Place a new spud washer over the flush valve tailpiece. Lower the tank onto the base so the tank bolts go through the holes. Reinstall the tank bolts, gaskets, and nuts. Alternate tightening the nuts from side to side so they tighten evenly. Reinstall the supply tube coupling and fill valve. Turn on the water supply and check for leaks.

📖 WORK SMARTER

TIGHTEN BY DEGREES
You might give the toilet a flush to test it and notice a slight leak. If so, turn off the supply valve. If there is a leak along the supply valve, tighten the fittings an additional quarter turn. If the leak is around the base of the tank, check the washers in the tank to make sure they're seated properly. If the washers appear to be properly seated, tighten the tank nuts another quarter turn.

Curing a sweating tank

PROJECT DETAILS

SKILLS: Measuring and cutting polystyrene foam, applying waterproof mastic
PROJECT: Curing a sweating toilet tank

TIME TO COMPLETE

EXPERIENCED: 20 min.
HANDY: 40 min.
NOVICE: 1 hr.

STUFF YOU'LL NEED

TOOLS: Pencil, straightedge, scissors, utility knife
MATERIALS: Paper, polystyrene foam, waterproof mastic

Humid weather can cause condensation to form on the outside of the tank. You will have to buy a kit to insulate the tank and stop it from sweating, but you can do the job yourself. Remember, you will not be able to use the toilet overnight while the mastic is drying.

Prepare the toilet
Turn off the water to the toilet at the supply valve. Flush the toilet and remove as much water as possible from the tank with a sponge and bucket. Completely dry the inside with an old towel or rag.

Keep the toilet tank from sweating with an insulation kit you can install yourself.

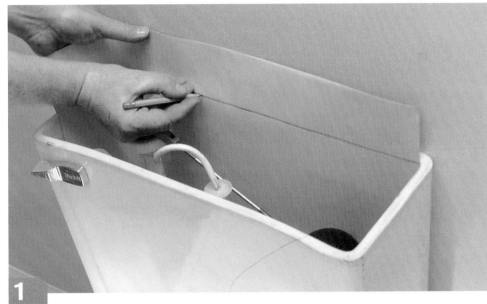

1 MAKE THE TEMPLATE
Make a pattern out of a sheet of paper placed over the rear wall of the tank. Mark the edges with a pencil and cut the lines with a straightedge.

2 CUT THE FOAM
Lay the pattern you created on top of a sheet of polystyrene foam. Fasten it with tape or pins so it won't move when you cut it. Use a utility knife to cut along the pattern. You now have a rear wall insulation panel for the tank.

3 APPLY WATERPROOF MASTIC
Press the panel into place against the rear wall. Repeat the process for the front and all sides of the tank. Let the mastic dry overnight before refilling the tank.

Replacing a toilet seat

S tyle and comfort are two of the many reasons for changing the toilet seat. The seat or cover can become cracked or damaged. Appearance is the usual reason for changing the seat and cover. With an adjustable wrench and screwdriver, this is very easy because you don't have to shut off the water.

Replacing your toilet seat and cover is an easy upgrade to the look of the whole bathroom.

GOOD IDEA

KNOW YOUR TOILET SEAT
People often have to make extra trips to the store when replacing toilet seats because they don't realize there are two basic styles—round, which is 16 inches front to back, and elongated, which is 18 inches front to back. Measure before you go or bring the old seat to the store.

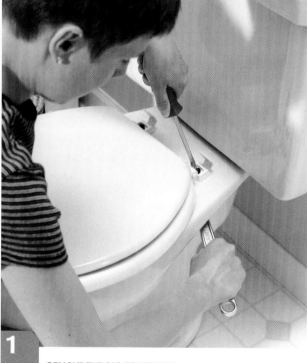

1

REMOVE THE OLD TOILET SEAT
Pry open the bolt caps. Use a screwdriver and adjustable wrench to remove the anchor bolts. Turn the bolt with the screwdriver while holding the nut steady. Lift off the old seat. Clean around the mounting holes with a scrub pad to remove any sediment or debris.

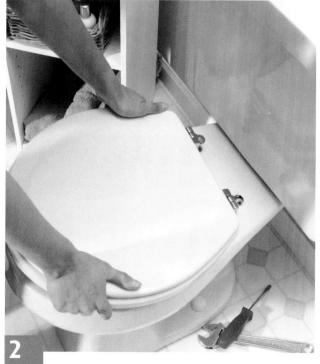

2

INSTALL THE NEW SEAT
To install a seat with metal hinges, align the holes of the toilet with the hinge bolts of the seat. Drop the bolts through the holes in the bowl. Fasten the nuts hand-tight and adjust the seat so it's centered properly. Tighten (but don't overtighten) with an adjustable wrench. (If you're installing the same type of seat you removed, reverse the procedure in step 1.)

5

TOILETS

Removing an old toilet

5

TOILETS

PROJECT DETAILS

SKILLS: Disconnecting plumbing fittings

PROJECT: Removing an old toilet

TIME TO COMPLETE

EXPERIENCED: 20 min.

HANDY: 40 min.

NOVICE: 1 hr.

STUFF YOU'LL NEED

TOOLS: Adjustable wrench, ratchet wrench and sockets, hacksaw, putty knife, rubber gloves

MATERIALS: Rags, sponge, bucket, towel

SAFETY ALERT

POTENTIAL BIOHAZARD

The water in the toilet bowl may contain harmful bacteria. Wear rubber gloves when cleaning or removing the bowl. Wash your hands thoroughly with an antibacterial soap afterward.

WORK SMARTER

RAISING ISSUES

If you're laying a new floor, remove the toilet, so you don't have to trim around it. You'll get a cleaner and neater looking installation. The catch is that the new floor will lift the toilet by its finished thickness, but not the soil pipe. In that case, you may have to install an extension flange, which is readily available at your local home center.

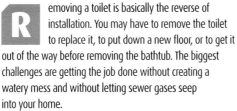

Removing a toilet is basically the reverse of installation. You may have to remove the toilet to replace it, to put down a new floor, or to get it out of the way before removing the bathtub. The biggest challenges are getting the job done without creating a watery mess and without letting sewer gases seep into your home.

1 Turn off the water supply at the shutoff valve. Flush the toilet until the tank is empty. Wipe up any water remaining in the tank and bowl with rags and a sponge. Always wear rubber gloves when cleaning wastewater. Disconnect the supply tube with an adjustable wrench.

2 Remove the tank bolts with a ratcheting socket wrench.

3 Lift the tank off the bowl. Be careful when you remove the tank, especially if you plan to reuse it; most toilets are made of porcelain, which is easily damaged.

4 Remove the toilet base. Pry open the floor bolt caps at the base of the toilet. Use a socket wrench to remove the nuts from the floor bolts. If a nut is rusted solid, cut down (along the side of the bolt) through the nut with a hacksaw. Then, you can easily remove the nut. Straddle the toilet and gently rock it from side to side to break the wax seal; lift it off the bolts and set it on its side on an old towel. Water may spill from the toilet trap.

5 Scrape the old wax from the toilet flange with a putty knife. Plug the drain opening with a rag to prevent sewer gases from escaping and entering the house while you work.

Installing a toilet

PROJECT DETAILS

SKILLS: Connecting plumbing fittings
PROJECT: Installing a toilet

TIME TO COMPLETE

EXPERIENCED: 30 min.
HANDY: 45 min.
NOVICE: 1 hr.

STUFF YOU'LL NEED

TOOLS: Two adjustable wrenches, ratchet wrench and sockets, screwdriver, hacksaw, tubing cutter
MATERIALS: Toilet, toilet seat, "no-seep" wax ring, plumber's putty, felt marker, pipe compound, supply tube

5

TOILETS

BUYER'S GUIDE

SUPER DUPER FLANGE

Closet flanges take a lot of abuse and can crack or break. If you don't want to pull out the old one and do a new connection job, use an adapter sometimes called a super flange that fits over the old model and makes a secure connection for the toilet. There are other adapters available as well. Check them out at your local home center.

I f you're installing a new toilet in a new location, you'll need to run (or have someone run) a water supply line and a drainpipe, which must be connected to the drain/vent system in compliance with code. (See Chapter 10, "The DWV System," page 175.) Even if you're just replacing an existing toilet, you should replace the water supply tubing as well.

Some parts are extra

Most of the parts you need to install the new toilet will come with it—except the toilet seat, which is a separate item on almost every model, with the exception of some one-piece models. The wax ring—which comes in two sizes—is also not part of the package. The manual that comes with the new toilet will tell you the correct size to buy.

Supply tubes come in a variety of styles. A solid copper chromed supply tube is shown in the following project because there are additional steps involved with that type of supply tube. If you don't feel up to the bending of the supply tube necessary when installing a solid one, buy a braided supply tube instead. They are equally as durable, and are much easier to install. to see a variety of tubes available see page 165.

1

SET THE MOUNTING BOLTS

If you're reusing the old flange, it's a good idea to replace the 3½-inch flange bolts. Purchase two 3½-inch-long closet bolts at your local home center. If you're replacing the flange, it must be screwed into a wooden floor. Self-tapping concrete screws are used for concrete.

2

PLACE THE WAX RING ON THE TOILET

The "no-seep" wax ring size will vary with the size of the flange. Be sure to purchase the proper size. A 3-inch neck will fit a 3-inch closet elbow, and a 4-inch neck will fit a 4-inch closet elbow. If the closet elbow is 4 inches and the neck is 3 inches in diameter, purchase a 4×3 reducer.

Be careful when handling the toilet. It may look strong, but it can chip or crack if dropped.

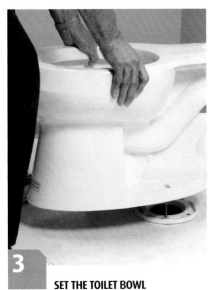

3

SET THE TOILET BOWL

Straddle the toilet bowl and lift, using your legs and not your back. Toilets are heavy, so get some help. Set the toilet over the anchor bolts and sit on the toilet, rocking it back and forth to seat the wax ring.

4

TIGHTEN THE NUTS

Draw the nuts down over both anchor bolts until they are hand-tight. Shim as necessary to maintain level. Use an adjustable wrench and—moving from one side of the toilet to the other—alternate the tightening of each nut a half-turn at a time until it's snug. Don't overtighten.

5

CUT THE FLANGE BOLT TO SIZE

Use a mini hacksaw to cut the flange bolt so only ¼ to ½ inch extends above the bolt. This will allow the cap to fit snugly. Most bolts have snap-offs every ½ inch or so, but you should still cut through so you don't bend the bolt.

6

INSTALL THE BOLT CAP

Some types of caps will snap over the bolt. Others have to be filled with plumber's putty and seated over the anchor bolt.

7

SET THE TANK ANCHOR BOLTS

Place the tank anchor bolts in the holes of the tank to help guide the tank onto the bowl.

8

PLACE THE TANK ON THE BOWL

Lift the tank and place it over the bowl. You may need some help with this. Guide the tank bolts into the corresponding holes on the toilet bowl.

9

TIGHTEN THE TANK BOLTS

Hold an adjustable wrench over the tank bolt nut while you tighten the bolt with a screwdriver. Don't overtighten; you can crack either the tank or the toilet bowl.

10

INSTALL THE SHUTOFF VALVE

Set the valve over the compression ring and draw the nut to it. Tighten the nut until hand-tight. Use two adjustable wrenches to tighten until snug—one to hold back the valve and the other to tighten the compression nut.

11

MEASURE THE SUPPLY TUBE

Hold the tank supply tube so it's in place. Let the extra pipe extend past the shutoff valve. Mark the pipe for cutting. Leave enough pipe so it will fit snugly inside the shutoff valve outlet. Cut the supply pipe with a tubing cutter.

If your think your plumbing skills are limited you can use a raided supply line instead of the solid supply line shown above. Be sure your supply line and shutoff valve are compatible before leaving the store.

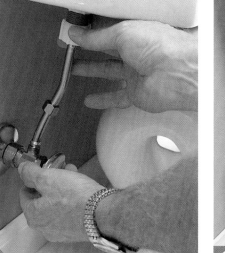

12

CONNECT THE SUPPLY PIPE TO THE TANK

Seat the end of the pipe against the tank. Draw up the tank nut. Hand-tighten until snug. Slide the compression nut over the other end, then place the compression ring over the end of the pipe. Seat the end in the outlet of the shutoff valve.

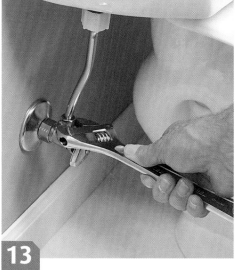

13

TIGHTEN THE COMPRESSION NUT

Use an adjustable wrench to carefully tighten the compression nut. Don't overtighten. Turn on the water supply and check for leaks along the supply line, visually and by touch. Flush the toilet and check for leaks around the base of the tank. If there is a leak, tighten the connections a half-turn.

REAL WORLD

GET THE RIGHT SIZE TOILET

In order to avoid buying a toilet that needs to be returned, or worse, that is non-returnable, determine the size toilet needed before going to the store. The distance the drain is from the wall will determine the size of the toilet. Ninety percent of toilets are made for a drain opening 11 to 12 inches from the wall. The rest are either 9 to 10 or 13 to 14 inches away.

5

TOILETS

Appliances

This chapter deals with appliances that you may find in a basement or utility room; for kitchen appliances, see chapter 8. The major utility appliance in a home is the water heater, which is indispensable yet sure to act up from time to time. With a bit of maintenance—even if you just flush it for 15 minutes or so once a year—you can significantly lengthen the life of your water heater. If something does go wrong, repairs are not difficult; and replacing a water heater is a project within the reach of a capable homeowner. This chapter will also show how to troubleshoot a clothes washer and dryer and replace a sump pump.

Maintaining a water heater

PROJECT DETAILS

SKILLS: Attaching wire to a terminal, operating plumbing fittings
PROJECT: Maintaining a water heater

TIME TO COMPLETE

EXPERIENCED: 20 min.
HANDY: 20 min.
NOVICE: 20 min.

STUFF YOU'LL NEED

TOOLS: Garden hose, screwdriver, bucket
MATERIALS: None

SAFETY ALERT

BE WARY OF EXPOSED WIRES
Always use care when working around exposed wires. If possible, turn off the electrical supply at either the switch box or the circuit breaker.

T oday's water heaters are designed to last 10 years. Many come with 10 or 12 year warranties. However, you can significantly extend the life of your water heater with regular maintenance.

Standard water heaters are designed to be easily maintained. Access panels allow you to remove and replace worn parts. If you need to replace any parts, make sure you replace them with parts that match the make and model of the existing water heater. A plate attached to the outside of the water heater usually has product information.

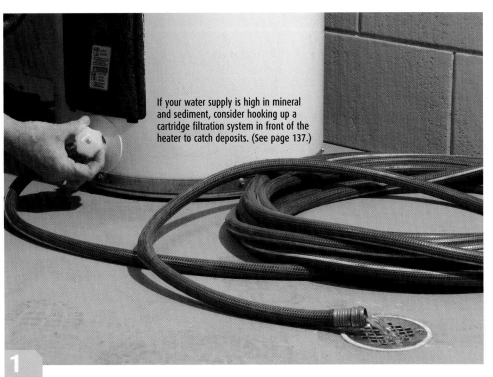

If your water supply is high in mineral and sediment, consider hooking up a cartridge filtration system in front of the heater to catch deposits. (See page 137.)

1 DRAIN THE HEATER

Turn off the electricity or shut off the gas. Find the water heater drain near the base of the water heater. Connect a standard garden hose to the outlet. Place the other end of the hose near a floor drain or in a large bucket. Leave the water supply on. Removing any sediment in the bottom of the heater by opening the drain spigot to flush the water heater system until the water runs clear, usually less than 3 or 4 gallons.

WORK SMARTER

WATER HEATER MAINTENANCE TIPS

Water heaters are workhorses unless you don't take care of them; then they'll reward you with a cold shower!

- Flush the system at least once a year. Sediment from the water supply builds up in the tank and makes it heat less efficiently. Sediment is more of an issue in gas heaters because the burner is at the base of the unit and has to heat through the gunk to get to the water.

- Check the elements in an electric water heater. There are two of them, and the top one is usually the first to fail.
- Don't test the pressure-relief valve; once it's been opened, it will need to be replaced.
- Check the flue on a gas water heater at least once a year to make sure the ducts are properly aligned and the tape is secure.

APPLIANCES

6

Installing an on-demand water heater

An on-demand water heater can easily be mounted under a kitchen sink or off to the side, in a place where looks don't matter. When you turn the hot water tap on, the flow turns on a heating element that heats the water as it runs through copper tubes. When the faucet goes off, so does the heat saving you a lot of money in heating costs.

If you are not experienced working with electricity, hire an electrician or consult a book like The Home Depot's *Wiring 1-2-3*. To meet code, you will need an electrical shutoff switch within sight of the unit. Run armored cable or conduit (as shown). Make sure your breaker or fuse box has an extra circuit before starting. You'll need one free breaker for a 120-volt heater or two free breakers for a 240-volt unit. Time needed to run wire or pipe is not included in the estimate.

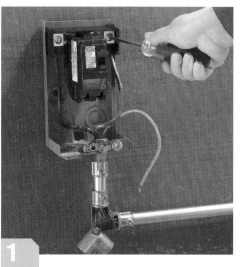

1

RUN POWER FOR THE UNIT

The heater will be either a 120- or a 240-volt circuit, and it must be a circuit wholly devoted to the heater. Either voltage requires 8-gauge wire, and the section exposed to the area under the sink must be armored cable or conduit. If the manufacturer's instructions call for installing larger cable or thicker wire, be sure you do so.

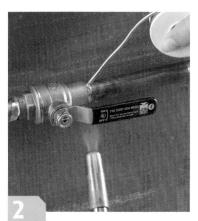

2

IF YOU'RE INSTALLING THE HEATER UNDER AN EXISTING SINK

Turn off the water line. Drain the line by opening a faucet at a lower point somewhere in the house. Solder a cutoff valve onto the pipe stub that comes from the floor or wall. Solder a second valve onto what's left of the line that runs to the faucet, cutting the line as necessary to allow room for the heater. (For more on soldering copper pipe, see page 166.)

3

SCREW THE UNIT TO THE WALL

Follow manufacturer's instructions. Connect the water supply line to the cold in-feed fitting by soldering copper pipe or via high-pressure flex connections, as shown here. Wrap Teflon tape around the threads. Hand-tighten, then use a wrench. Connect the line going to the faucet to the hot water outlet using the same materials.

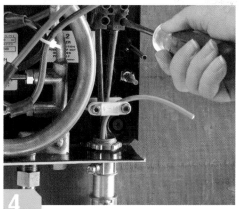

4

WIRE THE UNIT

Follow the manufacturers instructions on wiring exactly. Often, on a 240-volt circuit, the white wire connects to one of the hot terminals, and the black to the other hot terminal—they're often labeled L1 and L2. The ground wire will go to the grounding screw on the unit. On a 120-volt unit, splice the white supply wire to the white wire in the unit, and splice the black wire to the black. Cover with wire nuts and tape the nuts in place.

APPLIANCES

6

Adjusting the water temperature

PROJECT DETAILS

SKILLS: Removing access panel and using a screwdriver
PROJECT: Adjusting the thermostat on a water heater

TIME TO COMPLETE

EXPERIENCED: 10 min.
HANDY: 10 min.
NOVICE: 10 min.

STUFF YOU'LL NEED

TOOLS: Screwdriver
MATERIALS: None

SAFETY ALERT

PREVENT SCALDING!
Don't set the thermostat too high. Water can scald a person quickly. Water that is 150 degrees scalds in just half a second. Water that is set at 140 degrees scalds in just one second. It will take water at 120 degrees four minutes to scald a person.

Adjust the temperature of the water heater yourself. Wait one hour and test the temperature of the water at a remote faucet. If you need to make another adjustment, do it in 10-degree increments. Be aware that increasing the water temperature may shorten the life of the unit; lower settings can lengthen the life of the water heater. You will also see an increase on your utility bill if you increase the water temperature. You should follow the manufacturer's suggested temperature setting.

1 TURN OFF THE ELECTRICITY AND REMOVE THE ACCESS PANEL
Shut off power to an electric water heater by flipping a breaker at the service panel. Then test to make sure power is off. Pull back any insulation to expose the thermostat.

2 ADJUST THE SETTING
Use a screwdriver to change the thermostat in 10-degree increments. Close up the panel, restore power, and check the water temperature after one hour. Repeat until it's where you want it.

CLOSER LOOK

ADJUSTING THE THERMOSTAT ON A GAS WATER HEATER
It's easy to adjust the temperature on a gas water heater. The thermostat is on the outside of the tank and can be easily adjusted with the control knob. Change the setting in 10-degree increments. Wait an hour and test the temperature of the water at a remote faucet. Readjust another 10 degrees if you want. Don't set the temperature too high; that will shorten the life of your water heater. You'll also see an increase on your energy bill.

6

APPLIANCES

Relighting a gas water heater

PROJECT DETAILS

SKILLS: Ability to light a gas pilot
PROJECT: Relighting gas water heater pilot lights

TIME TO COMPLETE

EXPERIENCED: 10 min.
HANDY: 15 min.
NOVICE: 30 min.

STUFF YOU'LL NEED

TOOLS: Long wooden fireplace matches or a barbecue lighter
MATERIALS: none

SAFETY ALERT

NEVER IGNORE GAS ODORS!
If you think you smell natural gas odor, call the gas company immediately. Don't turn on any light switches! Open all the windows and leave the house.

C old water pouring out of the hot shower tap is an annoying surprise, to say the least. You may need to flush the sediment out of the system. (See "Maintaining a Water Heater," page 96.) Or you may just need to relight the pilot as you would on a gas stove. There will be detailed instructions for relighting your water heater on a plate located on the side of the tank next to the pilot and thermostat control knob. Long wooden matches or a barbecue lighter will easily reach the pilot through the access opening. Don't use a propane torch; it will melt the thermocouple. If the pilot does not stay relit, replace the thermocouple. (See pages 100–101.)

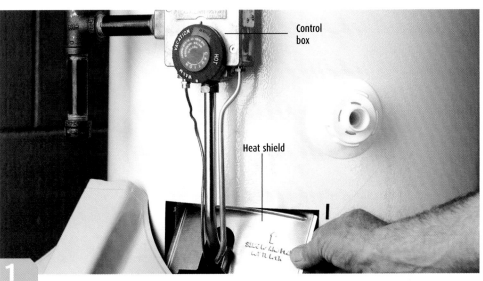

Control box

Heat shield

1 REMOVE THE COVER PANEL

Lift off the access panel at the bottom of the tank. This is where the gas line enters the water heater tank and where the pilot is located. Remove the heat shield and look inside to see if there is a flame. If not, shut off the gas at the supply valve. Disperse excess gas by blowing gently into the opening before you relight the pilot.

Top control box knob

For a more detailed look at the pilot light mechanism, see "Replacing a Gas Thermocouple," pages 100–101.

2 RELIGHT THE PILOT

Turn the knob on top of the control box to the "pilot" position. (See inset at left.) Hold a lit fireplace match or barbecue lighter to the pilot access opening below. Press and hold down the "reset" button on the control box for 60 seconds after the pilot ignites, then turn the control knob to the "on" position. The main burner should ignite. If it doesn't, turn the control knob to the "off" position. You may need to replace the thermocouple (next page).

6

APPLIANCES

Replacing a gas thermocouple

The water heater isn't working if cold water comes from a hot water tap. Remove the access panel and check to see if there's a flame at the pilot light. Try relighting (previous page). If the pilot light will not stay lit, the thermocouple may be the problem.

The thermocouple is a thin copper line with a tip that rests in the flame of the pilot light. It runs from the burner to the control box on the outside of the water heater. The thermocouple shuts off the gas when the pilot light goes out. A worn thermocouple has to be replaced.

While replacing the thermocouple, you should also clean the burner and tubes. Unscrew the burner from the tube. Use a stiff wire or paper clip to clean out debris clogging the burner holes. Shake out any debris that has fallen into the chamber. You may want to use a vacuum cleaner to remove any debris remaining in the tubing and the burner chamber.

Access panel cover

1 **TURN OFF THE GAS**
Locate the gas control knob on the top of the control box. Turn it to the "off" position, then wait five minutes for gas to dissipate. Remove the access panel cover.

2 **DISCONNECT THE BURNER**
After removing the access cover, if there is one behind the access panel cover, use an adjustable wrench to remove the connectors for all three tubes connecting the burner to the control box.

Be sure to have the model number and manufacturer of your water heater to ensure you get the correct replacement thermocouple. If you have any doubts about getting the right part, take your old thermocouple with you when shopping.

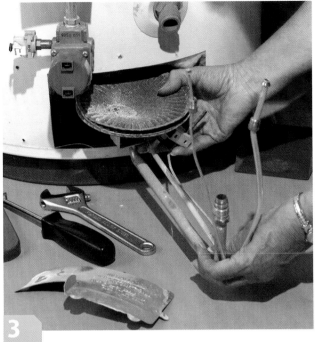

3 REMOVE THE BURNER

Remove the burner access panel and slide the burner out.

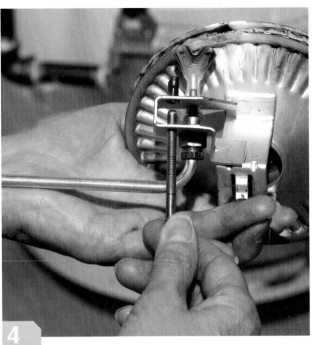

4 REMOVE THE OLD THERMOCOUPLE

Unsnap the old thermocouple from its mounting bracket and replace it with one of the same model and length.

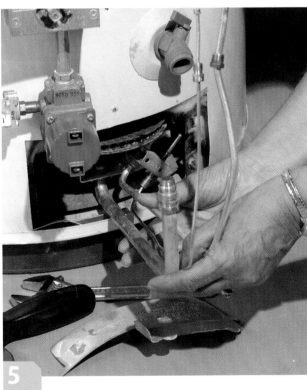

5 INSERT THE BURNER AND THERMOCOUPLE

Slide the burner unit back into the water heater. The flat end of the burner tube will slip into a slot in the water heater bracket. Carefully bend any excess thermocouple tubing into a coil that is at least 2 inches wide. If there are any kinks in the line, you'll have to replace it—again.

6 RECONNECT THE LINES

Align the tubes and reconnect them to the control box using an adjustable wrench. Test all the newly connected fittings for leaks. (See step 8, page 112.) Relight the pilot (see "Relighting a Gas Water Heater," page 99).

Troubleshooting an electric water heater

PROJECT DETAILS

SKILLS: Ability to disconnect wires with a screwdriver and read a continuity tester
PROJECT: Troubleshooting electric water heaters

TIME TO COMPLETE

EXPERIENCED: 10 min.
HANDY: 15 min.
NOVICE: 30 min.

STUFF YOU'LL NEED

TOOLS: Screwdriver, continuity tester
MATERIALS: None

SAFETY ALERT

WATER HEATER OVERHEATING
Turn on all hot water faucets in the house to relieve pressure buildup. Turn off the circuit breaker. If you suspect a faulty thermostat, see pages 105–106 for how to replace it.

Before you call the plumber, troubleshoot your electric water heater. You can do it with a screwdriver and a continuity tester.

Water heaters heat the water in an insulated cylinder with a heating element—smaller units will have one element; larger ones may have two. The temperature within the tank is controlled by one or two thermostats attached to the outside.

Upper or lower?

A simple way to troubleshoot is to turn on a faucet in the house and let the water run for a while. If you only get a large amount of lukewarm water, chances are the upper element or the thermostat is not working. (See pages 103–104 for replacing the element and pages 105–106 for replacing the thermostat.) A small volume of hot water at the faucet means the lower thermostat or the element is not working. (See pages 103–106.)

Access panel

1

REMOVE THE ACCESS PANEL
Turn off the water heater circuit breaker at the main electrical panel. Remove the access panel from the water heater. Remember that large-capacity water heaters may have two access panels.

2

DISCONNECT WIRES
Use a screwdriver to disconnect the wires to the water heater element terminals.

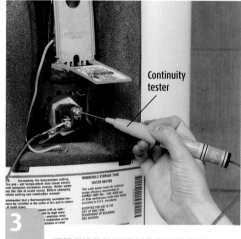

Continuity tester

3

TEST THE ELEMENT FOR CONTINUITY
A continuity tester tells you if a circuit is complete. A heating element is like a circuit. If the light comes on, the element is OK. If not, it needs to be replaced.

Replacing an electric water heater element

PROJECT DETAILS

SKILLS: Attaching wire to a terminal, removing fittings with a wrench or pliers
PROJECT: Replacing an electric water heater element

TIME TO COMPLETE

EXPERIENCED: 30 min.
HANDY: 50 min.
NOVICE: 1.5 hrs.

STUFF YOU'LL NEED

TOOLS: Voltage tester, element wrench or water-pump pliers, silicone grease, garden hose
MATERIALS: Heater element

GOOD IDEA

SAVE YOURSELF SOME TIME
Most plumbers replace the thermostat when they replace a heating element on a water heater. (See "Replacing a Water Heater Thermostat," pages 105–106.)

arger water heaters have an upper and lower heating element. Separate thermostats control each one. If your hot water doesn't get hot enough, the upper element is usually the problem. If you run out of hot water too quickly, replace the lower heating element.

Screw-in or flange?
Depending on the heater, the elements will either screw in or attach with a flange.

Don't blow it!
When working on an electric water heater, the first step is to turn off the power. Don't restore power until the job is done. Also make sure the heater is full of water before you restore power; otherwise you will destroy the element.

Wrap masking tape around the jaws of pliers to protect against damaging the surface of the aerator.

1 REMOVE THE AERATORS
Replacing a water heater element loosens sediment in the tank, which can go through the pipes and clog faucet aerators. Remove the aerators with water-pump pliers. Protect the aerator surface by wrapping tape around the jaws of the pliers.

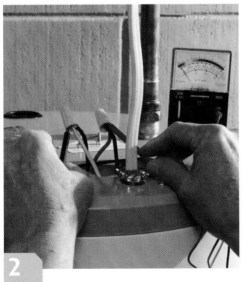

2 TEST FOR VOLTAGE
Turn off the power to the water heater at the circuit breaker in the main electrical panel. Use a voltage meter to make sure the power is off. Shut off the water flow to the water heater at the supply valves.

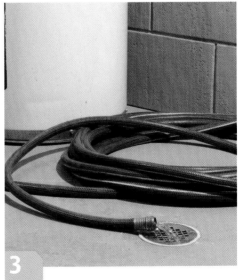

3 DRAIN THE TANK
Connect a garden hose to the water heater drain. Place the end of the hose near a floor drain. Open the drain valve to drain the water in the tank. Close the valve and remove the hose when it's empty.

6

APPLIANCES

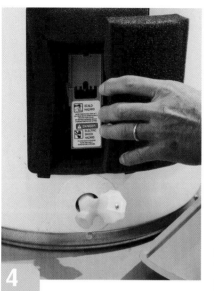

4 REMOVE THE ACCESS PANEL

Remove the access panel to access the heating elements.

5 DISCONNECT THE WIRES

Loosen the terminals connecting the wires to the heating element and remove the wires.

6 REMOVE THE HEATING ELEMENT

Removal is easy with an element wrench, or you can use water-pump pliers or an adjustable wrench. Turn the heating element counterclockwise to remove it.

The tank must be filled with water before the electricity is turned on — otherwise the heating element will melt.

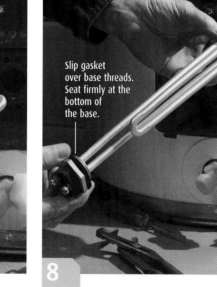

7 INSTALL A NEW GASKET

Coat both sides of the new element gasket with heat-resistant silicone grease and slide it over the heating element to the base.

Slip gasket over base threads. Seat firmly at the bottom of the base.

8 SCREW THE NEW ELEMENT INTO THE TANK

Screw the new element into the tank with the element wrench, then hook up the wires in the same order you removed them.

9 RESTORE THE SYSTEM

Turn on the water supply and open all faucets in the house. When there is a steady flow through the hot side, turn the faucets off. Replace the access panel. Restore power to the water heater by turning on the circuit breaker. Press the "reset" button to activate the unit.

6

APPLIANCES

Replacing a water heater thermostat

A faulty thermostat or high-temperature cutoff in an electric water heater can allow the water in the tank to heat well past recommended safe temperature ranges. Water heated above 120 degrees can cause serious burns.

The same thing can happen if the high-temperature cutoff is defective. The thermostat and high-temperature cutoff are often linked into one unit. If they are separate, follow a basic rule of water heater maintenance: Replace both elements while you're at it. The parts are inexpensive, and you'll save time and an extra trip to the home center.

If your thermostat and high-temperature cutoff are separate, replace both elements.

1

TURN OFF THE POWER
Disconnect the power to the water heater by turning off the circuit breaker at the main panel. If you haven't mapped your breaker box, shut off all the breakers one-by-one until you find the heater switch. Since you've gone to all the trouble to find the right breaker, mark it so you don't have to search next time.

GOOD IDEA

EVERYBODY NEEDS A BLANKET
Older water heaters can gain a new lease on life when you fit them with an insulating blanket of fiberglass. Kits that slip over the entire heater are simple to install and keep heat from escaping into the basement or garage.

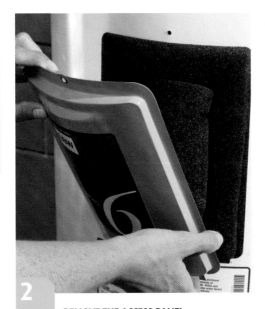

2

REMOVE THE ACCESS PANEL
Use a screwdriver to remove the screws from the access panel. Lift off the panel.

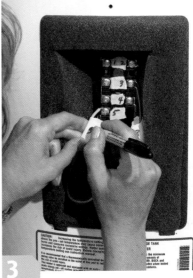

3

LABEL THE WIRES AND TERMINALS
Before removing the thermostat, number the wires and terminals. This will help you reconnect each wire to the proper terminal.

DOUBLE CHECK FOR SAFETY!
Be careful when working with electric water heaters. Most household appliances use 120 volts, which can give you quite a jolt. Electric water heaters require 240 volts. This is enough to do serious harm and could even be fatal. Always turn off the power at the circuit breaker in the main panel or remove the fuse. Use a voltage meter or a neon tester to make sure the power is off.

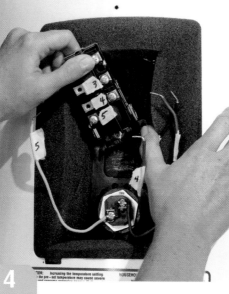

4

LIFT OUT THE THERMOSTAT
Disconnect the old thermostat from the mounting clip and lift it out. Replace it with a new thermostat of the same model.

5

CONNECT THE WIRES
Install the new thermostat to the mounting clip. Reconnect the wires by the numbers you wrote on them in step 3.

6

RESTORE THE SYSTEM
Set the thermostat to the manufacturer's recommended temperature. Make sure the tank is full. Restore power to the water heater at the circuit breaker. Press the red "reset" button on the thermostat.

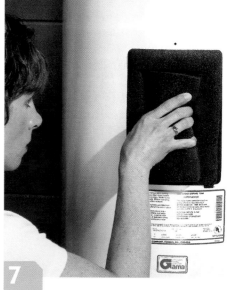

7

REPLACE THE ACCESS PANEL
Replace insulation and reinstall the access panel.

Water heaters

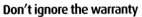

W ater heaters are easy to forget about. They do their work in the dark corners of basements or supply closets and aren't given much thought until a rush of cold water ruins a morning shower. Even with proper maintenance, your water heater will eventually need to be replaced. Here are some considerations when looking for a replacement:

Gas or electric?
Either a gas or electric water heater will supply your hot-water needs efficiently. Choosing one over the other is a matter of what kind of service is available to your home and what makes the most economic sense. Make a list of the different appliances and fixtures in your home that are supplied with hot water, then talk it over with a salesperson at your local home center.
- If you are adding a dishwasher, jetted tub, or other new appliance, you may need a heater with a larger capacity.
- Make sure your electrical system can handle the wattage requirements of your heater.

Insulation is a factor
Insulation is installed to maintain water temperature inside the water heater, reducing energy costs. Choose a water heater insulated with polyfoam over fiberglass batting. Thicknesses vary from 1 to 3 inches in the higher-efficiency water heaters. Insulation type and thickness are key factors in determining the length of the warranty.

Don't ignore the warranty
Warranties vary in length. Six to 12 years on the tank is the usual life span. Check the limitations of the warranties of different manufacturers. The life of the water heater will depend on environmental factors; hard water shortens its life.

The energy factor
Water heaters must bear a yellow Energy Guide sticker required by the National Appliance Energy Conservation Act of 1987. The sticker will display the units of kilowatt-per-year usage for electric models, therms-per-year usage for natural gas, gallons per year for propane, and first-hour rating.

Rate of recovery is not listed, but should be considered when purchasing a water heater, because it determines the amount of rise in temperature per gallon of output (how quickly it heats the water).

Size matters—electric
A family of up to four in a home with two full bathrooms, a clothes washer, and a dishwasher should have a 65-gallon tank with a 4,500-watt heating element. A family of five with the same appliances should have an 80-gallon tank and a 5,500-watt model.

Size matters—gas
A family of up to four in a home with two full bathrooms, a clothes washer, and a dishwasher needs a 50-gallon tank with a 40,000-BTU burner unit. A family of six with the same appliances needs a 50- to 75-gallon tank and a 40,000-BTU model. A family of up to seven needs a 50- to 75-gallon, high-input tank, but should have a 52,500-BTU unit.

Gas
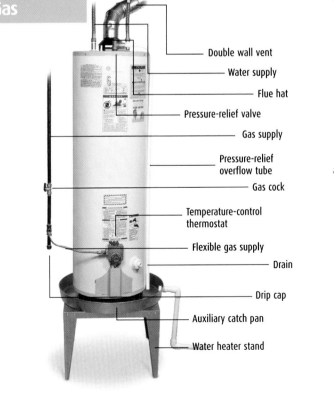

- Double wall vent
- Water supply
- Flue hat
- Pressure-relief valve
- Gas supply
- Pressure-relief overflow tube
- Gas cock
- Temperature-control thermostat
- Flexible gas supply
- Drain
- Drip cap
- Auxiliary catch pan
- Water heater stand

Electric
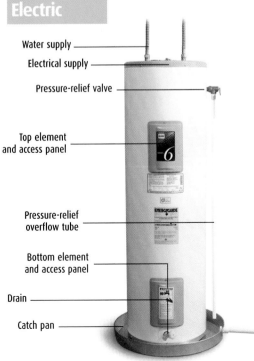

- Water supply
- Electrical supply
- Pressure-relief valve
- Top element and access panel
- Pressure-relief overflow tube
- Bottom element and access panel
- Drain
- Catch pan

Installing an electric water heater

1

SET THE WATER HEATER IN PLACE
Use a level to check the unit for plumb in two directions, and level it with wooden or plastic shims.

Hauling out an old water heater is usually the hardest part of the installation process.

📖 **WORK SMARTER**

REMOVING THE OLD WATER HEATER: IT'S AS EASY AS 1-2-3

1 Turn off the electrical power to the water heater at the main circuit breaker; if you have fuses, remove them. Remove the access panel to the thermostat. Use a voltage tester across the terminal connections to make sure there is no power to the water heater. Turn off the water supply. (If there are two valves, turn them both off.)

2 Connect a garden hose to the tank discharge valve; place the end of the hose in the floor drain or a bucket. Open the valve and drain the water out of the tank and supply lines. Remove the hose. Disconnect the piping. If the piping has been soldered into place, use a hacksaw or tubing cutter to cut the pipe. Be sure to make straight cuts.

3 Remove the electrical supply access plate at the top of the water heater. Disconnect the wires one at a time, label the supply wires as you go. Get some help removing the water heater. Sediment builds up in the body over time, so it could be even heavier than the new one.

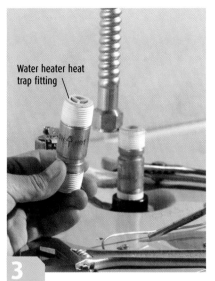

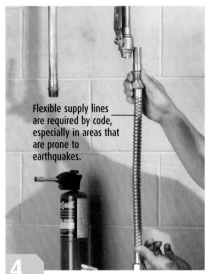

2
SWEAT SOLDER THE SHUTOFF VALVE TO THE END OF THE COLD WATER SUPPLY PIPE

Use a propane torch and lead-free solder to connect the valve to the supply line. The valve must be in the open position when you solder. (See pages 166–167.)

Cut a 2×4 to support the shutoff valve while soldering.

3
WRAP THE THREADS OF THE WATER HEATER HEAT TRAP FITTING WITH TEFLON TAPE OR COAT WITH PIPE COMPOUND

Attach the blue-coded fitting to the cold-water inlet and the red-coded fitting to the hot-water outlet. These fittings are directional; they have arrows that show the proper installation. Tighten with two adjustable wrenches.

Water heater heat trap fitting

4
INSTALL THE WATER SUPPLY

Use two adjustable wrenches to connect the pipe from the pipe run to the water heater. Turn the main shutoff on and open all line valves. Open all the faucets in the house and run the water until it flows steadily from the faucets. Close the faucets.

Flexible supply lines are required by code, especially in areas that are prone to earthquakes.

The tank must be full of water before you restore power. The elements will burn out in seconds when exposed to air.

GOOD IDEA

SAVE AT THE METER

The water heater heat trap fittings in step 3 may have to be purchased separately, but they are highly recommended to conserve energy.

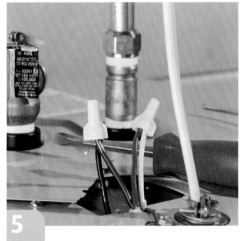

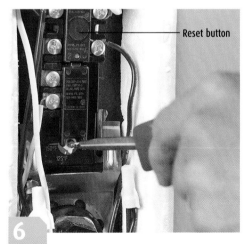

$ BUYER'S GUIDE

Reset button

Rigid foam insulation

5
REMOVE THE ELECTRICAL ACCESS PLATE

Always turn off the power to the unit before you do any electrical work. Connect the electrical supply according to the manufacturer's instructions using wire nuts. Connect the bare copper or ground wire to the ground screw. Replace the electrical access plate. Remove the thermostat access plate.

6
ADJUST THE THERMOSTAT

Recommended settings are 120 to 125 degrees. Now open a faucet near the heater, turn on the water supply, and fill the tank until the faucet is flowing. The tank must be full before you restore power. When the tank is full, restore power and press the reset button on the panel.

INSULATION IS THE KEY

A new water heater is lined with rigid foam insulation to conserve heat so you won't need an insulating blanket to keep the water hot. The newest models also have LED lights wired to the upper and lower elements, so you can see if the element is working.

6

APPLIANCES

Installing a gas water heater

PROJECT DETAILS

SKILLS: Connecting plumbing fittings, stripping wire, and attaching wire to a terminal
PROJECT: Installing a gas water heater

TIME TO COMPLETE

EXPERIENCED: 45 min.
HANDY: 1 hr.
NOVICE: 2 hrs.

STUFF YOU'LL NEED

TOOLS: Continuity tester, carpenter's level, propane torch, two adjustable wrenches, two pipe wrenches, hacksaw or tubing cutter, screwdriver, garden hose, fireplace match or grill igniter
MATERIALS: Gas water heater, acid-free flux, plastic shims, Teflon tape, water heater heat trap fittings, copper supply lines, liquid soap, sponge, bucket

GOOD IDEA

SAVE AT THE METER

The water heater heat trap fittings in step 5 may have to be purchased separately, but they are highly recommended to conserve energy.

Gas water heaters require a gas supply, a cold water supply, and a flue connection to carry away harmful gases (see pages 113, 166, and 173). Today's homes tend to be airtight, so make sure you have adequate venting. Carbon monoxide—a byproduct of combustion—can be fatal when inadequate venting allows it to build up in the home. Call your local utility immediately if you suspect the water heater is not working properly.

Disconnect the supply wires one at a time and label each one so you can rewire without guessing.

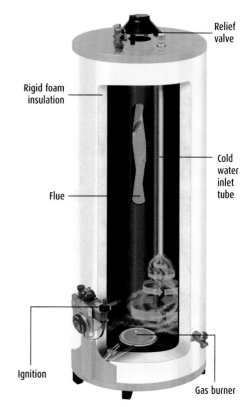

Relief valve

Rigid foam insulation

Cold water inlet tube

Flue

Ignition

Gas burner

1 REMOVE THE OLD WATER HEATER
Turn off the water and gas supply valves to the tank. Turn off the power. Remove the electrical supply access plate at the top of the water heater. Check the connections with a continuity tester to make sure the power is off. Attach a garden hose to the drain valve and empty the tank. Using two pipe wrenches, disconnect the gas line at the union fitting if the pipe is galvanized, or at the flare fitting if the gas supply line is copper.

2 DISCONNECT THE WATER LINES
Using two adjustable wrenches or pipe wrenches, disconnect the piping above the tank. If the piping has been soldered into place, use a hacksaw or tubing cutter to cut the pipe. Make sure the cuts are straight.

APPLIANCES

6

3

DETACH THE GAS EXHAUST VENT FROM THE FLUE HAT

Remove the screws connecting the vent to the water heater using a screwdriver or nut driver. Save your back—get some help removing the old water heater. They fill with sediment, so the old one may be heavier than the new one.

4

SET THE NEW WATER HEATER

Install the water heater in an area where it won't be cramped. There should be at least 6 inches of clearance around it for ventilation. Don't set it next to flammables. Turn the water heater so there is unobstructed access to the burner and controls. Place a carpenter's level on the side of the water heater and level it with plastic shims. Connect the flue hat to the gas exhaust vent. (See page 113.)

6

APPLIANCES

5

WRAP THE WATER HEATER HEAT TRAP FITTING THREADS

Use Teflon tape on the pipe threads. These fittings are directional and must be installed properly. Both have arrows showing the correct direction for installation. Attach the blue-coded fitting to the cold water inlet with the arrow facing into the water heater. Attach the red fitting to the hot water outlet with the arrow pointing away from the water heater. Tighten using two pipe wrenches or adjustable pliers.

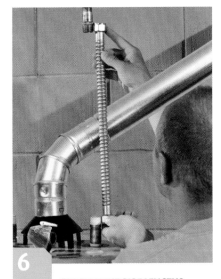

6

CONNECT THE PIPE LENGTHS

Measure and cut the water line connections to length. Precut lengths of flexible copper pipe are available at your local home center if you don't want to use rigid copper pipe.

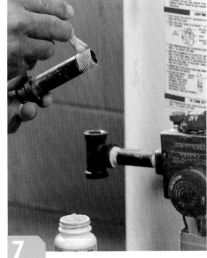

7

CONNECT THE GAS SUPPLY LINE

Clean all threads with a wire brush and rag. Apply piping compound to the threads of the black pipes as you connect them. Assemble and tighten each fitting with two pipe wrenches. The union fitting should be the last fitting you install because it connects the new line to the existing line. Once finished, open the gas supply valve.

8

TEST THE GAS LINE FOR LEAKS

Fill a sponge with liquid dishwashing soap and water. Apply it to the new fitting and look for bubbles. It's the same process used for finding a leak in a car tire. If there's a leak, bubbles will form on the surface; and you'll have to refit the joint. Test all connections.

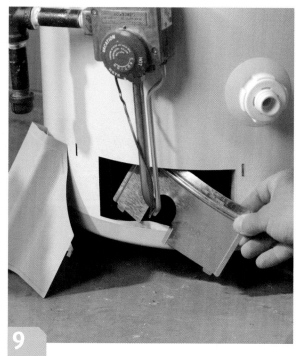

9

REMOVE THE BURNER ACCESS PANEL

This panel covers the burner chamber and prevents debris from entering.

10

LIGHT THE PILOT

Use a fireplace match or a grill igniter to light the pilot. (See page 99.) Replace the burner access panel and set the control at 120 to 125 degrees. Make sure the pilot light just touches the thermocouple.

11

TURN THE CONTROL KNOB TO THE "ON" POSITION

You should hear the burner ignite. If it doesn't, relight the pilot following the manufacturer's instructions to the letter. Then adjust the thermostat to the desired setting.

Installing a flue hat

The combustion of natural gas produces harmful fumes. Without a means of removing these gases, they would build up in the house. The flue hat serves as a funnel to collect these gases and carry them away from the house through metal duct pipe.

Vents vary

Vent duct for flues comes in three varieties: "A," which is single wall; "B," which is double wall; and "C," which is triple wall. Check local codes for the one that is approved in your area.

Test for draw

Test to be sure your flue is drawing fumes out of the house: Light a match, blow it out, and immediately hold it under the flue. If the smoke is not sucked up and out, the flue is not drawing. Also install a carbon monoxide detector in the room. If there are any problems call the gas company to come and inspect.

1 INSTALL THE VENT LINE

Measure, cut, and assemble the vent from the flue hat to the roof vent stack. Make sure horizontal sections have a slope of ¼ inch of rise for every foot of length to efficiently carry fumes away from the house.

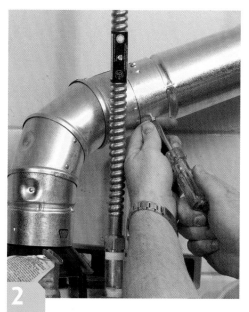

2 ATTACH THE DUCTWORK

Connect the ductwork by driving ⅜-inch sheet metal screws into the vent every 3 to 4 inches around the duct. You will need at least three screws per joint.

3 CONNECT THE DUCT TO THE FLUE HAT

Drive a ⅜-inch sheet metal screw through the duct connecting it to the flue hat. Some codes require copper pipe for the pressure-relief valve. (See page 114.)

6

APPLIANCES

Installing a pressure-relief valve

PROJECT DETAILS

SKILLS: Connecting plumbing fittings and CPVC pipe
PROJECT: Installing a relief valve and drain line

TIME TO COMPLETE

EXPERIENCED: 20 min.
HANDY: 40 min.
NOVICE: 1 hr.

STUFF YOU'LL NEED

TOOLS: Pipe or adjustable wrench
MATERIALS: Pressure-relief valve, Teflon tape or piping compound

When water is heated, pressure builds up in the tank. If this pressure is too great, a rupture could occur. A pressure-relief valve serves as a check valve to automatically open and relieve the pressure. Most water heaters now come with one; but if yours doesn't, you'll have to install one, and occasionally they need to be replaced. Consult your local home center to find the valve that will fit your water heater.

Never use more than two Teflon wraps; more will get in the way.

1

PREPARE THE FITTING THREAD
Wrap the threads of the pressure-relief valve clockwise with Teflon tape or apply piping compound.

2

ATTACH THE VALVE TO THE WATER HEATER
Use a pipe wrench or an adjustable wrench to connect the relief valve to the opening in the water heater. Measure the distance from the relief valve to the floor. Cut lengths of CPVC pipe to match the ones you're replacing, as long as they extend to within 3 inches of the floor. Connect the pipe and elbow to the pressure-relief valve. (See pages 169–170.)

BUYER'S GUIDE

TAKE EXTRA PRESSURE OFF THE SYSTEM
Water heater safety tanks provide relief from pressure that can build up in a contained system like your water heater. Pressure can damage fittings and fixtures, as well as shorten the life of appliances. Symptoms are water dripping from the pressure-relief valve, frequent dishwasher repairs or breakdowns, dripping faucets, periodic hot water pressure surges, and puddles of water at the base of the water heater. Rapidly heated water can also cause scalding.

Safety tanks are designed to be installed in-line on the inlet (cold water) pipe side of the water heater. Typically, they are attached at a location along the line with a tap saddle that supports the weight of the tank. You will have to provide support for the pipe to accommodate the extra weight.

Tankless water heater

REPLACING A WATER HEATER? YOU MAY WANT TO THINK TANKLESS

Common in Europe, tankless (on-demand) water heaters are beginning to make their mark in the United States and Canada. If you're adding a bathtub and shower to your home or need to upgrade the size of your water heater, tankless may be the way to go. On-demand heaters come in sizes small enough to mount in a kitchen cabinet and large enough to handle almost any size home. In milder climates, some can even be placed outdoors. Tankless water heaters not only guarantee a constant supply of hot water, they also take up far less space than a conventional water heater. While they are more expensive than standard water heaters, their savings in energy and low maintenance might quickly make up the difference in cost.

If water entering a unit is too cold, a tankless heater may have difficulty heating adequately. If you live in a cold region, ask a salesperson whether a tankless water heater will work for you.

HOW DO THEY WORK?

Tankless heaters flow water through a set of coiled copper pipes. The water is heated by a gas burner as it passes through the coils. Water heater tanks, on the other hand, maintain water at a constant temperature, even when hot water is not being drawn. Heat loss in the tank can be as much as 4 percent per hour. To maintain a constant water temperature in the tank, a thermostat will activate to heat the water. This requires an increase in gas and electric usage, resulting in higher energy costs.

WHAT ABOUT CAPACITY?

Tankless water heaters eliminate the need for maintaining a constant water temperature, supplying heated water only when there is a demand. They can supply continuously heated water at 105 degrees to 115 degrees at rates of 2 to 3 gallons per minute. Most conventional water heaters, on the other hand, will eventually run out of hot water when demand is high, and they require time to recharge.

WHAT IS THE LIFE EXPECTANCY?

Because tankless water heaters are not constantly heating water, they may have a longer life expectancy than conventional water heater tanks. Conventional water heaters are constantly running and have life expectancies of 2 to 10 years. Tankless water heaters may have life expectancies of more than 20 years.

Tankless water heaters eliminate the need for maintaining a constant water temperature. Because they are not constantly heating water they will often have a life expectancy twice that of conventional water heaters.

Fixing a slow-filling clothes washer

6

APPLIANCES

PROJECT DETAILS

SKILLS: Connecting plumbing fittings
PROJECT: Fixing a slow-filling clothes washer

TIME TO COMPLETE

EXPERIENCED: 15 min.
HANDY: 20 min.
NOVICE: 1 hr.

STUFF YOU'LL NEED

TOOLS: Water-pump pliers, screwdriver or tweezers, small wire brush or old toothbrush, small bowl
MATERIALS: Inlet screens, white vinegar or cleaning solution

BUYER'S GUIDE

CHECK THE HOSES!

Hoses become brittle after several years. Instead of waiting for them to bubble, crack, and fail, buy a new set. Look for "nonburst"-type hoses. A reinforced cover prevents the hose from bursting. They're a little more expensive than the regular hose; but if a hose bursts, you're not going to appreciate the money you saved.

Does it take too long for the washer to fill? This may be a sign that the inlet screens are filled with sediment.

Hard water results in sediment buildup, caused by excess quantities of calcium carbonate and magnesium from soil and limestone.

Inlet screens prevent the sediment from entering the components of the washer and causing damage to the internal parts. Clogged parts can be expensive to replace and time-consuming to repair. Cleaning the screens is an easy project for a beginning do-it-yourselfer. While you're at it, replace the hoses with the "nonburst" braided type for a longer lasting repair.

Keep damaging sediment out of washer components by keeping the inlet screens clean.

1 DISCONNECT THE FILL HOSES

Unplug the washer and pull it away from the wall so you'll have enough room to work. Turn off the hot and cold water to the unit at the shutoff valves. Remove the hoses from the back of the washer using water-pump pliers. Drain any water left in the lines into either a bucket or the floor drain. If water continues to drip out of the lines, you may need to repair the shutoff valves; sediment may build up on the faucet washers because of lack of use.

2 PRY OUT THE INLET SCREENS

Use tweezers, a screwdriver, or a pick to remove the inlet screens. These screens prevent debris from entering the washer. Work carefully—if you damage a screen, you will need to replace it. You can find replacements at your local home center. If the screens are undamaged you can clean and reuse them.

Clothes washers and dryers

🌐 **REAL WORLD**

IF IN DOUBT, UPGRADE

Wiring in old homes can be suspect because electrical codes may not have been strictly followed or enforced. Also, deterioration of the wire and receptacle over time can create potential fire hazards. If there is any uncertainty as to the quality of system, it should be upgraded. It's important to ensure that the circuit breaker can accommodate the amps required by modern-day appliances, like washers and dryers.

WATER AND ENERGY EFFICIENCY

Washer and dryer design is regulated by standards set by the U.S. Department of Energy and the U.S. Environmental Protection Agency. These standards define requirements for energy efficiency and water conservation. New washer designs use half the water of older models, while requiring 30 to 40 percent less energy.

TOP- OR FRONT-LOADING

Choose from top-loading and front-loading washers. Front loaders tend to perform better, are gentler on clothes, and use less water and energy than top loaders. But top loaders are easier to load and unload.

WHAT SIZE, PLEASE?

Your first decision will probably be about the size of drum you need. Sizes of washers and dryers are measured in cubic feet. Large families may want to have a 3-cubic-foot drum or larger. Capacities of 2.5 to 3 cubic feet will meet most needs. Extra-large dryers have capacities of 5 to 7 cubic feet. Smaller-capacity models are available for homes and apartments that have space limitations. The compact models may use less energy and require less space, but you'll have to do more loads of laundry to get the same amount of clothes done.

Stainless-steel drums won't chip or rust like porcelain-coated drums. A plastic drum won't either, and it costs less than the other two.

ACCESSORIES

Manufacturers offer a number of features. Some have automatic detergent dispensers and automatic temperature controls. Three spin-and-wash speed cycles are common, but you can choose as many as five.

People who are sensitive to detergents may want multiple-rinse cycle options, such as warm rinses and extra-rinse cycles. Stackable units save space, and cost-conscious people will probably want a time-delay feature to take advantage of off-peak utility rates.

Moisture detectors in dryers help save energy. A sensor in the dryer detects the moisture level in the load and turns the dryer off when the clothes are dry. Some allow you to set for various degrees of dampness, so you can remove clothes for ironing.

Installing a washing machine

PROJECT DETAILS

SKILLS: Using a level and connecting plumbing fittings
PROJECT: Installing a washing machine

TIME TO COMPLETE

EXPERIENCED: 45 min.
HANDY: 1 hr.
NOVICE: 1.5 hrs.

STUFF YOU'LL NEED

TOOLS: Carpenter's level, water-pump pliers, hacksaw
MATERIALS: Washing machine, washer hoses, PVC primer, PVC cement

Washing machines are easy to install, especially if you're replacing the old unit with a new one. All you have to do is hook up the drain and supply lines, level it, plug it in, and wash a load of laundry. If you're installing in a new location, you may need to run plumbing pipes and set up an electrical outlet. The washer can drain into a utility sink or into a standpipe, as shown in step 1.

Washing machines aren't particularly heavy, but they are awkward, bulky, and very likely to be installed in a basement or some other out-of-the-way corner. You'll want to have some helpers around or make sure the delivery people get the unit into its final position. You can rent a furniture truck or a wheeled dolly to make the work a little easier on your back.

GOOD IDEA

WALK THE WALK

If you're installing a washing machine in a new location, make sure you've walked the delivery route and measured openings so there won't be any surprises when the unit is delivered.

Make sure you have plenty of help on hand to get your washing machine to the location where it will be installed.

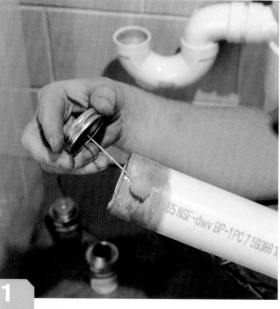

1 CONNECT THE STANDPIPE

Install a standpipe to a P-trap connected to the drainage and vent system. (See pages 149–150.) The standpipe must have a greater diameter than the hose, and the top should be above the washer's water level to prevent overflow.

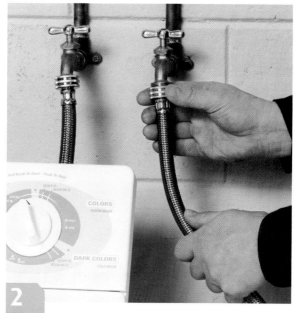

2 HOOK UP THE WASHER SUPPLY HOSES

Connect the hot and cold water lines using water-pump pliers. Connect the waste line to the washer and run it to the standpipe. Turn on the water valves and run the clothes washer. If there are any leaks, tighten the connections.

6

APPLIANCES

3 LEVEL THE CLOTHES WASHER

Once the machine is in place, you'll want to make sure it's seated securely on the floor and is perfectly level to keep it from "walking" and banging loudly while you're doing the family wash. Place a carpenter's level or a bubble level on top of the washer. Level the unit by adjusting the legs and securing the locknuts against the frame.

Do all the work at the back of the machine (hooking up the supply hoses and waste line) before you set and level the washer.

🔍 CLOSER LOOK

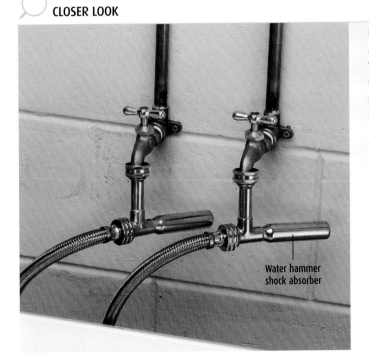

Water hammer shock absorber

INSTALL WATER HAMMER SHOCK ABSORBERS ON NOISY PIPES

The banging sound of air trapped in pipes is both noisy and annoying. The stress can also damage pipes over time. Water hammer shock absorbers eliminate the problem. Because they are sealed, they can be installed vertically or horizontally. Turn off the hot- and cold-water supply valves. Disconnect the supply hoses from the valves with water-pump pliers. Connect the shock absorbers to the valves and reattach the supply hoses. Turn on the water and enjoy living with pipes that don't bang when water is turned on or off.

Installing a dryer vent

PROJECT DETAILS

SKILLS: Connecting ductwork and drilling a hole

PROJECT: Installing a dryer vent

TIME TO COMPLETE

EXPERIENCED: 45 min.
HANDY: 1.5 hrs.
NOVICE: 2 hrs.

STUFF YOU'LL NEED

TOOLS: Power drill, hole saw, tape measure, screwdriver, caulking gun, level
MATERIALS: Dryer vent, silicone caulk, wood screws, hanger straps, foil tape

 orced heat, whether produced by natural gas, propane, or electricity, dries the clothes. It's important to remove this moist air from the house because it may be mixed with hazardous gases such as carbon monoxide, a byproduct of combustion. Vent pipe is normally made of 4-inch diameter, rigid sheet metal.

Don't use flexible ducts

Flexible vinyl cannot be used because it doesn't support its weight and lint that collects in low spots presents a fire hazard. Seal joints with foil duct tape. **Never use sheet metal screws; they will catch lint.**

Don't run a duct into a chimney, a crawlspace, or under a floor. The lint will build up and create a potential fire hazard.

1 CUT THE VENT HOOD OPENING

The hood will need to be accessible from inside. Measure the location and find out where the hood will be from the inside. Translate it to its outside location. Drill a pilot hole and check inside to make sure the hole is in the right place. Plug and redrill if necessary. Use a 4¼-inch hole saw to cut the hood opening.

2 INSTALL THE VENT HOOD

Insert the duct pipe through the hole. Attach the hood to the siding with wood screws. Caulk around the edges of the hood to seal against the elements.

APPLIANCES

6

3 CONNECT TO THE HOOD DUCT

The location may require an elbow to the hood duct. You may have one or two elbows back-to-back to the run. Attach the duct lengths to the elbow.

4 SECURE THE DUCT

Attach straps to support the duct. Apply foil tape around the joints to seal them and help support the duct. Use a carpenter's level and set horizontal sections with a fall of ¼ inch per foot to prevent moisture from collecting.

5 INSTALL THE DUCT INTO THE DRYER VENT OUTLET

Insert an elbow over the dryer outlet. Connect the duct pipe to the elbow. (See inset.) Slide the dryer into place. Level using a carpenter's or bubble level. Adjust the legs and lock into place by tightening the locknut against the dryer.

⊘ SAFETY ALERT

WHY YOU CAN'T USE SCREWS!

Sheet metal screws are not approved by code for use in areas where dust or lint collects, so cannot be used to connect the duct pipe and fittings. The ends of the screws will stick into the duct and catch lint. The lint will build up over time and block the flow of harmful gases. Without anywhere to go, gases such as carbon monoxide will vent into the house. The back pressure created by the blockage can also shorten the life of the motor.

APPLIANCES

6

Replacing a sump pump

PROJECT DETAILS

SKILLS: Connecting plumbing fittings
PROJECT: Replacing a sump pump

TIME TO COMPLETE

EXPERIENCED: 20 min.
HANDY: 40 min.
NOVICE: 1 hr.

STUFF YOU'LL NEED

TOOLS: Screwdriver, water-pump pliers, carpenter's level, tubing cutters
MATERIALS: Sump pump, discharge pipe if needed, plastic or composite shims

A sump pump removes excess water from a basement and sends it through a discharge line that exits the house. Test the system once a year by pouring a couple gallons of water into the sump pit to activate the pump. This project shows you how to replace a pedestal-style sump pump with a submersible pump. If your basement has no existing pit and sump pump, see the next two pages for installing a new one.

REMOVE THE OLD PUMP AND INSTALL A NEW ONE

Unplug the sump pump and disconnect the discharge line entering it. You may need to use two pairs of water-pump pliers. Make sure the new pump sits level in the pit; use plastic or composite shims, if needed. Reuse the old piece of discharge line from the old pump, or cut a new piece. Connect the outlet pipe to the main discharge line, either by tightening a union or by slipping on a rubber fitting and tightening the hose clamps. Plug the cord into a grounded outlet. Test by filling the pit with water until the pump is activated.

BUYER'S GUIDE

GUIDE WATER AWAY

If water continues to come back into the system, it may be because the exterior drain is too close to the house. Make sure discharge water is guided away from the foundation.

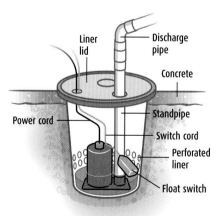

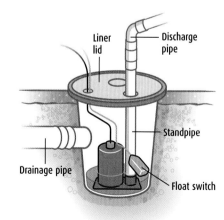

TWO SUMP PUMP SETUPS

In an older home with no drainage pipe, or if you will install a sump pump in a home that has none, water that travels just below (and sometimes on top of) the concrete floor seeps into a perforated liner (above left). Many newer homes have a drainage pipe that leads into a non-perforated liner (above right). Both types use a sump pump to send water through a discharge pipe.

Installing a new sump pump

PROJECT DETAILS

SKILLS: Operating a jackhammer and connecting plumbing fittings
PROJECT: Installing a sump pump

TIME TO COMPLETE

EXPERIENCED: 2 hrs.
HANDY: 4 hrs.
NOVICE: 6 hrs.

STUFF YOU'LL NEED

TOOLS: Electric drill, keyhole saw, jackhammer, caulking gun, water-pump pliers, trowel, screwdriver, nut driver, level, adjustable wrench, PVC primer and cement, gloves, eye protection
MATERIALS: Sump pump and assembly, PVC drain pipe and fittings, caulk, gravel, concrete, pit lines, electrician's tape, rubber seal

WORK SMARTER

RENT A BIG HAMMER

Breaking concrete to install a sump pit requires a jackhammer or a heavy-duty hammer drill and sledgehammer. If you decide to tackle a pit installation yourself, visit your local rental center.

I f your basement has an existing sump pump, see the previous page for how to replace it. (If you have a sump pump pit but no sump pump, see the illustration on the bottom of page 122 to determine which setup you need.)

To install a new pump, you're going to have to break through the concrete slab and dig a pit. Before you attack the slab with a jackhammer, check with your municipality or water company to make sure you will not break into a sewer line or water supply line.

Locate the lines

The sewer line should have a visible cleanout, which will indicate the direction it's running. Identifying branch sewer line locations may be a little more difficult. Look for risers to help identify them. The water service line might be difficult to locate in slab construction. Most service lines enter the home 4 to 6 feet away from the sewer line. Contact the local water company; they'll tell you where service comes in.

Mark out the pit

The sump pit should be located at the lowest point on the concrete floor and near an exterior wall so the discharge piping won't be too long. Use a carpenter's level to identify the low point. Mark out the opening for the pit liner, allowing an extra 6 inches for gravel fill.

Break out the concrete

Wear heavy clothing and gloves to minimize vibration, cover your eyes with protective goggles, and give yourself plenty of light to work by. Use the electric jackhammer to cut around the perimeter and break out the center area in small chunks. (Smaller chunks are easier to haul upstairs and out of the house.)

Set the liner

Remove the soil from the hole to the depth of the pit liner. Set the liner in the pit and level it flush to the concrete surface. Fill around the liner with coarse gravel to within a foot of the surface. Seal around the outside of the pit with concrete. Finish the concrete surface to match the existing floor, using a trowel.

When the concrete is dry, you can begin installing the pump.

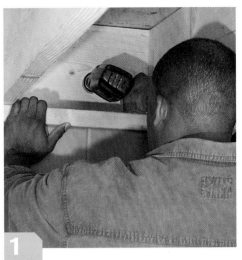

1 CUT A HOLE IN AN OUTSIDE WALL FOR THE DISCHARGE PIPE

Use a keyhole saw to drill a hole the same diameter as the discharge pipe recommended by the manufacturer. Measure and cut a section of PVC pipe to extend through the wall with 6 inches extending outside and enough extending inside to install an elbow.

Connect extension here

2 SEAL THE OUTSIDE OF THE PIPE

Caulk around the pipe with a caulking gun. Connect an extension to the pipe long enough to carry water away from the house; if it's too close, the water will seep back through the foundation.

6

APPLIANCES

3

ATTACH THE SUMP PUMP TO THE DISCHARGE STANDPIPE

You will need to assemble the unit; the sump pump and the discharge fitting will not normally be preassembled. Connect the two.

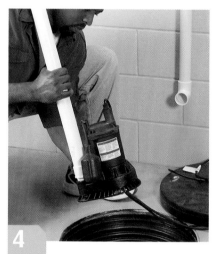

4

INSTALL THE SUMP PUMP

Set the sump pump on the bottom of the pit.

5

SET IT ON A SOLID SURFACE

Make sure the gravel base is solid enough to keep the pump from shifting. If it is not, place a small, flat concrete block or some bricks under the pump. Set the pump so the float is several inches from the liner.

6

LEVEL THE PUMP

Place a bullet level on top of the pump housing. Level the pump using a flattened copper pipe or plastic shims. Check the discharge pipe to make sure it's also level vertically.

CLOSER LOOK

STOP CONSTANT RUNNING WITH A CHECK VALVE

If your sump pump constantly turns on and off when there's no water to pump, the water left in the discharge pipe may be flowing back into the pit. The solution is a check valve that prevents the backflow. Check valves are available at your local home center.

7

CONNECT THE DISCHARGE PIPE

Install the check valve with the arrow pointing up. Slide the rubber coupling over the end of the check valve. Place a hose clamp over it and tighten, using a screwdriver or a nut driver. Measure and cut PVC pipe that extends to the pipe through the basement ceiling joist or the wall. Test-fit the line and fittings first. Make sure all the connections are snug. Make adjustments as needed. Use hangers to support longer runs. Cement the PVC (pages 182–183). Once the cement has dried, slide the rubber seal over the end and tighten it.

8

POWER IT UP

Run the power cord along the discharge pipe, securing it with electrician's tape. Adjust the float to the level recommended by the manufacturer. Plug the pump cord into a nearby GFCI-protected receptacle. Test the sump pump by emptying a 5-gallon bucket into the liner, turning it on, and watching it in action.

WORK SMARTER

MINIMIZE VIBRATION

Installing a rubber seal between the pump and the discharge pipe minimizes vibration created when the sump pump is running.

APPLIANCES

6

Supply pipes and filters

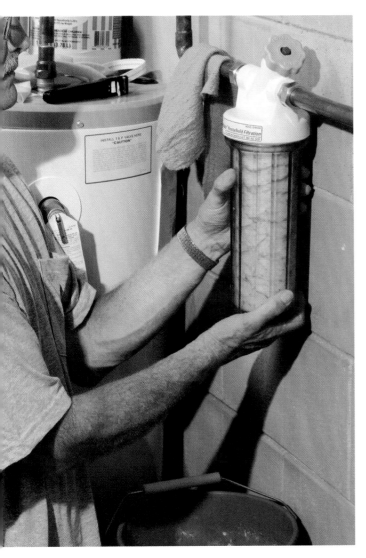

Most of the time, water supply pipes provide you with a reliable stream of water. Occasionally, however, a pipe may burst or develop a leak at a fitting. Or your pipes may make vibrating noises, sweat in the summer, or freeze during a hard cold snap. This chapter shows permanent solutions to these problems. Here you'll also find instructions for installing and maintaining water filters, as well as a hot-water dispenser. For information on running new supply pipes—a project that calls for careful planning and adhering to local codes—see chapter 9.

Protecting pipes from freezing

PROJECT DETAILS

SKILLS: Cutting and fitting various types of insulation around pipes
PROJECT: Protecting pipes from freezing

TIME TO COMPLETE

EXPERIENCED: Variable
HANDY: Variable
NOVICE: Variable

STUFF YOU'LL NEED

TOOLS: Carpenter's level, hair dryer or heat lamp, watering can, towel, bucket
MATERIALS: Polystyrene foam, pipe insulation tubes, hot water

Freezing climates pose a threat to both outdoor and indoor plumbing. Water expands when it freezes, fracturing pipes and valves. You may be required to bury pipe below the frost line; check with your building department. Or, drain all outdoor pipes in the fall, either by installing drain valves at the lowest points or by blowing the pipes out with a compressor. You should also protect indoor pipes that are exposed to exterior walls.

No need to freeze

You can prevent pipes from freezing by not running supply lines in exposed areas or against exterior walls, wrapping pipes with sleeve-type foam insulation, or protecting them with an insulation wrap, such as heat tape. Be careful when using heat tape, however. It can deteriorate over time and pose a fire hazard. You should inspect it occasionally and replace it if it is worn.

Pipe insulation

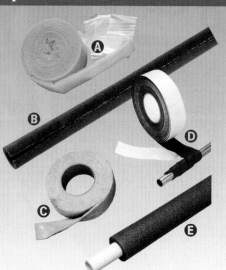

Ⓐ Fiberglass insulation,
Ⓑ Synthetic rubber insulation for copper,
Ⓒ Foam and fiberglass insulation, Ⓓ Pipe tape, and Ⓔ Foam insulation for CPVC that won't soften or damage pipe

SAFETY ALERT

NEVER PLACE NEW HEAT TAPE OVER OLD!
Remove old heat tape before wrapping the pipe with new tape. Placing new heat tape over old creates a potential fire hazard.

1

PROTECT SHALLOW BURIED PIPES
It may help to cover shallow pipes with a sheet of polystyrene foam to insulate pipes. Codes may also require that pipes be protected from damage with a board laid on top. For extra protection, drain a shallow line before winter arrives, if possible.

2

INSTALL A FREEZE-PROOF HOSE BIB
A new freeze-proof hose bib has a long stem so it can shut off water inside the house, where it is far less likely to freeze. Seal the area around the hose bib with a gasket and/or caulk so cold air cannot get in.

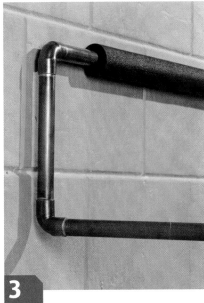

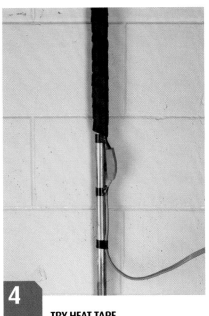

3
INSULATE PIPES ALONG EXPOSED EXTERIOR WALLS

Pipes installed against exposed exterior walls can freeze during winter months. Insulate them with a foam jacket. This protects the pipes from freezing and is an excellent way to conserve energy. Hot water pipes tend to lose heat rapidly, so wrapping them will help maintain water temperature.

4
TRY HEAT TAPE

Heat tape or cable wraps around or attaches to pipes and plugs into a standard outlet. Use only UL-approved materials and follow the manufacturer's instructions carefully.

5
LEAVE THE FAUCET OPEN

We can't always plan or build for temperature extremes. Should your area experience unusually cold temperatures, use this stop-gap method for preventing pipes from freezing. Leave faucets that are connected to piping on outside walls open so water trickles from them. This is not energy efficient, but it will get you through a day or two of extremely cold weather. Also, leaving the cabinet doors open will help keep pipes warm.

Some types of insulation will soften and damage CPVC. Check manufacturer's instructions and use only foam-type insulation on plastic pipe.

CLOSER LOOK

THAWING FROZEN PIPES

If you forget to do something to prevent your pipes from freezing and one pipe is frozen, there's still a solution. Turn off the water from the main shutoff valve. Inspect the pipe for damage. Look for ruptures along the pipe that may have been caused by expansion of the freezing water. If you find a rupture, fix it. (See "Emergencies—Quick Fixes for Leaking or Burst Pipes," pages 131–132.) If the pipe does not appear to be fractured, drain out any water in the line by opening a downstream faucet. Use Ⓐ, a hair dryer or heat lamp to thaw the pipe. Or Ⓑ, place a bucket under the pipe, wrap the pipe with an old towel, and pour hot water over the towel to thaw out the pipe. Once the pipe is thawed, have someone turn on the water supply while you inspect the pipe for leaks and damage.

Fixing noisy pipes

PROJECT DETAILS

SKILLS: Connecting plumbing fittings and wrapping pipe
PROJECT: Fixing noisy pipes

TIME TO COMPLETE

EXPERIENCED: 10 min.
HANDY: 15 min.
NOVICE: 20 min.

STUFF YOU'LL NEED

TOOLS: Water-pump pliers, utility knife
MATERIALS: Water hammer shock absorbers, pipe foam insulation tubes, vibration clamps

I f your car starts making strange sounds, your first thought is to get it repaired. The same should apply to your house. Banging or vibrating pipes are more than an annoyance; they may eventually damage the piping.

Noise that starts when you open your faucet may be a sign that the seat washer is defective, causing vibration or rattling. Replacing the washer may solve the problem.

High water pressure may cause pipes to bang. See the next page for solutions.

Clamps and hangers

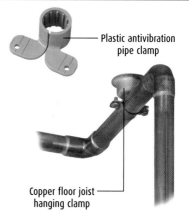

Plastic antivibration pipe clamp

Copper floor joist hanging clamp

1 INSTALL WATER HAMMER SHOCK ABSORBERS ON NOISY PIPES

Turn off the hot and cold water supply valves. Disconnect the supply hoses from the valves using water-pump pliers. Connect water hammer shock absorbers to the valves and attach the supply hoses to the shock absorbers. Water hammer shock absorbers come in many styles with different installation requirements. They can be attached anywhere you have noisy pipes.

2 APPLY INSULATION TO PREVENT NOISE FROM VIBRATING PIPES

Have a helper turn on the water supply to the section of line you suspect is causing the noise, while you find the source of the banging. Once you find it, wrap foam insulation around the pipe at the point of impact. There are a variety of clamps and hangers available that will stop pipes from vibrating. (See "Clamps and Hangers" above.)

Dealing with thermal expansion and high water pressure

PROJECT DETAILS

SKILLS: Connecting plumbing fittings
PROJECT: Installing a thermal expansion device

TIME TO COMPLETE

EXPERIENCED: Variable
HANDY: Variable
NOVICE: Variable

STUFF YOU'LL NEED

TOOLS: Screwdriver, water-pump pliers, tubing cutters, water pressure tester, other plumbing tools if you will install an expansion tank or new valve
MATERIALS: Thermal expansion device

I f you have banging pipes or a sharp burst of pressure when you first turn on a faucet, you may have either generally high water pressure or sporadically increased water pressure due to thermal expansion. Excess water pressure is not just annoying; it can shorten the life of a water heater, or even damage it outright. Other plumbing features, like sensitive parts of faucets or backflow prevention devices, may also be damaged by high water pressure. Plumbing codes often require that thermal expansion be addressed with special devices.

Generally high water pressure is a problem caused by your water supplier. Thermal expansion occurs because water expands when it is heated, increasing the pressure in hot-water lines. Often the highest water pressure occurs at night, when heated water builds up in the pipes for several hours. Fortunately, there are some simple solutions.

TEST THE WATER PRESSURE AND TEST FOR THERMAL EXPANSION
Turn off all the faucets and other water users in the house. Screw a special tester like the one shown onto a hose bib that is near where water enters your house. Turn on the hose bib. The pressure indicated on the tester is the general water pressure delivered to you by your utility. If you have high water pressure, contact your water supplier for the best solutions.

BUYER'S GUIDE

EXPANSION TANK
An in-line expansion tank is attached to the incoming main water supply, much like a new whole-house water filter (see page 136).

SHUTOFF VALVE WITH RELIEF VALVE
Or, replace a main shutoff valve with a special combination shutoff and relief valve. It operates like a standard ball-type shutoff valve, but also works to relieve pressure due to thermal expansion.

TOILET BALLCOCK VALVE
This may be the simplest solution. Replace an existing toilet tank valve with this special ballcock valve (see page 83). It works like a standard toilet valve, but also provides relief from thermal expansion.

Fixing sweating pipes

PROJECT DETAILS

SKILLS: Cutting foam insulation and measuring lengths
PROJECT: Fixing sweating pipes

TIME TO COMPLETE

EXPERIENCED: 15 min.
HANDY: 20 min.
NOVICE: 30 min.

STUFF YOU'LL NEED

TOOLS: Tape measure, serrated kitchen knife
MATERIALS: Pipe foam insulators

7

SUPPLY PIPES AND FILTERS

Pipes sweat in areas of high humidity. Most basements tend to be damp, so you may have sweating pipes there.

The combination of the humidity in the area and water running through the pipes will cause condensation to form on the surface of the pipe. Operating a dehumidifier in the basement may solve the problem. Covering the pipes with foam tubing insulators will also prevent the buildup of condensation on the surface of the pipes. Tube insulators are available in most home centers and come in standard diameters to fit over indoor water lines.

Foam tubing insulators will keep humidity from reaching the pipes and causing condensation to form on the surface.

Install a vibration clamp here

1

MEASURE THE PIPE

Use a measuring tape to measure the length and diameter of the pipe you wish to insulate. Go to your local home center and purchase pipe insulators to fit the diameter of the pipe. These usually come in packages of a standard length. Use a serrated knife, such as a kitchen knife, to cut the insulation to length.

2

CUTTING CORNERS

To cover 90-degree bends in the pipe, cut a 45-degree notch in the tubing. This will allow you to fit the tubing around the elbow.

3

WRAP INSULATION AROUND THE PIPE

Separate the insulation along the seam. Slip it over the pipe. Press the seam back together to seal.

Emergencies—Quick fixes for leaking or burst pipes

inding a leak is a job in itself. You might be amazed at how far water can travel before reappearing to ruin a wall or ceiling. Water can travel across joists and other surfaces. You may have to cut into walls and ceilings to find the source.

Most leaks occur at pipe fittings. Fractures result from corrosion, dents, or freezing.

Temporary fixes include epoxy and clamps. Permanent solutions involve cutting the pipe and installing dresser couplings. Never install a temporary fix behind a wall, because it will fail; and when it does, you'll be in the same trouble all over again.

If you don't want reoccurring problems, be sure that any fixes you make behind a wall are permanent.

BUYER'S GUIDE

PATCHING THE LEAK

Quick fixes can be made for small leaks and wet surfaces with Ⓐ plumber's epoxy putty. More serious leaks require more drastic measures, but solutions abound. Try 1/16-inch-thick neoprene rubber or a bicycle tube patch with Ⓑ hose clamps, Ⓒ sleeve clamps, or Ⓓ dresser couplings.

TIME SAVER

A QUICK FIX FOR A LEAKING PIPE

Plumber's epoxy is a good quick fix for a small leak at a pipe joint. Turn off the water supply upstream of the leak. Tear off two pieces of the claylike ribbon. Knead enough plumber's epoxy putty to cover the surface around the leak. Apply the putty according to the manufacturer's instructions. Turn on the water and inspect for leaks. Remember, this is only a temporary fix, so make sure you make a permanent repair to the line.

7

SUPPLY PIPES AND FILTERS

1

PREPARE THE SURFACE FOR A SLEEVE CLAMP

Clean the area around the rupture. Use a flat metal file on any sharp edges that may cut through the patch. Measure the length of the area you will need to patch and the diameter of the pipe. Buy the appropriate patching supplies at your local home center.

2

CUT THE PATCH TO THE RIGHT LENGTH

Use scissors to cut out the size of the neoprene rubber patch you will need to repair the leak. For a pinhole leak, cut a 1-inch square. For a fracture, cut a patch that is 1 inch wider and 1 inch longer than the split in the pipe.

3

TIGHTEN THE CLAMPS TO SEAL THE LEAK

Wrap the pipe with the neoprene rubber. Secure the piece with hose clamps. This type of patch will work for most small fractures. You may need to cut out the broken section of a larger fracture. Install either a dresser coupling or a sleeve clamp to fix this type of leak.

WORK SMARTER

REMEMBER QUICK FIXES ARE ONLY TEMPORARY!
It's easy to convince yourself that a quick fix on a leaking pipe is the final solution. It's not; quick fixes are temporary. If you don't take time to go back and properly repair the leak, you'll forget about it. Before you know it, the fix will have failed or developed a new leak. Don't be tempted to apply another temporary measure. You'll be spending more time applying a new bandage than it would have taken to go back and do the job right the first time. Don't procrastinate!

Purifying water

I f your water comes from a public utility, it is probably safe. If you have any doubts about water safety, contact your utility company to find out how it can be tested. If your water comes from a well, it should be tested regularly. Your local department of health should be able to tell you how to get it tested, as well as which pathogens to look out for.

If you worry about lead in your water, you can purchase a home lead-testing kit. If your water has dangerous levels of lead, contact your water supplier or your health department.

In most cases, the problem is not safety but bad taste, bad smell, or staining and inefficient cleaning. See the chart at right for the most common problems and their solutions.

If you just want better-tasting water, the simplest solution may be to install a charcoal filter that mounts on the end of the kitchen faucet. However, it can be a bit cumbersome, and will need to have its filter changed fairly often. An under-sink water purifier (pages 134–135) or a whole-house water filter (page 136) will take a few hours to install and will require little maintenance.

Types of filters

PROBLEM	SOLUTION
Chlorine odor and taste	Simply placing the water in a container in the refrigerator overnight will get rid of most chlorine taste. To get better-tasting water right away, install a carbon filter.
Rotten-egg smell	This is often a problem particularly with well water and is caused by high sulfur content. You can minimize the problem with a filter that attaches to a showerhead. Installing a carbon filter plus a water softener will help. For severe problems, have a professional install a chlorinization feeder system.
Soap scum often makes bathtub rings or leaves a residue on clothing, or water does not lather well when you are cleaning	You have hard (i.e., mineral-laden) water. A water softener will probably solve the problem, or at least make it less severe.
Particles come out of faucets or clog aerators and showerheads	You likely have old galvanized pipes that are getting clogged with mineral deposits. If possible, replace at least some of the old pipes with new copper or PEX pipes. A carbon or particle filter will help as well.
Rust stains	A charcoal filter or water softener will usually solve the problem.
You fear bacteria or chemical pollution	In addition to consulting with local health authorities, a reverse-osmosis filter will take care of many potential health concerns.

BUYER'S GUIDE

CHOOSING AND USING A WATER SOFTENER

Soap scum, rust stains, and reduced lathering ability of detergent and soap are all signs of hard water. A water softener runs water through a brine solution to clean out most minerals that cause problems. The resulting water will clean well but may not taste good, so you may want to install a bypass line for drinking water.

You can install a water softener yourself, but it is often worth the extra cost to hire a water softener company to install the machine and take care of any maintenance. You or the company will need to fill the softener's bin with salt pellets or a slab of salt periodically.

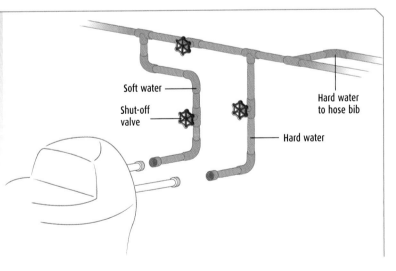

Soft water —
Shut-off valve —
Hard water to hose bib
Hard water

Installing an under-sink water purifier

PROJECT DETAILS

SKILLS: Connecting plumbing fittings
PROJECT: Installing a water purifier

TIME TO COMPLETE

EXPERIENCED: 30 min.
HANDY: 1 hr.
NOVICE: 1.5 hrs.

STUFF YOU'LL NEED

TOOLS: Power drill and bits, screwdriver, two adjustable wrenches, tubing cutter
MATERIALS: Water purifier, compression fittings, bucket, wood screws

I f you don't like your water's taste or have another water problem, see the previous page for information on water filter options. Also consult with a plumbing expert at your home center to find the type of filter that is most common in your area. In most cases, a carbon filter will improve your water's taste and smell.

The under-sink water purifier shown here mounts on the cabinet and is easy to hook up, as long as you get parts that fit your supply pipes or tubes. Hook it up to the cold-water line, so you will have good-tasting water every time you turn on the cold tap. You can also buy a unit that provides a separate source of drinking water; this type is a more difficult project, because you must install a separate spout.

TIME SAVER

GIVE YOURSELF ROOM TO WORK
If the space under your cabinet looks like mine, working under it is about as impossible as finding anything. Clear out the area, so you have room to work. When you finish, take a second to organize under the sink. Install trays so it will be easier to find items. If you have young children, install childproof locks on the doors and keep poisonous or caustic items in another area.

GOOD IDEA

KEEP A SPARE NEARBY
The filters need to be changed regularly in order for the unit to be effective. The kit usually comes with a special wrench to remove the cartridge. Hang that wrench near the unit so you don't have to hunt for it when it's time for a new filter.

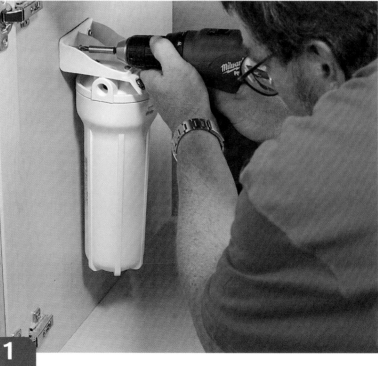

1

POSITION THE WATER PURIFIER
Set the bracket so the bottom of the purifier hangs at least 3 inches above the cabinet floor. This will allow you to remove the cartridge easily. Predrill the holes, then attach the bracket to the wall with wood screws. You may find it easier to attach the bracket with the cartridge removed.

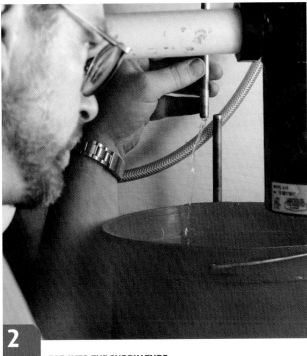

2 TAP INTO THE SUPPLY TUBE

Place a bucket under the water line. Turn off the shutoff valve for the line. Use a tubing cutter to cut into the supply line at least 3 inches above the shutoff. Drain the line into the bucket. If you have a braided supply tube (see page 50), you may need to consult with a plumbing salesperson to find the parts you need.

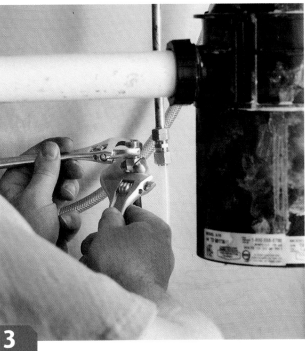

3 INSTALL A COMPRESSION FITTING ON EACH END OF THE CUT LINE

Insert the lines to and from the water purifier into the compression fitting. (See steps 4 and 5 on page 139.) Tighten the compression nuts for the fittings using two adjustable wrenches.

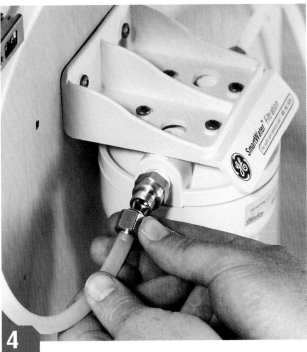

4 CONNECT THE INLET AND OUTLET LINES TO THE WATER PURIFIER

Slide the compression nuts over each line. Place compression rings (ferrules) over each end. Insert the lines into the water purifier and tighten the nuts using an adjustable wrench.

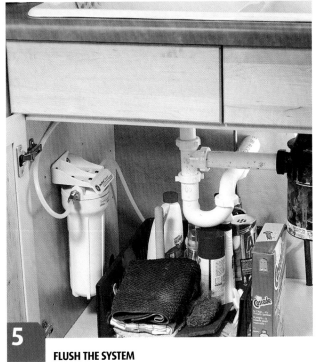

5 FLUSH THE SYSTEM

Install the cartridge and turn the water back on. While you're checking for leaks, flush the system until the water runs clear.

Installing a whole-house water filter

PROJECT DETAILS

SKILLS: Cutting into a water line and installing new fittings
PROJECT: Installing a whole-house water filter and a shutoff valve

TIME TO COMPLETE

EXPERIENCED: 45 min.
HANDY: 1.5 hrs.
NOVICE: 3 hrs.

STUFF YOU'LL NEED

TOOLS: Tools for working with whichever type of water supply pipe you have, water-pump pliers
MATERIALS: Water filter, pipe fittings as needed, shutoff valve, jumper wire with clamps

See page 133 for common water problems and the types of filters to solve the problems. If you only want better-tasting drinking water, you may choose to install an under-sink water purifier, as shown on pages 134-135. A whole-house water filter, as shown below, will treat all the water in your house if you install it on the main supply pipe. If you want to treat only your hot or your cold water, install it on a hot- or cold-water pipe that exits the water heater.

There should be a shutoff valve on either side of the filter. If you don't have one on the supply side then install one (as shown in step one) in addition to the valve on the house side. Tell your salesperson the type and size of pipe you will be attaching the filter to and get all the fittings you need; they may come in a kit from the filter manufacturer.

1

CUT PIPE AND INSTALL A NEW SHUTOFF VALVE
Shut off water to the house. Near a shutoff valve, break into the supply line. (If you have galvanized or plastic supply pipe, see pages 169–174.) Follow manufacturer's instructions and make sure you cut away enough pipe to accommodate the filter, the new shutoff valve, and any connecting fittings. Install a shutoff valve on the house side of the line. If you are sweating the valve, as shown, remove the insides of the valve before applying heat.

2

ASSEMBLE THE PARTS AND MARK FOR CUTTING
Dry-fit as many fittings as possible. You may need an adapter on either side of the filter in order to join to your size and type of pipe. Hold the final piece of pipe in place and mark it for cutting.

3

INSTALL THE FILTER
Most filters install using compression fittings. For each connection, slide on a nut, then the compression ring (ferrule). Slide the rings tightly in place and tighten the nuts. Turn the water back on and test for leaks.

4

ADD A JUMPER CABLE, IF NEEDED
If your electrical service panel has its main ground wire attached to a pipe (rather than to a rod driven into the ground), then the filter will interrupt the ground path and remove an important safety device. Install grounding clamps on either side of the filter and run a thick wire from clamp to clamp. Tighten securely.

7

SUPPLY PIPES AND FILTERS

Changing a filter cartridge

PROJECT DETAILS

SKILLS: Connecting plumbing fittings
PROJECT: Changing a water filter cartridge

TIME TO COMPLETE

EXPERIENCED: 10 min.
HANDY: 15 min.
NOVICE: 20 min.

STUFF YOU'LL NEED

TOOLS: Filter or strap wrench, bucket, sponge
MATERIALS: Filter cartridge, O-ring, silicone grease

Concern about minerals and sediment in the water supply has increased the installation of sediment filtration systems. The in-line cartridge filtration system is a popular style (see page 133 for other options). These systems require filter replacement every 100 to 1,000 gallons. Follow the manufacturer's instructions for setting up a cartridge replacement schedule. Only use solutions recommended by the manufacturer for cleaning the inside of the cartridge housing.

Keep your drinking water consistently clean by changing your filter every 100 to 1,000 gallons.

GOOD IDEA

KEEP SOME SPARES ON HAND
Save on trips to the store by buying extra filters for your cartridge. You'll be able to change the filters on schedule, keeping the water free of sediments, and you'll save time spent running unnecessary errands.

1 TURN OFF THE FILTER VALVE
If there is no valve, turn off the water at the main shutoff valve. Place a bucket under the cartridge. Release the water pressure in the line by opening a downstream valve. Some styles will have a pressure-relief valve you press to release pressure.

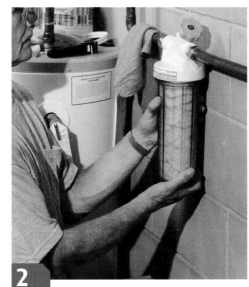

2 REMOVE THE CARTRIDGE HOUSING
Grasp the housing body with both hands and unscrew it counterclockwise. Use a water filter wrench or strap wrench to remove the housing if it is too tight to remove by hand. Remove the old filter cartridge.

3 CLEAN THE HOUSING
Follow the manufacturer's recommendations for cleaning the housing. If the housing has an O-ring, replace it with a new one. Coat the O-ring lightly with silicone grease. Place the new cartridge in the housing and connect it. Tighten by hand.

7

SUPPLY PIPES AND FILTERS

Installing a hot-water dispenser

PROJECT DETAILS

SKILLS: Connecting plumbing fittings and attaching wire to a terminal
PROJECT: Installing a hot-water dispenser

TIME TO COMPLETE

EXPERIENCED: 1 hr.
HANDY: 1.5 hrs.
NOVICE: 2 hrs.

STUFF YOU'LL NEED

TOOLS: Power drill and bits, center punch, hammer, knockout punch, adjustable wrench, screwdriver
MATERIALS: Hot-water dispenser, saddle tee or compression tee valve, wood screws

BUYER'S GUIDE

SADDLE TEES AND LOCAL CODE
Even though they often come with the kits, saddle tees may not meet code requirements in your area. In that case, you will have to install a compression tee valve on the supply line to get water to the hot-water dispenser.

H ot-water dispensers supply 190-degree water, so making soup, coffee, or tea is a snap. Instant hot-water dispensers are small electric water heaters that supply a single tap. The system connects directly to the cold water supply under the sink. Water is heated in the dispenser by an electric coil.

Check local codes before installing a hot-water dispenser. Some communities require the electrical outlet to have a ground fault circuit interrupter. Most codes allow the dispenser to be connected to the same outlet that supplies power to the disposer, as long as the receptacle is split.

WORK SMARTER

NOT ENOUGH HOLES IN THE SINK?
Install a one-touch faucet so one hole can be used for the hot-water dispenser. Plug the other hole or install a sprayer or drinking water dispenser.

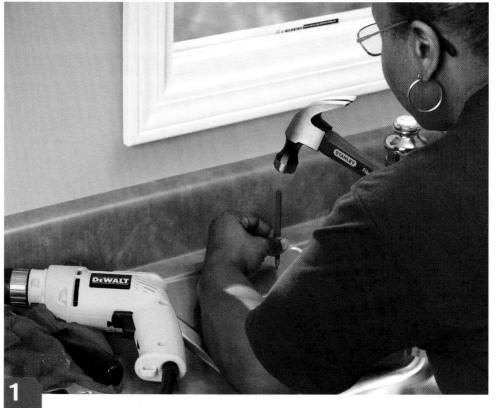

1 MARK THE DISPENSER LOCATION
Decide where you want to install the hot-water dispenser, making sure the area is flat and large enough. Measure the area for the center and mark with a center punch. Drill a hole at the mark.

7

SUPPLY PIPES AND FILTERS

2

CUT A HOLE IN THE SINK
Connect the knockout punch through the hole. Tighten the bolt using an adjustable wrench. Continue to tighten until the hole is cut. Remove the knockout, insert the hot-water dispenser spout through the hole, and connect.

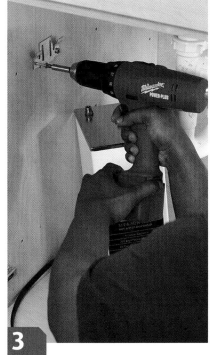

3

MOUNT THE DISPENSER BRACKET
Set the bracket so the bottom of the dispenser hangs at least 3 inches above the cabinet floor. Predrill the holes, attach the bracket to the wall with wood screws, then attach the dispenser.

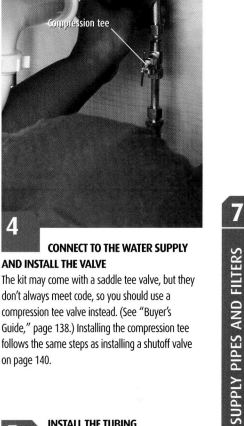

Compression tee

4

CONNECT TO THE WATER SUPPLY AND INSTALL THE VALVE
The kit may come with a saddle tee valve, but they don't always meet code, so you should use a compression tee valve instead. (See "Buyer's Guide," page 138.) Installing the compression tee follows the same steps as installing a shutoff valve on page 140.

5

INSTALL THE TUBING
Connect the supply tubing from the supply valve to the dispenser. Then, connect the tubing from the dispenser to the spout. Open the valve and inspect for leaks. Plug the dispenser into an electrical outlet.

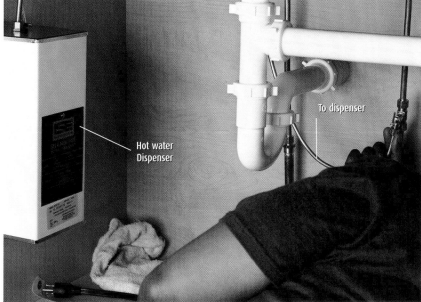

Hot water Dispenser

To dispenser

Shutoff valves

PROJECT DETAILS

SKILLS: Connecting plumbing fittings
PROJECT: Installing a new shutoff valve

TIME TO COMPLETE

EXPERIENCED: 1 hr.
HANDY: 2 hrs.
NOVICE: 3 hrs.

STUFF YOU'LL NEED

TOOLS: If you have galvanized pipe, two pipe wrenches
MATERIALS: New ball-type shutoff valve, Teflon tape, perhaps a new union and nipples (short lengths of pipe)

CLOSER LOOK

REPAIRING AN OLD VALVE
If there is no nearby union or for some other reason it is difficult to replace a valve, you can try to repair it. Shut off the water prior to the valve. If a globe valve does not fully shut off water, replace the washer, much as you would for a compression-style faucet (see pages 32–33). If water leaks out the nut just below the handle of a gate or globe valve, first try tightening the nut, but don't overtighten or you could crack the nut. If the leak persists, remove the stem and replace the string packing. If a gate valve does not fully shut off water, you may be able to buy a replacement gate, but you probably need to replace the valve.

You should be able to easily and completely shut water off in your house. See page 10 for the most common locations of shutoff valves. Unfortunately, older valves, which were usually of the gate or globe variety, develop leaks, may not shut off the water completely, and may reduce your water pressure. A newer ball valve has none of those problems, so consider installing one, as shown below.

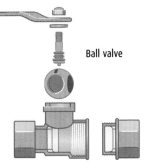

Gate Valve

Ball valve

Globe valve

THREE TYPES OF SHUTOFF VALVE
A gate valve has a gate that either pivots to allow water to flow past it, or that raises up to allow water to flow beneath it. A globe valve has a step with a rubber washer at its end; when the washer is pressed into the valve body, water is shut off. A ball valve has a ball with a hole in it; when the handle is rotated a quarter turn, water flows through the hole.

Replacing a shut-off valve

1

REMOVE THE OLD VALVE
Shut off the water. Cut into the line. If you are working with galvanized pipe, see pages 173–174. If possible, disassemble a nearby union. Remove the old valve. If you have to install a new union, wrap the male threads with Teflon tape, slide on the nut, and tighten the nut using a pipe wrench.

2

ASSEMBLE ALL THE PARTS
Use two pipe wrenches to tighten all the fittings and the valve. Wrap all the male threads and tighten each component as you go. Turn on the water and check for leaks.

Sinks

Chapter 8 highlights

 ith the variety of stylish, high-profile sinks available today, it's easy to make any kind of design statement you wish.

New colors, shapes, and features have revolutionized design in both style and function.

Material considerations

Materials now available include porcelain, fired clay, porcelain-coated cast iron and steel, stainless steel, and more. Even the old standard—stainless steel—is the focus of a resurgence in popularity with the perfecting of the brushed stainless-steel surface. Other new alternatives include quartz-acrylic and solid-surface drop-in sinks. Quartz-acrylic sinks are popular among many homeowners and designers because they are attractive, durable, and heat resistant. Solid-surface drop-in sinks are sought now because of their longer warranties and aesthetically pleasing, seamless look.

Sink installation tips

A new sink and faucet installation will do wonders for an older bathroom.

- If space is tight below (and it usually is), do as much work above ground as possible. Install the faucets and most of the trap before you set the sink into the counter. The job of connecting fittings from beneath the counter will be much easier.
- The drain holes on a double sink make perfect handholds for setting the sink into the countertop opening. If there is ample room to work underneath, you may choose to install the trap after installing the sink.
- Square up the faucet body on the sink top before you go below and tighten it up.

- Flexible, braided supply line is a great alternative to copper because of its ease of installation (see page 50). Follow the instructions for hooking up compression fittings carefully to prevent leaks.
- Don't use pipe compound on compression fittings; compound keeps the fitting from connecting tightly and can cause leaks.
- Pipe compound and Teflon tape act as sealants, but they also lubricate the threads so you can fully tighten the connections. Don't use too much—no more than one pass with compound or two wraps of tape—or you may not get a good connection.
- A PVC trap is light, easy to use, and more flexible to work with than a chrome trap.
- There are two kinds of joint compound—with and without Teflon. Compound with Teflon is better for general use because it can be applied on plastic, brass, copper, steel, PVC, ABS, and CPVC. Joint compound without Teflon can damage plastic pipe.
- Plumber's putty is not recommended for use on cultured marble or plastic sinks or fittings; it can discolor surfaces and weaken fittings. Follow the manufacturer's instructions and/or use silicone products.
- Metal strainer basket assemblies are superior to the plastic kind; they last longer and are less prone to leaking.
- If the drain isn't exactly where you need it to be, you can usually combine 90-degree and 45-degree elbows and short pieces of straight pipe to make the connection. P-traps and extensions with flexible sections may also help.
- If the stub coming out of the wall or floor for the drain is metal or an incompatible plastic and you want to install PVC or ABS, rubber transition fittings are available to make the connection.

Escutcheon plates prevent bugs from getting inside your walls and moving from one part of the house to another.

GOOD IDEA

USING ESCUTCHEON PLATES

Escutcheon plates fit around the drainpipe covering the hole where the drain line enters the wall or floor. Where plumbing is visible, such as under a wall-hung lavatory, they add a finishing touch. Using escutcheon plates inside cabinets isn't always required but they do help seal the hole. Two basic types are available in both metal and plastic.

Split-ring escutcheon plates fit around a pipe that is already in place.

Solid-ring escutcheon plates slip onto the pipe before the drain is assembled.

8

SINKS

Installing a countertop sink

PROJECT DETAILS

SKILLS: Carpentry and connecting plumbing fittings
PROJECT: Installing a countertop sink

TIME TO COMPLETE

EXPERIENCED: 1 hr.
HANDY: 1.5 hrs.
NOVICE: 2 hrs.

STUFF YOU'LL NEED

TOOLS: Tape measure, scissors, carpenter's pencil, power drill and bits, saber saw, caulk gun, putty knife, screwdriver, utility knife
MATERIALS: Countertop sink, fixtures, cardboard template, masking tape, rag, silicone caulk

Sinks show their age over time. Cracks, scrapes, chipping, dents, and persistent stains take their toll. The time will come when you need to install a replacement and perhaps go for a new look in your kitchen.

Choosing a sink style depends on your personal taste and the size of your kitchen. The colors, shapes, and features offered today give you a vast choice to meet your practical needs and design choices. Now is the time to get a fixture that really does the job.

Connect the fixtures first

Connect the faucets and other fixtures to the sink before you install it. It will be much easier to install them out of the cabinet. Wait to install the drain so you can use the drain holes as handholds when you set the sink in place. You also may want to install most of the trap (see pages 149–150).

1 CREATE A TEMPLATE

If the sink doesn't come with a template, create one by laying the sink face down on a sheet of cardboard and drawing a line around the edge. Lift off the sink and draw a second line ¾ inch inside the first line. Cut along the second line with scissors.

TOOL SAVVY

CUT IT SHORT
High-speed cutting tools make short work of cutting holes in drywall and are a perfect alternative to using a saber saw for cutting out a countertop.

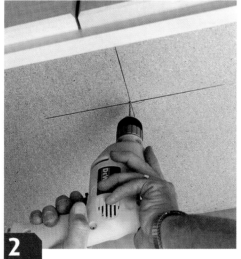

2 MARK THE CENTER OF THE CABINET FROM UNDERNEATH
Drill a hole large enough to fit a nail through it.

3 MARK THE CENTER OF THE TEMPLATE
Push a nail through the center of the template. Align the center of the template over the hole in the countertop. Push the nail through the countertop to anchor the template into place. Center the template and check to make sure the edges are square so the rim will lie entirely on the surface.

8

SINKS

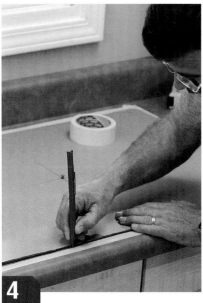

4

TRACE THE OUTLINE OF THE TEMPLATE ON THE COUNTERTOP
Remove the template and place tape over the line. Replace the template, center it, and draw the outline of the template on the tape. Remove the template.

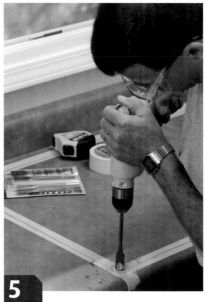

5

DRILL A ¾-INCH HOLE INSIDE THE CUTOUT LINE
Use a power drill and spade bit to make a starter hole for the saber saw.

6

INSTALL BRACES BENEATH THE COUNTERTOP
The braces will support the section to prevent it from binding while cutting.

7

CUT ALONG THE LINE USING A SABER SAW
Use a blade designed to cut countertops without chipping the surface. Test-fit the sink in the opening. Trace the rim lightly on the countertop.

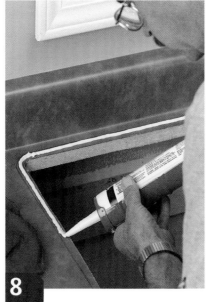

8

APPLY A BEAD OF SILICONE CAULK INSIDE THE LINE
Remove the sink and apply silicone caulk around the opening in a steady, continuous bead between the mark and the opening.

9

PLACE THE SINK IN THE OPENING
Press the sink firmly into the silicone caulking, then level and clean. Connect the faucets and the drains. Test for leaks.

10 CLEAN AWAY EXCESS SILICONE

Trim silicone caulking with a plastic putty knife for a professional look.

1 SET THE SINK

Follow the steps for installing a countertop sink through step 7, check for fit, then caulk the rim and lower the sink into place.

2 TIGHTEN THE CLAMPS BENEATH THE SINK

Align the sink and from below place clamps on the rim lip that projects down. Tighten the clamps alternately moving around the bowl of the sink so that the sink is tightened evenly.

8

SINKS

Removing an old sink

OUT WITH THE OLD

Like many plumbing projects, removing the old sink can be the toughest part of a replacement job. Fittings may be rusted or fused tight, and it can be tricky getting around under the counter. If it's a cast-iron sink, it will be heavy, so have some help available for removal.

1 Before you begin, make sure the new fixture will fit properly into the old hole.

2 Turn off the water supply valves to the hot and cold water faucets. Place a bucket beneath the drain trap. Loosen the slip nuts and remove the trap. (See "Installing a Single-Bowl, PVC P-trap," pages 149–150.)

3 Remove the bucket and place a shallow tray or rags beneath the sink supply lines to catch water that may remain in the water supply lines.

4 Remove the coupling nuts connecting the supply tube to the faucet tailpiece.

5 Disconnect additional plumbing for disposers (see pages 156–157), dishwashers (see pages 158–159), and sink sprayers (see pages 51–52).

6 Slice through the caulking around the rim using a utility knife.

7 Lift the sink from the countertop using the drain hole as a handhold.

8 Look for water damage to the countertop and clean any excess caulking from the rim before you install the new sink. If there is countertop damage, consider getting a new countertop as well.

Call your local waste removal service for instructions on disposal of the old sink.

Installing an undermount sink

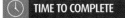

PROJECT DETAILS

SKILLS: Good plumbing and tiling skills

PROJECT: Installing an undermount sink

TIME TO COMPLETE

EXPERIENCED: 1 hr.
HANDY: 2 hrs.
NOVICE: 3 hrs.

STUFF YOU'LL NEED

TOOLS: Water-pump pliers, screwdriver, drill, saber saw, tiling tools

MATERIALS: Undermount sink, bullnose or other trim tiles to fit around the sink or other countertop material

A countertop sink, as shown on pages 143–145, simply rests on top of the countertop. This makes for easy installation, but the sink's flange can catch crumbs. For the easiest cleanup, an undermount sink can't be beat. However installation is a good deal more difficult because the countertop around the sink will be visible, and it must seal water out. Plan an installation like this carefully; you may choose to have a pro install it.

If you hire a company to install a solid-surface countertop, you can purchase a top with a molded sink, as shown at right. If you are having a granite slab top installed, the company will cut and finish a hole for the sink. Consult with the company to see if you should attempt the sink installation yourself, or if they will install it for a nominal charge.

You can purchase an undermount sink made of stainless steel, enameled cast iron, or other materials. Just make sure you know how you will attach the sink firmly. In some cases, the sink is mounted to the underside of the countertop using special screws and brackets. In other cases, the sink is first installed onto the cabinet, then the countertop is built on top of it.

UNDERMOUNT SINK WITH SOLID-SURFACE (CORIAN) COUNTERTOP

ANATOMY OF A STAINLESS-STEEL SINK MOUNTED UNDER A TILED COUNTERTOP

Here is one undermount option. For an installation like this, the hole is carefully cut in the substrate, which is made of ¾-inch plywood topped with ½-inch cement backerboard. The sink is screwed, via mounting brackets, to the plywood, and it may be supported by the cabinet as well. Bullnose tiles, which have one rounded edge, are installed around the hole, and thin pieces of tile are cut to fit below. The joint between the tiles and the sink must be filled with grout and then sealed with silicone caulk.

4"×4" field tile

½" concrete backerboard

4"×4" bullnose tile

¾" plywood

Mounting bracket

Installing a basket strainer

A void inexpensive plastic basket strainers. They will do the job in the short term, but for the long term, metal is the way to go. Strainers should be replaced when they leak consistently, chip, crack, or become stained and tarnished.

1 APPLY PUTTY TO THE SINK STRAINER HOUSING
Form a rope with plumber's putty. Wrap the rope around the underside of the strainer housing and press so it adheres to the strainer.

2 SET THE HOUSING INTO THE SINK DRAIN HOLE
Press the housing firmly into the drain hole.

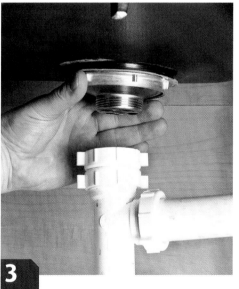

3 CONNECT TO THE SINK
Place a rubber gasket over the threads, then slide on a flat washer. Hold the gasket and washer in place while you hand-tighten the locknut.

8

SINKS

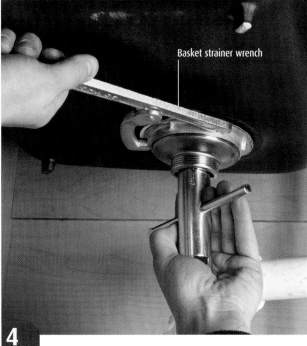

4 HOLD THE STRAINER BODY IN PLACE WHILE TIGHTENING THE LOCKNUT

Use a basket strainer wrench or water-pump pliers to tighten the locknut. **DO NOT OVERTIGHTEN.** Remove any excess putty that oozes out the bottom and top of the drain.

Basket strainer wrench

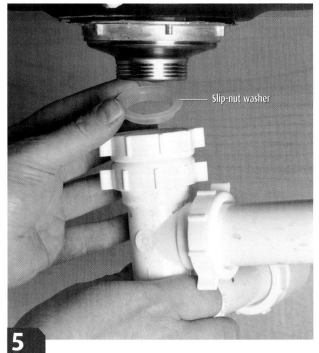

5 INSERT THE SLIP-NUT WASHER INTO THE DRAIN TAILPIECE

The washer should sit inside the tailpiece with the flange of the washer extending over the top.

Slip-nut washer

6 ADJUST THE TAILPIECE

Make sure the tailpiece is seated snugly against the strainer body.

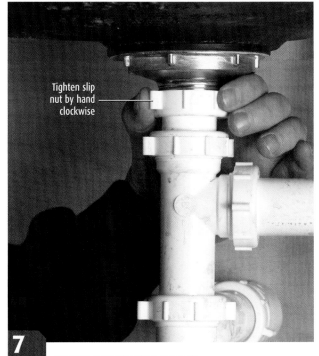

7 CONNECT THE TAILPIECE SLIP NUT

Slide the slip nut up to the threads of the strainer body and hand-tighten. Wipe away any excess putty. Turn on the water. Inspect for leaks. Tighten if necessary.

Tighten slip nut by hand clockwise

8

SINKS

Installing a single-bowl, PVC P-trap

PROJECT DETAILS

SKILLS: Connecting plumbing fittings
PROJECT: Installing a PVC P-trap

TIME TO COMPLETE

EXPERIENCED: 20 min.
HANDY: 40 min.
NOVICE: 1 hr.

STUFF YOU'LL NEED

TOOLS: Felt marker, tubing cutter, water-pump pliers
MATERIALS: PVC P-trap (U.S.), ABS P-trap (Canada), slip-joint tailpiece

Canada watch

DWV systems in Canada use black ABS (acrylonitrile butadiene styrene) for running drain lines instead of white PVC. Techniques for cutting, connecting, and cementing ABS are similar to PVC. (See "Connecting ABS Pipe," page 186.)

O lder installations sometimes have an S-shaped trap, but that can cause drain water to siphon back into the sink. Codes now require that a trap be P-shaped, or that an S-shaped trap travel at least three horizontal inches at the highest point. (In Canada, you must use only a P-trap.) The trap serves as a safety device by preventing noxious gases from backing up the sewer pipe and entering the house. Sewer gases not only pose a health hazard, they can also be explosive.

How the P-trap works

The curved portion of the trap holds standing water. Every time the drain is used, water is flushed through the trap and is replaced with fresh water. Solids will adhere to the trap over time and eventually clog the drain or possibly damage the trap—which means it's time to install a new one.

WORK SMARTER

WHAT'S A SLIP JOINT ANYWAY?
Slip joints allow fixtures, such as strainer baskets, to be joined to drainpipes without making permanent connections. This means parts can be removed for easy replacement. A smaller pipe with slip nuts at each end is inserted into a larger pipe, and the seal is made by the pressure that results from tightening the slip nuts to the threaded ends of the larger pipe.

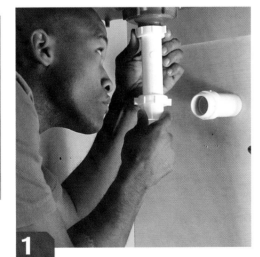

1 CONNECT THE TAILPIECE TO THE SINK DRAIN
Hand-tighten the slip nut.

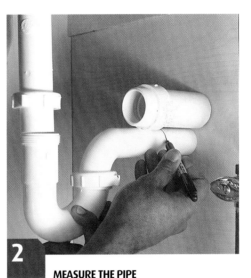

2 MEASURE THE PIPE
Test-fit the P-trap. Mark the P-trap inlet so it will seat inside the end of the drainpipe. Remove the P-trap. Cut the inlet of the trap to length using PVC pipe cutters. Insert the inlet into the pipe socket. Slide the slip nut over the end of the inlet and tighten by hand.

Hand-tightening is usually sufficient for a pressure connection. Use pliers gently to stop leaks, if necessary.

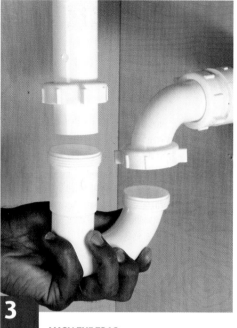

3

ALIGN THE TRAP

Make sure the trap will set flush against the outlet and inlet pipes. Adjust the pipe if necessary.

Slip nuts

4

TIGHTEN THE SLIP NUTS

Hand-tighten the nuts. Turn on the water. Stopper the drains, fill the sink bowls, then unstopper and look for leaks. Tighten nuts if necessary.

GOOD IDEA

ESCUTCHEON PLATES HELP TO FIGHT BUGS!
Escutcheon plates fit flush around the pipe where the drain line enters the wall or floor. They do add a finishing touch where plumbing is visible, such as under a wall-hung lavatory. Escutcheon plates also seal the drainpipe hole and can prevent drafts or unwanted insects from entering your home.

▲ Split-ring escutcheon plates fit around a pipe that is already in place.

▲ Solid-ring escutcheon plates slip onto the pipe before the drain is assembled.

CLOSER LOOK

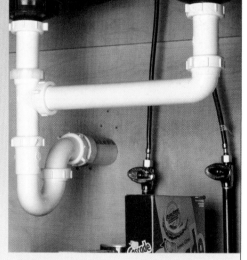

CONNECTING OPTIONS FOR DOUBLE-BOWL SINKS

Two bowls can be served by one P-trap. Conversion kits are available at your local home center. One style has the P-trap centered between the bowls with a connecting tee and separate lengths running to the sink drains. **Centering the P-trap does not meet code in Canada.** Another style has the P-trap aligned beneath one of the drains with a vertical tee connecting to the second bowl. Though the installation procedure is the same as for a single-bowl sink, make sure the horizontal run has a fall of ¼ inch per lineal foot toward the tee connector. Otherwise solids will settle along the horizontal pipe and eventually stop or impede the flow of wastewater.

8

SINKS

Installing a double-bowl sink with garbage disposer

PROJECT DETAILS

SKILLS: Connecting plumbing fittings
PROJECT: Installing a double-bowl sink and garbage disposer

TIME TO COMPLETE

EXPERIENCED: 1 hr.
HANDY: 2 hrs.
NOVICE: 3 hrs.

STUFF YOU'LL NEED

TOOLS: Water-pump pliers, hacksaw or PVC saw for a plastic trap, screwdriver, drill, spud wrench
MATERIALS: Garbage disposer, double-bowl sink, plumber's putty, perhaps an air gap, perhaps extra trap parts

his is perhaps the most common drain arrangement for a kitchen sink. A garbage disposer is installed on one of the bowls, and the dishwasher's drain line empties into the garbage disposer. However, check with local codes for some of the specifics. For instance, some codes require that the dishwasher drain run to a dishwasher tailpiece attached to the bowl without a garbage disposer, rather than into the disposer. Some codes call for an air gap, and others simply say that you must loop the dishwasher drain up near the top of the sink. Some codes require that each bowl have its own trap (see the next page).

You'll save yourself back strain and frustrations if you do as much of the installation before you install the sink, with the sink upside down on a pair of sawhorses. You will probably want to install the faucet at the same time as the drain assembly (see pages 51–52).

INSTALL THE STRAINERS
On one of the bowls, install a regular basket strainer (see page 147). To install the basket, press a rope of plumber's putty under the flange and hold it in place while you add the washers and tighten the nut. A spud wrench makes this easy, but you can also use a large pair of water-pump pliers.

INSTALL THE GARBAGE DISPOSER
If you will run the dishwasher drain into the disposer, punch out the knockout in the drain fitting and shake it out of the disposer. Slip on the disposer's mounting hardware, which includes a mounting ring and a thick rubber gasket. To mount the disposer, hold it in correct alignment, push it down over the strainer, and twist to securely fasten it. Most manufacturers of disposers include specific installation instructions for their models.

8

SINKS

3 INSTALL AN AIR GAP

If codes require, slip an air gap through a hole in the sink and tighten a nut to hold it in place. You may either connect the dishwasher's drain to the air gap at this point, or do so after the sink is installed if that would be easier. Also run a drain line from the air gap to the garbage disposer. Tighten all hose clamps.

4 ASSEMBLE THE TRAP

You will likely need to cut one or two pieces to make all the parts fit. Make sure each piece goes straight into a fitting; if it is at an angle, the joint may leak. For most joints, you will need to slip on a nut, then the rubber or plastic washer, before making the connection. Install the tailpiece onto the non-disposer bowl and run a straight piece over to the disposer. Add the trap. Once all the parts are assembled, tighten all the nuts.

Up to code

If codes require that each bowl have its own trap, consult with a plumbing inspector to make sure you configure the trap parts correctly. In the setup shown, a y-fitting emerges from the wall, and the traps tie into the wye. Make sure that all horizontal pipes are sloped downward.

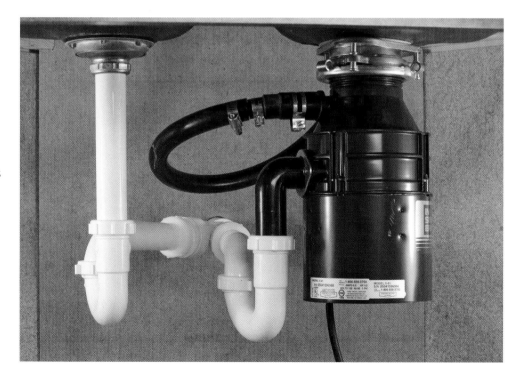

8

SINKS

Installing a wall-hung lavatory sink

PROJECT DETAILS

SKILLS: Carpentry and connecting plumbing fittings
PROJECT: Installing a wall-hung lavatory sink

TIME TO COMPLETE

EXPERIENCED: 2 days
HANDY: 2 days
NOVICE: 2 days

STUFF YOU'LL NEED

TOOLS: Keyhole saw, hammer, tape measure, carpenter's pencil, power drill and bits, ratchet wrench and sockets, caulk gun, screwdriver, utility knife
MATERIALS: Wall-hung sink, mounting bracket, anchor bolts, 2×10 wood blocking, water-resistant drywall scrap, drywall tape and compound, paint, faucets and fittings, drainpipe and fittings, rag, silicone caulk

If you install a wall-hung lavatory sink, you have to install wooden blocking between the wall studs to mount the support bracket for the fixture. Without the blocking, the sink could be pulled off the wall.

Pick your height

Lavatory sink heights vary between 30 and 38 inches, depending on individual needs. Position the blocking for the mounting bracket so the sink will hang at a height that is comfortable for you. Locate the studs and cut away the existing drywall so you can install the blocking. Run the hot and cold water supply and drain lines to the fixture.

Manufacturers will often include a template to help you align the height and position of the sink on the wall.

1 CUT AWAY A 16×16-INCH SECTION OF DRYWALL AND NAIL OR SCREW THE BLOCKING INTO PLACE
Use a keyhole saw to remove the drywall. Nail the 2×10 between the studs so it's flush with the leading edge of the studs. Cut a piece of water-resistant drywall to cover the hole. You may be able to use the piece you cut away. Finish the drywall and paint it. Once dry, attach the mounting bracket.

2 PREPARE TO SET THE LAVATORY SINK
Attach the faucet and drain before mounting the sink. Run the supply line with stop valves. Install the drain line and P-trap. Set the sink on the bracket. Secure it to the bracket with anchor bolts. Connect the supply line to the faucet and the drain to the P-trap. Open the valves. Check for leaks. Tighten leaking fittings if necessary. **Legs for most wall-mounted sinks can be purchased as an option.**

8

SINKS

Installing a pedestal sink

PROJECT DETAILS

SKILLS: Connecting a faucet and a trap
PROJECT: Installing a pedestal sink

TIME TO COMPLETE

EXPERIENCED: 1.5 hrs.
HANDY: 2.5 hrs.
NOVICE: 3.5 hrs.

STUFF YOU'LL NEED

TOOLS: Water-pump pliers, hacksaw or PVC saw, screwdriver, adjustable wrench, drill, small level, wall patching tools
MATERIALS: Pedestal sink, trap, faucet with pop-up assembly, 2×8 for brace, screws, drywall piece, wall-patching materials, silicone caulk if needed

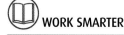

WORK SMARTER

DIFFERENT MOUNTS

Some sinks are mounted on a bracket rather than lag-screwing into a mounting brace. For this style, attach all the fixtures and plumbing before you hang it on the bracket. Mark for the pedestal holes, but complete the drain and supply hookups before you attach the pedestal to the floor.

Most pedestal sinks are supported only secondarily by the pedestal; the sink itself hangs from a bracket that is attached to a framing member in the wall, much like a wall-hung sink, as shown on the previous page. Installing the framing and patching the wall afterward will likely take more time than installing the sink. You will probably want to install the brace, patch the wall, and paint before you install the sink.

If the pedestal is wide and the plumbing is installed in a tight arrangement, you may choose to hide all the plumbing behind the pedestal. Or you can hide only the trap and allow the supply lines to show on either side. In that case, you may want to buy fancy-looking stop valves and install solid chrome supply tubing instead of braided supplies.

1 INSTALL THE MOUNTING BRACE

Follow manufacturer's instructions for locating the sink brace. Cut a hole in the wall spanning from stud to stud and cut a piece of 2×8 to fit snugly between the studs. At this point, you may also choose to move the stop valves closer to the trap, in order to hide them behind the pedestal. Attach the brace with angle-driven screws. Patch the hole, sand smooth, and paint.

2 ATTACH THE MOUNTING BRACKET

Assemble the sink on top of the pedestal and hold against the wall to mark for the position of the mounting bracket. Anchor the bracket by driving screws into the 2×8 inside the wall. Check that the bracket is level as you attach it.

The pedestal on a pedestal sink appears to be freestanding, but it can be anchored to the floor with lag screws.

8

SINKS

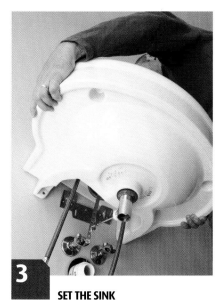

3 SET THE SINK

Install the faucet, most of the trap, and the pop-up assembly onto the sink (see pages 57–58). Set the sink onto the bracket. Check that the pedestal will fit; you may need to adjust the position of the bracket.

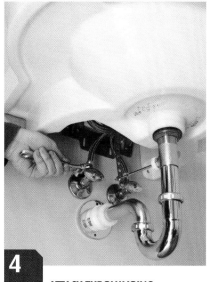

4 ATTACH THE PLUMBING

Connect the trap and the supply lines. Turn on the water and check for leaks.

5 SLIP IN THE PEDESTAL

You may need to gently lift the sink a bit as you slide the pedestal in place. Check again for leaks.

8

Other mounting options

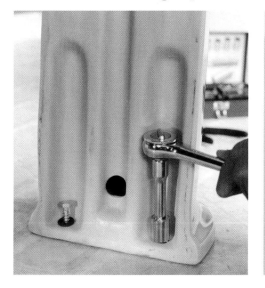

INSTALL THE PEDESTAL LAG BOLTS

Some pedestals attach to the floor using screws or bolts. Snug the screws, but don't tighten too much or you could crack the pedestal.

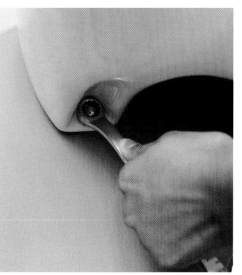

CONNECT THE BASIN TO THE WALL

If the sink attaches with screws, first drill pilot holes, then insert and alternately tighten the screws until just snug—don't overtighten.

GOOD IDEA

TO CAULK OR NOT TO CAULK?
Depending on the shape of your pedestal, you may choose to caulk where it meets the floor. This will make it easier to clean the floor, but the caulk will need to be removed if you need to take out the pedestal to make a plumbing repair. You could choose to remove the pedestal when doing a thorough floor cleaning. You will likely want to apply caulk where the sink meets the wall, otherwise debris can quickly gather there. Use silicone caulk.

SINKS

Installing a garbage disposer

 PROJECT DETAILS

SKILLS: Connecting plumbing fittings and attaching electrical wires to terminals
PROJECT: Installing a garbage disposer

TIME TO COMPLETE

EXPERIENCED: 30 min.
HANDY: 45 min.
NOVICE: 1.5 hrs.

STUFF YOU'LL NEED

TOOLS: Screwdriver or disposer wrench, hacksaw or tubing cutters, water-pump pliers
MATERIALS: Garbage disposer, plumber's putty

A garbage disposer requires an electrical source that is controlled by a wall switch. If you don't have one under the sink, you will need to install one. Check with local codes before installation. Some communities have codes that don't allow disposers because of limits on sewer capacity. They may also require an air gap for a disposer and a dishwasher.

If you have a septic system, install a disposer specifically designed for use with a septic tank. Too much food waste can interfere with the normal decomposition of septic waste.

How much horsepower?

In-home disposers operating at less than ½ horsepower are not usually recommended for households of more than two people. A 1-horsepower disposer is an ideal choice for larger households and tougher jobs.

TIME SAVER

SAVE THAT BRACKET
Are you replacing an existing garbage disposer with the same brand? You may be able to use the existing mounting bracket to make the job easier and quicker.

NOTE: Installation may vary depending on whether or not your drain line comes out of the wall or the floor. Know which you have and ask the sales associate about the right procedure.

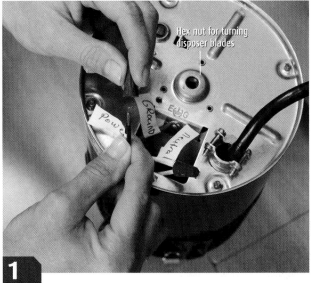

1 WIRE THE DISPOSER
The disposer may come with the appliance cord attached. If not, you will have to connect one. Remove the cover plate beneath the disposer. Most cords and disposers have the same colored wires. Connect white to white, black to black, and the green wire to the disposer's ground screw. If the colors are different, read the manufacturer's instructions for wiring.

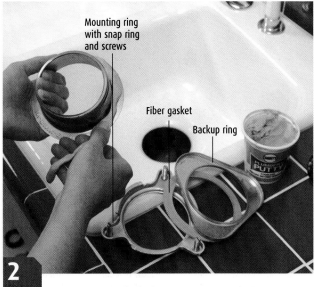

2 APPLY PLUMBER'S PUTTY
Press a rope of plumber's putty onto the underside of the drain flange. Insert the flange into the drain hole and press down evenly. Install the backup ring, fiber gasket, and mounting ring from beneath the sink.

8

SINKS

3   INSTALL THE MOUNTING RING

Tighten the mounting screws for the upper mounting ring. Alternate the tightening of the screws to pull the ring up evenly against the sink.

4   MOUNT THE DISPOSER

Place the disposer into the mounting ring. Make sure the outlet of the disposer is facing the drainpipe connection. Turn the lower ring clockwise until the disposer is supported by the mounting assembly.

5   CONNECT THE OUTLET TO THE P-TRAP

Measure the discharge pipe and use a hacksaw or tubing cutter to cut it to length. Install the discharge pipe to the outlet of the disposer. Attach to the drain line with slip nuts.

6   TIGHTEN THE MOUNTING LUG

Insert a screwdriver or disposer wrench into the mounting lug on the lower mounting ring. Turn clockwise until the disposer is locked into place. Tighten all slip nuts snug using water-pump pliers. Run water into the sink. Turn on the disposer and check for leaks. Tighten fittings if necessary.

GOOD IDEA

CONNECT A DISHWASHER
Be sure the disposer you purchase has a knockout for a dishwasher. Remove the knockout for the dishwasher connection on the disposer. Connect the dishwasher discharge line to the disposer using hose clamps (see pages 151–152). If local codes require an air gap between the dishwasher and the disposer, see page 159 on how to install one.

WORK SMARTER

GETTING SOME LEVERAGE
Sometimes the trickiest part of mounting the garbage disposer is the moment when you lift it up and lock it into the mounting rings. The pros will stack a couple of thick telephone books under the unit so they won't have so far to lift. You can do the same thing with scrap lumber or a toolbox.

8

KS

Installing a dishwasher

PROJECT DETAILS

SKILLS: Connecting plumbing fittings and attaching electrical wire to a terminal
PROJECT: Installing a dishwasher

TIME TO COMPLETE

EXPERIENCED: 1 hr.
HANDY: 1.5 hrs.
NOVICE: 3 hrs.

STUFF YOU'LL NEED

TOOLS: Power drill, hole saw, level, screwdriver, adjustable wrench, tubing cutter
MATERIALS: Wire nuts, hose clamps, drain hose, flexible copper tubing and compression fittings, drain tailpiece with inlet, air gap

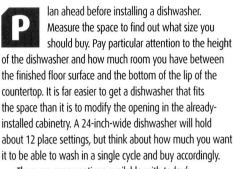

Plan ahead before installing a dishwasher. Measure the space to find out what size you should buy. Pay particular attention to the height of the dishwasher and how much room you have between the finished floor surface and the bottom of the lip of the countertop. It is far easier to get a dishwasher that fits the space than it is to modify the opening in the already-installed cabinetry. A 24-inch-wide dishwasher will hold about 12 place settings, but think about how much you want it to be able to wash in a single cycle and buy accordingly.

There are many options available with today's dishwashers. Dishwashers have light cycles for washing delicate or lightly soiled dishes, normal cycles for everyday usage, rinse cycles to remove food, and energy-saver cycles for drying. Better-quality dishwashers are clad tightly in insulation, to render them nearly noiseless.

Energy-conscious buyers should inspect the yellow Energy Guide label for the efficiency rating. The lower the number, the less energy the dishwasher will use over a one-year period.

As you push the dishwasher into place, make sure the water supply line and drain hose do not become kinked. Also keep an eye on the electrical cable to make sure it is not pinched or damaged by any sharp metal edges.

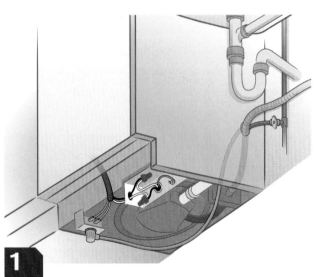

1

PREPARE THE OPENING
Consult your dishwasher's installation guide for specific information, but a typical opening looks like this. The space between cabinets should be just the right size (usually 24 inches wide and 34 inches tall). There needs to be an electrical cable—preferably armored cable because of the vibration of the machine—connected to a circuit that has adequate amperage capacity. A water supply line typically is made of ⅜-inch copper tubing and is controlled by a stop valve under the sink. The drain line (which is usually already attached to the dishwasher) runs up to an air gap, if required by code, and attaches to a tailpiece (as shown in step 4) or to the garbage disposer.

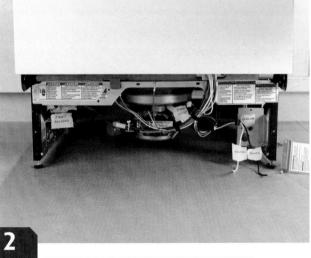

2

PREPARE THE DISHWASHER FOR INSTALLATION
Read the manufacturer's instructions for the location of the power supply and drainage lines—some will have separate holes for each line. Remove the bottom access panel to find the power cord connection, inlet solenoid valve, and drain outlet. Measure and mark the locations for the power, water supply, and drain line to run out of the cabinet and cut or drill holes in the wall of the sink cabinet to accommodate them. Slide the dishwasher into place and verify the location. Adjust the marks if necessary. Slide the dishwasher back out and set it aside to make more room to work beneath the cabinet.

8

SINKS

3

CONNECT THE LINES

Run the drain tubing, supply line, and power cord. Slide the dishwasher into place. Level the dishwasher by adjusting the threaded feet. A good way to check for level is to open and close the door—it will operate smoothly if the dishwasher is level. When level, tighten the locknuts. The mounting brackets for the dishwasher should also be aligned with the underside of the countertop and the side of the cabinet. Install the compression elbow on the dishwasher solenoid. Bend the supply line so it lines up with the elbow. Slide the compression nut over the tubing, then place the compression ring over the end. Connect the tubing to the solenoid using an adjustable wrench. Install a tee on the hot water supply. Measure and cut tubing to the tee. Connect with compression fittings. Turn on the water. Inspect for leaks, then tighten connections if necessary.

 WORK SMARTER

HOW TO INSTALL AN AIR GAP

Some local codes require an air gap between the dishwasher and the disposer. Mount the air gap in the countertop; if there is an extra hole available in the sink, mount it there. Connect a ⅝-inch drain hose to the ½-inch leg of the air gap with a hose clamp. Attach a ⅞-inch hose to the ¾-inch leg of the air gap. Make sure there are no low spots or kinks in either hose.

8

SINKS

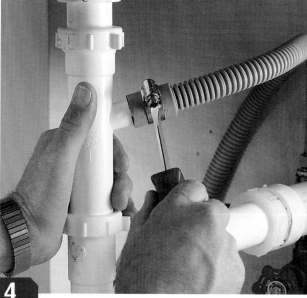

4

INSTALL THE DRAIN LINE

Replace the regular sink drain tailpiece with one that has a side inlet. Connect the drain line to the dishwasher outlet using hose clamps. Measure the hose and cut it to length so it connects to the inlet of the tailpiece. Connect the discharge hose to the inlet with another hose clamp. If local codes require an air gap, read the instructions to install one (see "Work Smarter" on this page).

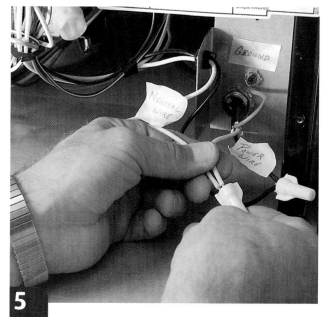

5

HOOK UP THE POWER

Match the wires: white to white, black to black, and green to the ground screw. If the colors are different, read the manufacturer's instructions for connecting the wires. Connect the wires with wire nuts. Plug the power supply cord into an electrical outlet installed under the sink cabinet. Run the dishwasher through a test cycle to make sure it works properly.

Installing an icemaker

PROJECT DETAILS

SKILLS: Connecting plumbing fittings
PROJECT: Installing a refrigerator icemaker

TIME TO COMPLETE

EXPERIENCED: 20 min.
HANDY: 40 min.
NOVICE: 1 hr.

STUFF YOU'LL NEED

TOOLS: Power drill and bits, screwdriver, adjustable wrench
MATERIALS: Icemaker kit, saddle tee or compression tee valve

I f you want a new refrigerator that includes an icemaker, you don't have to pay someone to hook it up. With a few plumbing and carpentry skills installation is an easy do-it-yourself project.

The only thing you need to be careful about is installing the tubing. Uncoil only the length of tubing you need. **Be careful not to kink the tubing, as you will then need to replace it.** Leave enough coiled tubing behind the refrigerator to allow you to move it away from the wall without stressing or crimping the tubing.

Leave enough tubing coiled behind the refrigerator so it can be moved without harming the tubing.

GOOD IDEA

CLAMPING STOCK
For pure, clear ice, purchase an in-line water filter for your icemaker. Locate it in an accessible place so you can change the filter on the recommended schedule. Follow the instructions that come with the kit.

Water filter

WORK SMARTER

USING A TUBING BENDER
Kinked copper tubing cannot be repaired, so it pays to take precautions against kinking. A tubing bender is a specialized tool that you will probably seldom use, but it is worth its small cost even if used for only one project. Without it, you simply cannot make a turn as tight as the one shown here. To use a tubing bender, simply slide it onto the tubing and position it wherever you are bending the tubing.

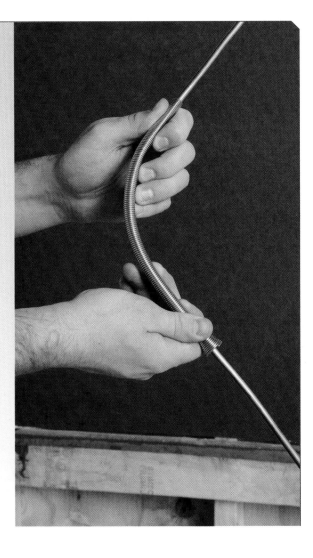

8

SINKS

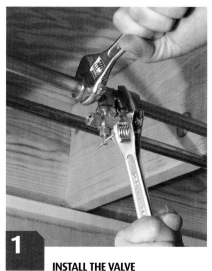

1 INSTALL THE VALVE

The kit may come with a saddle tee, but it doesn't always meet code, so you should use a compression tee instead. (See "To Code," below right.) Installing the compression tee follows the same steps as installing a shutoff valve (see page 140).

2 DRILL A HOLE IN THE FLOOR

The hole should be large enough for the tubing. Use a spade bit with a diameter of at least ⅜ inch and a power drill. From above, carefully uncoil the tubing and feed it through the hole. Feed enough tubing to run to the valve.

3 CONNECT THE TUBING TO THE VALVE

Insert the tubing into the valve and tighten the nut. Use an adjustable wrench to connect the compression fitting.

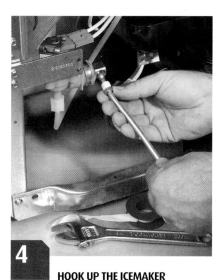

4 HOOK UP THE ICEMAKER

Remove the access panel at the back of the refrigerator. Unwind enough tubing to reach the supply valve; leave the rest coiled. Insert the tubing into the valve. Connect the fitting, turn on the water supply, and inspect for leaks.

To code

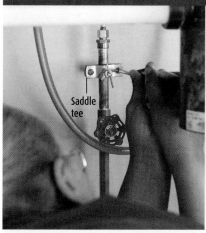

Saddle tee

Here are two products that can make icemaker installation easier; however, check first to be sure they are allowed by your local codes. A saddle tee valve (shown above left) is the easiest way to tap into a pipe. To install one type, simply clamp the valve over the pipe and then tighten a screw to puncture the pipe and supply water. Another type requires that you shut off the water and drill a hole in the pipe before installing the valve.

Plastic icemaker tubing (shown above right) is easier to work with and less likely to kink than copper. It connects via compression fittings similar to those for copper. Again check to make sure this product meets local codes.

The supply system

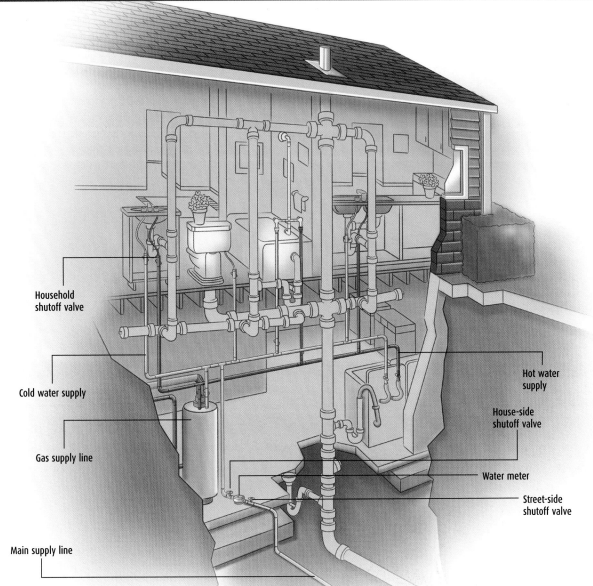

Household shutoff valve

Cold water supply

Gas supply line

Main supply line

Hot water supply

House-side shutoff valve

Water meter

Street-side shutoff valve

Chapter 9 highlights

he quality of the water that enters your house from a municipal water system or from a private well is your first concern. If your source is a public system, the responsibility for the safety of the drinking water is with the provider. Communities must abide by state and federal regulations concerning the potability and safety of drinking water. Standards for private well water are regulated by state and federal governments as well, but the owner of the well is responsible for water purity and maintenance of the well and its pumping system.

Through the service line

Water from the municipal water company typically enters your property from the main water line in the street through a main valve box with a shutoff valve (which you may or may not have access to) into a service line that runs to your home. Repair and maintenance of the service line—once it passes the stop-box valve—is the homeowner's responsibility.

To the water meter

The service line usually enters the house through a water meter owned and maintained (sometimes for a fee) by the municipality that measures the amount of water you use. Homes on a grade or slab have a utility area where the service line enters and where the water meter is located. Homes with basements usually have the water meter in the basement where the service line enters the house. The meter has a valve on each side. The valve on the street side is controlled by the provider. The valve on the home side is controlled by the homeowner and is called the main shutoff valve.

The main shutoff valve

The main shutoff valve is near the meter. Know its location and how to shut it off in case of an emergency (see page 10). It's a good idea to turn off the water at the main and drain the system before attempting major repairs or maintenance work. Local shutoff valves should also be installed near every fixture and appliance so you don't have to shut off the water to the entire house to fix the fixture or appliance.

Branching out

The sizes of the lines and branch piping in the house will depend on the demands of the appliances. The main supply line is usually ¾- or 1-inch pipe. A ¾-inch pipe is the standard size for most water heaters—usually the first connection to the water line as it enters the house. Internal branch lines to appliances and fixtures are usually made of ¾- or ½-inch copper, CPVC (chlorinated polyvinyl chloride) or, in some areas of the country, PEX (cross-linked polyethylene). (See "Rigid Supply Pipes," page 164.)

Branch lines from the main supply line are run in the subfloors and in the walls to the fixtures they serve. Branch lines should not be run along outside walls where freezing is common. Freezing can cause the pipes to rupture or burst.

The right pressure

Nothing in your supply system operates properly without the correct water pressure.

Correct pressure is usually 40 to 55 PSI, although pressure as low as 20 PSI can be acceptable. High water pressures, especially greater than 85 PSI, can cause damage. Test the water pressure at the service line with a gauge, which you can buy or rent. Install the gauge on the home side of the water shutoff valve. If water pressure is too high or too low, you may have to adjust the pressure reducing valve if one is present. Pressure Reducing valves are usually located in the house at the first point of entry of the main line. If one is not present you may have to contact your municipal supplier.

Slab construction

Homes built on a concrete slab have drain and supply lines buried beneath the slab. If there is a problem, the slab has to be broken through or tunneled under to get to the source of the problem.

Slab construction supply system

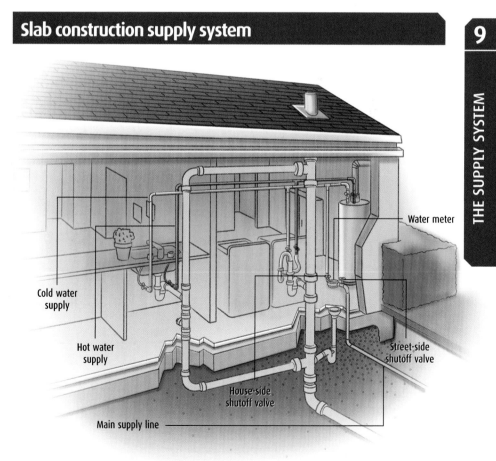

Cold water supply

Hot water supply

Water meter

Street-side shutoff valve

House-side shutoff valve

Main supply line

Rigid supply pipes

I f your home is older, you'll discover that many different plumbing materials were probably used—some of which meet code and some of which don't. Lead was common for supply lines 20 years ago, but much of it has been replaced with copper. You will find galvanized steel and cast iron. You will likely be able to replace the older materials with modern equivalents as long as they meet code requirements.

Copper, CPVC, and PEX
Copper and CPVC (chlorinated polyvinyl chloride) are the most common choices for supply piping. PEX (cross-linked polyethylene), an easy-to-connect, flexible plastic pipe, is common in warmer areas of the country where frost is not an issue. (Check local codes.) Galvanized pipe still meets code but is difficult for the home plumber to use and not as durable. Each withstands the pressure of water being driven into the supply system from the service.

Copper pipes used for supply lines in the home are sold in three grades—M, L, and K—based on the thickness of the pipe wall. M is the thinnest and adequate for most home uses. L is required by code in commercial and some residential installations, and K (the thickest) is used for underground water service.

CPVC, with its resistance to high temperatures (up to 180 degrees) and high water pressures, is an ideal pipe for water supply lines. It's easier to work with and less expensive than copper.

Check with local authorities to find out if there are restrictions on using CPVC as supply lines.

Pipe replacement guide
Here's what you'll need to know when replacing pipe:
- All pipe is designated by a grade, which will tell you how it can be used in a system to meet code requirements.
- Rigid copper pipe is sized by its interior diameter (ID).
- Type L and K soft copper pipe is sized by its outside diameter (OD). Refrigeration soft copper is sized by its outside diameter but is not generally to be used for house water supply.
- Schedule 40 PVC (for drain lines) is ID. Other PVC is OD.
- Galvanized steel is ID. (If you're measuring the length of galvanized steel, include the depth of the socket it will screw into.)

To find the diameter of various types of pipes, see page 13. If you're unsure of the proper size or grade for a replacement piece, take it to the store so you can buy an exact duplicate or find a viable alternative that meets code.

Up to code
When you're researching code issues, go to your home center and see what's on the shelves. If there are long rows of one item and not much of another for the same application, you've learned something about common use in your area. You've still got to check local codes to confirm that all materials meet standards, but you now have a place to start.

WORK SMARTER

TESTING FOR LEAKS
Never cover plumbing pipes or fixtures before testing for leaks. You have two options for testing—air pressure and water.

Testing with water: Isolate the new lines, then turn on the water to both hot and cold supplies. Inspect for leaks at each junction.

Testing with air pressure: Isolate the line being tested from existing supply lines. Install a threaded adapter for a pressure gauge and an air compressor fitting. Force air into the pipes with an air compressor. Local building codes will define the test pressure and time the line needs to maintain the pressure.

You may need to have an inspector on site, depending on the size of the project. Set up an appointment if necessary.

SAFETY ALERT

GETTING THE LEAD OUT
Lead is acknowledged as a health hazard, but it's still present as supply pipes in many older homes. Lead pipes may not be a problem if they have been properly installed and are well maintained. Some communities add a trace of phosphate, which coats the inside of the pipes and prevents lead from leaching into the system. If you have any concerns about potential health issues and lead pipes in your home, have the system tested. The results will tell you if pipes need to be replaced with copper or CPVC. In the meantime, run water through the pipes for a few minutes in the morning to get the lead out.

If you are unsure of the proper size or grade for a replacement pipe, take it to the store so you can buy an exact duplicate or find a viable alternative that meets code requirements.

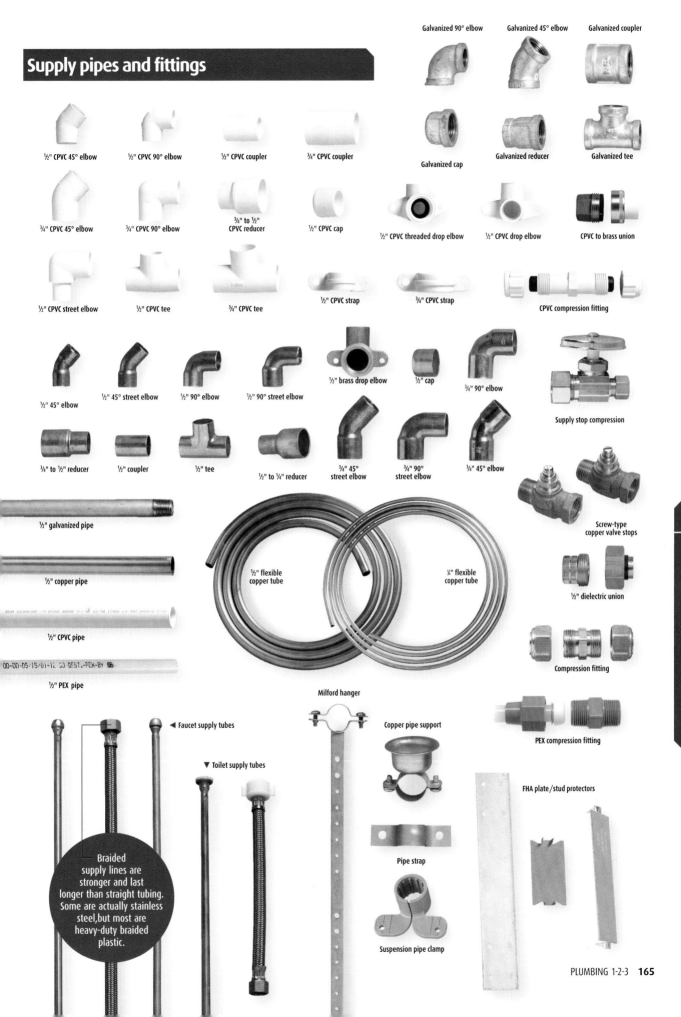

Galvanized 90° elbow

Galvanized 45° elbow

Galvanized coupler

½" CPVC 45° elbow

½" CPVC 90° elbow

½" CPVC coupler

¾" CPVC coupler

Galvanized cap

Galvanized reducer

Galvanized tee

¾" CPVC 45° elbow

¾" CPVC 90° elbow

¾" to ½" CPVC reducer

½" CPVC cap

½" CPVC threaded drop elbow

½" CPVC drop elbow

CPVC to brass union

½" CPVC street elbow

½" CPVC tee

¾" CPVC tee

½" CPVC strap

¾" CPVC strap

CPVC compression fitting

½" 45° elbow

½" 45° street elbow

½" 90° elbow

½" 90° street elbow

½" brass drop elbow

½" cap

¾" 90° elbow

Supply stop compression

¾" to ½" reducer

½" coupler

½" tee

½" to ¼" reducer

¾" 45° street elbow

¾" 90° street elbow

¾" 45° elbow

Screw-type copper valve stops

½" galvanized pipe

½" copper pipe

½" CPVC pipe

½" PEX pipe

½" flexible copper tube

¼" flexible copper tube

½" dielectric union

Compression fitting

PEX compression fitting

Milford hanger

◄ Faucet supply tubes

Copper pipe support

▼ Toilet supply tubes

FHA plate/stud protectors

Braided supply lines are stronger and last longer than straight tubing. Some are actually stainless steel, but most are heavy-duty braided plastic.

Pipe strap

Suspension pipe clamp

9

THE SUPPLY SYSTEM

Soldering copper pipes

9

THE SUPPLY SYSTEM

PROJECT DETAILS

SKILLS: Operating a propane torch, connecting plumbing fittings
PROJECT: Soldering copper pipes

TIME TO COMPLETE

EXPERIENCED: 10 min.
HANDY: 20 min.
NOVICE: 30 min.

STUFF YOU'LL NEED

TOOLS: Propane torch, spark lighter, emery cloth, round wire brush or 4-in-1 tool, flux brush, fire extinguisher, water, bucket
MATERIALS: Copper pipe, copper fitting, lead-free soldering paste (flux), lead-free solder, fire barrier, rag, bread

Soldering copper pipe fittings isn't difficult, but you'll need to practice before you're perfect. Once you've mastered the skill, you'll see why copper plumbing is appreciated for its professional look. Copper is a durable, clean, and functional connecting system.

Be a patient plumber

The most important thing with any fitting is that it doesn't leak. Your first few attempts may not be works of art, but soon you'll be soldering like a pro.

WORK SMARTER

KEEP YOUR COPPER DRY
Whether you're adding fittings to a system or starting from scratch, water in the line will keep the pipe from getting hot enough to make a secure solder joint.

1 Drain the line and open a faucet down the run to release steam.

2 Stuff a small amount of white bread into the pipe to absorb moisture; it dissolves when you run water later.

Don't ever apply heat directly to the solder. It will just melt away, and you'll never make a sealed joint.

GOOD IDEA

NO-FREEZE SOLUTION
In colder climates, run supply lines at a slight slope so they can be easily drained. Add bleeder caps at the low points so you can get rid of excess water.

 TOOL SAVVY

THE RIGHT COMBINATION
Wire brushes work well for cleaning fittings, but the 4-in-1 cleaning tool is a solderer's friend. It's a combination deburrer and cleaner for preparing ½- and ¾-inch copper pipe for soldering.

1

PREPARE THE INSIDE OF THE FITTING
Ream the inside of each fitting with a round wire brush. Clean, grease-free connections ensure a good seal.

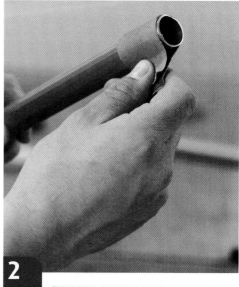

2

CLEAN THE OUTSIDE OF THE PIPE
Use emery cloth or steel wool to clean the outside of the pipe. Use a deburring tool or the handle of a pair of pliers to deburr the inside of the pipe. **Be careful—the edges may be sharp!**

3

APPLY FLUX TO THE PIPE

Apply a thin layer of lead-free soldering paste (flux) to the end of the pipe using a flux brush. The paste should cover about 1 inch of pipe. Insert the pipe into the fitting. Make sure the pipe is tight against the bottom of the fitting. Twist the fitting slightly to spread the flux.

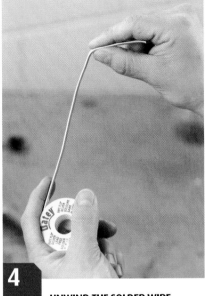

4

UNWIND THE SOLDER WIRE

You will need 8 to 10 inches of the wire extended from the spool. Bend the first 2 inches to a 90-degree angle.

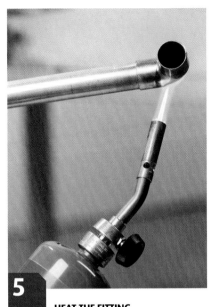

5

HEAT THE FITTING

Light the propane torch. Hold the tip of the flame against the middle of the fitting for 4 to 5 seconds or until the soldering paste begins to sizzle. Heat the opposite side of the fitting to ensure the heat is evenly distributed.

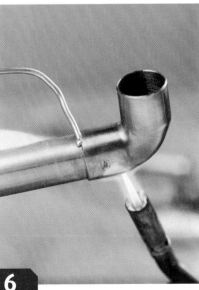

6

TOUCH THE SOLDER TO THE PIPE

If the solder melts, the pipe is ready to solder.

7

REMOVE THE FLAME FROM THE FITTING

Quickly insert ½ inch to ¾ inch of solder into the joint. Capillary action will draw the liquid solder into the joint. A properly soldered joint should show a thin bead of solder around the fitting.

8

CLEAN THE FITTING

Wipe away the excess solder with a rag. The pipe will be hot, so be careful while handling it. After the pipe and fitting have cooled, turn on the water and check for leaks. If the joint leaks, take it apart and resolder it.

Using a propane torch

To make it easy to turn on the flame, purchase a torch with a trigger-type igniter, as shown here. If your torch does not have an igniter, strike a match or a spark lighter, as shown at right, next to the nozzle until the gas ignites. Adjust the torch valve until the blue portion of the flame is 1 to 2 inches long.

Always read the manufacturer's operating instructions before using a propane torch. Make sure the area where you will solder is well-ventilated—propane torches can produce carbon monoxide. Inspect the area for potential fire hazards and isolate them by moving them or placing a fireproof barrier in front of them.

1 Inspect the seals on both the cylinder and nozzle for damage before you connect them. If either is damaged, do not use the damaged part. Follow the manufacturer's recommendation for disposal of the damaged piece.

2 When you're finished with the torch, turn the valve to the off position. Hand-tighten the seal to shut off the flow of gas. Do not overtighten the valve; you can damage the seals.

Spark lighter

TOOL SAVVY

SOLDERING IN PLACE SAFELY

Soldering isn't a difficult job when you're assembling a system on your workbench, but a lot of soldering projects require you to do the work against a wall, inside an access panel, or in the ceiling or floor joists. Fire is a constant danger whenever live flame meets combustible materials, so you've got to take some common-sense precautions. Purchase a flameproof barrier to hang on the surface behind the soldering position. Made of fire-retardant material, these barriers usually come with grommets to assist in hanging. Follow the manufacturer's instructions. Keep a fire extinguisher and a bucket of water near you when you work—just in case.

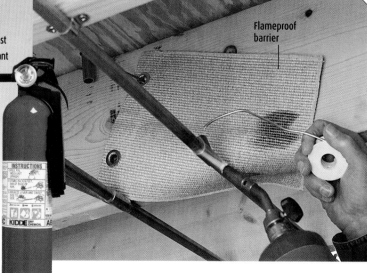

Flameproof barrier

9

THE SUPPLY SYSTEM

Connecting CPVC pipe

PROJECT DETAILS

SKILLS: Cutting pipe and connecting plumbing fittings
PROJECT: Connecting CPVC pipe

TIME TO COMPLETE

EXPERIENCED: 10 min.
HANDY: 20 min.
NOVICE: 30 min.

STUFF YOU'LL NEED

TOOLS: Pipe cutter, hacksaw, or miter saw and box; deburring tool
MATERIALS: Cleaner, primer, rags, cement

A s a general rule, CPVC is less expensive than copper but just as durable, and it withstands high temperatures and pressure in the supply system. It cuts easily with a tubing cutter or hacksaw, connections are easy, and assembly is quick. Check local codes to see if it is allowed for your plumbing project.

One easy way to ensure you have properly aligned the pipes and fittings before you glue them together is to first dry fit them. Once you have cut the pipes to length, use a pencil or marker and draw a line across the fitting to the pipe. Pull the pipe and fitting apart and then follow the priming and cementing steps listed. You can then use the marks on the pipe and fitting to align them.

Assemble quickly

Once you glue a fitting in place, it can't be removed—you have to cut it apart and start over. You can't twist fittings apart, and fine-tuning adjustments are impossible. Cut sections to length and test-fit the complete run before cementing the lines in place.

DO NOT use sparking or open-flame equipment (power drills or torches) near areas where solvent vapors may exist—the vapors are potentially explosive.

WORK SMARTER

TIPS FOR CONNECTING RIGID PLASTIC PIPE

- Use the correct primers and cements for the pipe you're installing. CPVC, PVC, and ABS are not interchangeable without transition fittings.
- Cure time depends on the cement used, the size and tolerance of the pipe and fitting, and the air temperature. You will weaken the bond by trying to speed or retard the cure.
- Keep the lid on cements and primers when not in use.
- Stir or shake cement before using.
- Use a ¼-inch dauber on small-diameter pipes, a 1½-inch dauber up through 3-inch pipe, and a natural-bristle brush, swab, or roller half the pipe diameter on pipes 4 inches and up. Do not allow daubers to dry out.
- DO NOT mix primer with cement. Do not use thickened or lumpy cement. Cement should have the consistency of syrup or honey.
- Do not handle joints until they are fully cured.
- All colored cements and primers will leave a permanent stain.

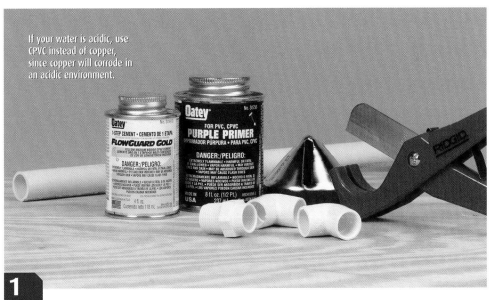

If your water is acidic, use CPVC instead of copper, since copper will corrode in an acidic environment.

1

PURCHASE PRIMER AND CEMENT

There are one-step cements available for CPVC that eliminate the need to use purple primer. But check local codes carefully to determine if primer is required. In some localities, you will fail inspection if you don't use it. Purple primer leaves a permanent and recognizable stain on the pipe, so everyone will know whether or not you've used it. Choose a dauber that is the proper size for the job. Daubers should be half the diameter of the fittings being joined so the job will take less time and cause less mess.

2 CUT THE PIPE

Use a plastic pipe cutter or a saw and miter box to ensure a square cut. Square cuts ensure that the pipe will seat properly in the fitting to produce a strong joint.

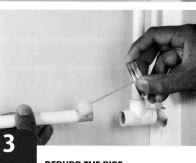

3 DEBURR THE PIPE

Removing burrs ensures even coverage with the primer and cement. Sanding can change the diameter and cause a poor fit, so use a deburring tool. Test-fit the pipe to the fitting; it should seat snugly in the fitting.

COAT THE SURFACES WITH PRIMER

Apply an even coat of primer to the pipe and the fitting. Primer softens the pipe to help seat it and reacts with the cement to make a permanent bond. Some manufacturers of CPVC pipe have explicit instructions for connecting them. Follow them to the letter.

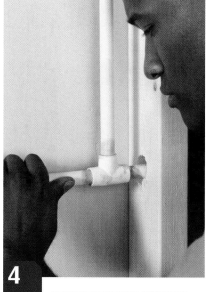

4 APPLY CEMENT AND ASSEMBLE THE PARTS QUICKLY BUT CAREFULLY

Apply an even coat of cement with a dauber to the pipe and fitting and insert the pipe all the way into the fitting until it stops. Twist a quarter of a turn to spread the cement evenly. Hold the pipe and fitting together for 10 seconds to prevent the heat from the cement from pushing the connection apart. Wipe off excess cement between the fitting and pipe with a clean rag.

⌕ CLOSER LOOK

PEX FLEXIBLE PLASTIC PIPE

PEX (cross-linked polyethylene) is a flexible plastic pipe used for hot and cold supply lines. While it is gaining wider national acceptance, PEX is primarily used in the southern United States and in parts of southern California. In these areas, it can also be used to run the main supply line from an outside water meter into a slab home.

Good resistance to deterioration, heat, and the high pressure required for supply, plus ease of assembly, make PEX an ideal choice for do-it-yourselfers in areas where it is approved for use. (Check local codes.)

Easy to assemble, the system uses two types of fittings:

■ Plastic compression-type fittings, which are tightened by hand and then given one full turn with pliers until snug. No tape or pipe compound is required.

■ Brass ribbed fittings, which are permanently sealed to the pipe with a crimping tool and crimp ring. (This method requires special tools and is usually a professional installation.)

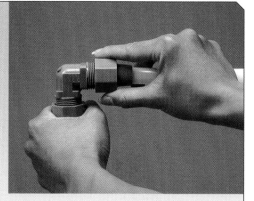

The pipe, which is available in rolls of 50 to 100 feet, is cut to length with a utility knife or a tubing cutter. It is flexible enough to turn corners that would require new connections and fittings with other types of plumbing. (Follow the manufacturer's instructions for maximum bends.)

Both the compression and crimped fittings are required by code to be accessible for inspection and repair and cannot be sealed in walls or ceilings. In order to make the fittings accessible, they are often grouped in manifolds with access panels installed in convenient locations.

Installing PEX pipe

PROJECT DETAILS

SKILLS: Making simple crimp and compression connections
PROJECT: Running and connecting about 50 feet PEX tubing with three or four fittings

TIME TO COMPLETE

EXPERIENCED: 30 min.
HANDY: 45 min.
NOVICE: 1.5 hrs.

STUFF YOU'LL NEED

TOOLS: Plastic tubing cutter, knife, crimp tool with gauge, water-pump pliers, drill
MATERIALS: PEX tubing, various fittings, clamps

This product is gaining acceptance in many parts of the country but is still against code in many areas. Cross-linked polyethylene (PEX) has emerged as the most common type of flexible plastic water supply pipe, replacing polybutylene (PB). It is available in a variety of sizes, and usually comes in rolls, though straight pieces are also available. It is durable even when used for hot water; in fact, it is often used for radiant heating systems. Check to be sure it is allowable by your local codes.

It is somewhat expensive, but the extra cost is often offset by its ease of installation. Though it cannot make tight turns, it can be snaked through much of a house without the use of fittings. And the fittings you do have to install are easy to connect.

PEX may be a good choice for remodeling work, because it can sometimes be fished through walls in much the same way as electrical cable—so you may be able to minimize damage to walls and ceilings. It is sometimes used to replace old galvanized pipe, for instance. After cutting some holes in walls, the old pipe can be cut with a reciprocating saw and pulled out, and PEX can be run through the same holes. You can even sometimes use an electrical fish tape to pull PEX through the holes.

Polybutylene crimp parts

Crimp tool

Crimp plug

Male elbow

Crimp rings

Crimp valve

Crimp elbow

Female adapter

Crimp tee

Drop ear elbow

Male adapter

PEX PARTS

There are two types of PEX fittings. Plastic compression-type fittings are tightened by hand and then given one full turn with pliers until snug. This type of connection is typically allowed only where it will be exposed; it cannot be hidden inside a wall or ceiling. Crimp connections use brass fittings, a crimp ring, and a special crimp tool, which can cost about $100. It will take a bit of practice to make crimp connections, but they are not difficult. And crimp connections are considered as solid as soldered copper, so they can be hidden inside walls.

A good variety of fittings is available to meet just about any need. In addition to tees and elbows, be sure to get drop-ear elbows for where pipe will protrude from the wall. You may also need transition fittings and adapters to join to other types of pipe.

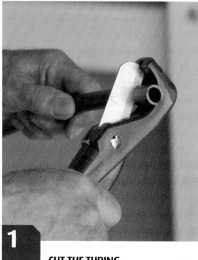

1 CUT THE TUBING

Whenever possible, run the tubing first and then cut it to length; use a tape measure when necessary. You can cut PEX with a knife, but a pair of heavy-duty cutters makes it easy to make straight, clean cuts. Take care to cut the pipe perpendicular; an end cut at an angle will not join as securely to a fitting.

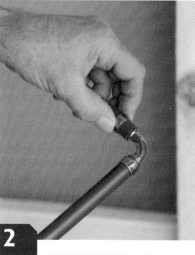

2 SLIP ON THE CRIMP RING AND FITTING

Slide the crimp ring onto the tubing, then insert the fitting. Slide the crimp ring ⅛ to ¼ inch from the end of the tubing; make sure it is in a position to grab onto the fitting inside the tubing.

3 CRIMP

Center the crimping tool jaws over the ring and check that the ring is perpendicular to the tubing. Hold the ring and the tool square with the tubing and squeeze to crimp the ring. Close the tool completely, one time. Do not crimp twice, or you may weaken the connection. If a ring is not securely fastened, cut the tubing and start again.

4 CHECK THE CONNECTION WITH A GAUGE

The crimp tool comes with a gauge for making sure the connection is secure. Slip the gauge over the crimped ring. The GO slot of the gauge should fit. If the ring is too large for the gauge, or if the NO/GO slot of the gauge indicates that the ring is too small, cut the tubing and try again with a new crimp ring.

RUNNING PEX

Be sure that the tubing is adequately clamped, supported, and protected. In the installation shown, a nailing plate is installed where the tubing runs through a stud. Clamps above and below a fitting ensure against excessive vibration. A drop-ear elbow is attached to a brace, so that a threaded pipe (either plastic, brass, chrome, or galvanized) can be attached; a stop valve can be tightly screwed onto this pipe.

Connecting galvanized or black steel pipe

PROJECT DETAILS

SKILLS: Connecting threaded metal pipe
PROJECT: Connecting galvanized or black steel pipe

TIME TO COMPLETE

EXPERIENCED: 5 min.
HANDY: 10 min.
NOVICE: 15 min.

STUFF YOU'LL NEED

TOOLS: Two pipe wrenches
MATERIALS: Pipe, fittings, pipe compound, rag, liquid dishwashing soap, sponge

Many years ago, galvanized pipe replaced lead in supply and drain applications, along with cast iron. Copper, PVC, CPVC, and PEX are now the most common choices. Black steel pipe is still used for gas lines.

Working with threaded galvanized or black steel pipe might seem simple, but it's a demanding job. You will need to keep track of what length and fitting goes where. It is also difficult to determine what lengths you need for the run. You may find that most of your time is spent running to your local home center. In the end, it is likely to be easier to measure carefully and have a home center or hardware store cut and thread the pieces for you.

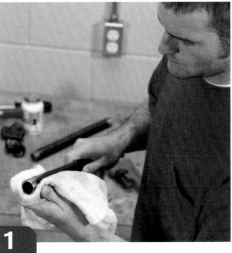

1

CLEAN THE THREADS OF THE PIPE AND FITTING
Use a rag to clean dirt and grease from the threads. This will ensure the best connection for the pipe and fitting.

2

APPLY PIPE JOINT COMPOUND TO THE PIPE THREADS
Connect the pipe to the fitting by holding the fitting in place with a pipe wrench and turning the pipe with the other wrench until it is snugly seated. Clean off any excess piping compound with a rag.

3

TURN ON THE GAS AND TEST THE LINE FOR LEAKS
If you are installing a gas line, it must be tested for leaks. Fill a sponge with liquid dishwashing soap and water. Apply it to the new fitting and look for bubbles. It's the same process used for finding leaks in a car tire. If there's a leak, bubbles will form on the surface, and you'll have to refit the joint.

9

THE SUPPLY SYSTEM

DIELECTRIC UNION
Whenever possible, switch to copper or plastic pipe when running a new line. To make the transition to copper, always use a dielectric union; otherwise, the joint will likely corrode and eventually leak. Solder one portion of the fitting onto the copper pipe and tighten the other portion onto the galvanized pipe. Tighten the union nut.

Tapping into a line

1
SHUT OFF THE WATER
If there is no union nearby, cut through the pipe with a reciprocating saw and a metal-cutting blade. You can also use a hacksaw. Unscrew the pipe on both sides.

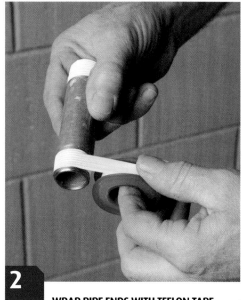

2
WRAP PIPE ENDS WITH TEFLON TAPE
Wrap male pipe threads with two or three windings of Teflon tape. (For black gas pipe, use yellow Teflon tape made for gas pipe.) Wrap the tape clockwise, so it will not come unwound as you screw the pipe into a fitting.

3
INSTALL A TEE AND PART OF A UNION
Screw on a short nipple, then a tee fitting (for the new line you will install), then another short nipple, then part of a union. For each connection, wrap the threads with Teflon tape and tighten with a pipe wrench before moving on to the next connection.

4
INSTALL THE REST OF THE UNION
Hold the other portion of the union in place and measure for the final section of pipe. You may need to have this piece custom-cut at a home improvement center or a plumbing supply source. Screw on the section of pipe, then the final part of the union. Finally tighten the union nut.

The Drain-Waste-Vent (DWV) System

The DWV (drain-waste-vent) system removes liquids, gases, and solid waste from your home through a series of drains and vents.

Where the sewage goes

Solid and liquid waste are drained away either to a septic tank on the property or into a municipal sewage system. Gases produced from the waste must be prevented from entering and remaining in the house—that's the purpose of the traps under the sinks and the vent system (see pages 176–177). The vent system also allows air into the drainage system so the wastewater and the gas can easily flow away from the house.

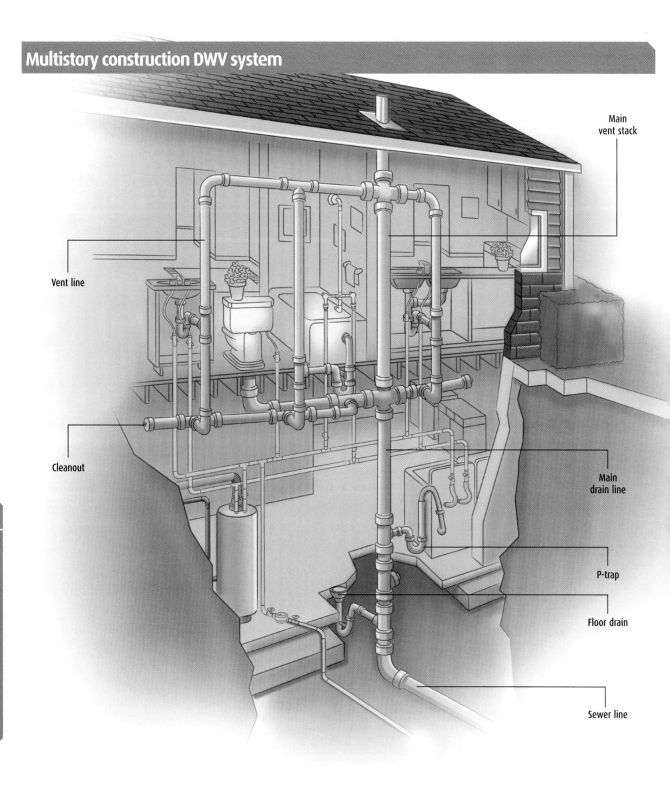

Main
vent stack

Vent line

Cleanout

Main
drain line

P-trap

Floor drain

Sewer line

Driven by gravity

Unlike the supply system, which uses water pressure to move water through the pipes, the drain system is installed at a slope and uses gravity to drain waste into the main sewage system. Water draining down a vertical pipe flows more quickly than from a horizontal one. Because of this rate of flow, deposits of grease and soap residue build up in horizontal pipes faster than in vertical pipes. To prevent deposit buildup, all horizontal pipes must be set and run at an angle called the "fall." The standard formula for calculating the fall is ¼ inch per foot over the course of the run. An 8-foot run, for instance, would have a fall of 2 inches from beginning to end.

Who's responsible?

The public sewage system is connected to your home through the main drain line. The main line serves as the trunk for the branch lines. The branch lines are tied to the main system by a large vertical pipe that leads down to the main drain and up through the roof to the main stack vent. You are usually responsible for all repairs on your side of the property line, which includes the service line. The municipality is responsible for repairs on the lines in the public rights-of-way.

Draining away

When wastewater leaves a sink or plumbing fixture, it enters a curved section of pipe called a trap. The trap is a U-shaped section of pipe installed between the fixture drain and the drain line that forces water to drain against gravity. They are often called P-traps or S-traps because of their shape when installed. As the sink, tub, or toilet drains, water is forced through the trap. When the fixture is empty, the trap holds the water, creating a seal to keep sewer gases from entering the house.

Bends are necessary in the branch lines because of the constraints of home construction. Elbows with gradual sweeping curves move the wastewater more smoothly through the system and prevent deposits from building at the elbows.

Cleanouts along the drain lines allow you to auger out blockages. There is probably a main cleanout where the drain exits the house. In slab construction, you may find the main cleanout outside next to the house.

Vents make it work

Without a constant air supply, a vacuum would be created in drain lines, and waste would not flow from the house. Air enters drain lines from the vent stack system that extends up through the roof. Each plumbing fixture should have its own vent line tied into the central vent system.

Air pressure also keeps sewer gases from breaking the seal made by wastewater in the drain traps. **If the water barrier in the trap is broken, sewer gases rich in unpleasant smells and potential health and fire hazards can enter the house.** Proper venting is rigorously enforced in plumbing codes by inspection and fines for violation.

Like drain lines, vent lines can become clogged. If the drain line gurgles or still seems sluggish after augering the main or branch line for a blockage, head up to the roof and auger down the vent to clear out the obstruction.

Anatomy of a P-trap

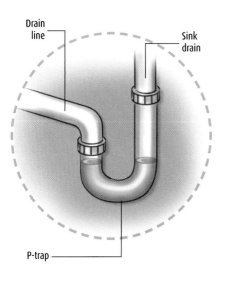

Drain line

Sink drain

P-trap

P-traps or S-traps are required by code wherever there is an open drain line that flows into the DWV system, such as from a sink, bathtub, shower or washing machine. It is constructed so that a water seal will form in the curve of the trap, preventing backflow of air or gas from the sewer line while permitting free flow of liquids through the system. A toilet has a built-in trap.

WORK SMARTER

USING ESCUTCHEON PLATES

Escutcheon plates fit around the drainpipe covering the hole where the drain line enters the wall or floor. Where plumbing is visible, such as under a wall-hung lavatory, they add a finishing touch. Using escutcheon plates inside cabinets isn't always required but they do help seal the hole. Two basic types are available in both metal and plastic.

◀ Split-ring escutcheon plates fit around a pipe that is already in place.

◀ Solid-ring escutcheon plates slip onto the pipe before the drain is assembled.

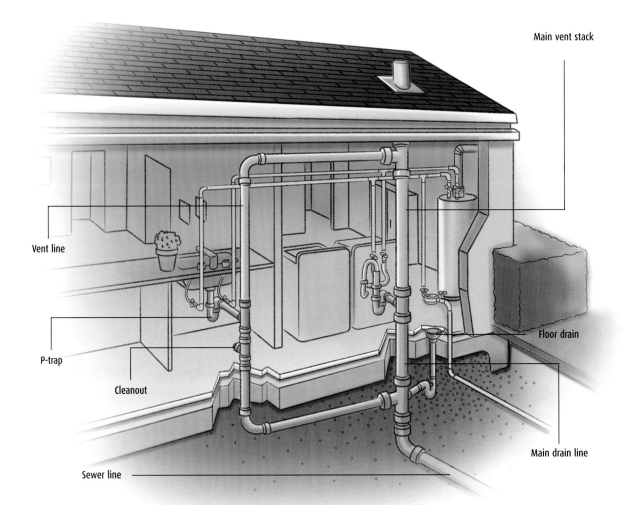

Main vent stack

Vent line

P-trap

Cleanout

Sewer line

Floor drain

Main drain line

DWV pipes and fittings

Different plumbing fixtures need different sizes of drainpipe because of flow requirements. Bathroom sinks have drainage flows requiring the pipe to be 1¼ inches in diameter; toilets require 3- to 4-inch lines; and sinks need 1½-inch pipes. The pipe size of the main drain is identified by its inside diameter (ID). Standard is usually 4 inches.

Types of drainpipes
The type of pipe used in the drainage system varies, depending on the age of the house. Vitrified clay, bituminized fiber, cast iron, ABS and PVC all have been used

at one time for the main sewer line. Vitrified clay can be damaged by tree roots, a major cause of replacement of main lines and sewer lines in older homes. Older homes typically have cast iron for the stacks and galvanized steel pipe for the runs.

Although the durability of cast iron makes it an attractive choice for the drainage system stack, it's difficult to work with. Galvanized steel also tends to have some limitations. It tends to corrode over time and requires more frequent replacement than other materials.

Newer homes use either PVC or copper pipe for DWV runs because they are virtually maintenance-free.

PVC coupling

PVC 90° elbow

PVC reducer

PVC cap

PVC 45° elbow

PVC p-trap

PVC Wye fitting or
y-fitting

PVC 90°
long sweep elbow

PVC slip joint elbow

PVC slip joint coupling

PVC Sanitary
Tee

PVC cleanout and plug

ABS coupling

ABS 90° elbow

ABS reducer

ABS cap

ABS 45° elbow

Wye fitting or
y-fitting

ABS 90°
long sweep elbow

ABS cleanout and plug

PVC pipe

ABS pipe

Cast iron pipe

Coupling band

GOOD IDEA

LAST THINGS FIRST

The size of the waste system piping gets larger as more fixtures dump into it. Usually you will want to run the waste lines first because they are the bulkiest and hardest to work with.

THE DRAIN-WASTE-VENT SYSTEM

10

How venting works

Whenever a plumber approaches a remodel job or a new installation, the first question he or she typically asks is, "How will the drainpipes be vented?" Depending on the situation, venting a new installation may be simple or it may be very difficult—but it must be figured out ahead of time. And any venting plan must be approved by a plumbing inspector. Local codes are very specific concerning how fixtures are vented. This may seem annoying at times, but the rules are there to ensure safe, smooth flow of wastewater.

There are four basic ways to vent. A separate vent, sometimes called a **true vent**, is the simplest to design but often the hardest to install: a vertical pipe that runs up through the roof. A true vent can have no water running through it. The upper portion of a stack serves as a true vent for top-floor fixtures. If there are no nearby vent pipes, the simplest solution is sometimes to install a new vent pipe.

A **common vent**, on the facing page, is when two fixtures, usually located on opposite sides of a wall, are connected to the same vent pipe. A fitting called a sanitary cross is often used to make this connection.

A **revent**, also called an auxiliary vent, is a common solution. The revent pipe typically runs up from the drain line and over to a true vent pipe. Revent configurations can get somewhat complicated, so you may need to have a plumber design yours. Codes stipulate how high a revent must run before it can make a horizontal turn.

Wet venting is a self-contradictory term, since a vent really should be dry. This method uses a portion of another fixture's drain line to double as a vent. Wet venting is sometimes allowed, if the pipe is large enough so that it will virtually never be filled with water.

Codes limit the distance between a fixture's trap and the vent. The larger the drain line, the larger the allowable distance. For instance, if you have a 1½-inch drain line, the vent may be allowed to be 3 feet away. With a 2-inch line, the distance increases to 5 feet.

In some cases, an air admittance valve is allowed, either to assist or to replace a vent pipe. This varies a good deal from locale to locale, so check with your building department.

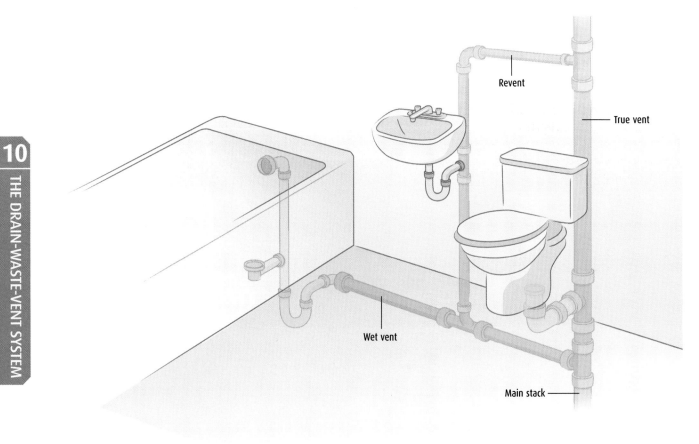

Revent

True vent

Wet vent

Main stack

Vent options

When planning the actual course your pipes will take, you need to take into account obstructions like windows and doors, as well as existing pipes. Here are some configurations that may make the installation easier.

Vent pipes are often somewhat smaller than the drain pipes they attach to. It used to be common to use special vent fittings, which did not have sweeping turns, but nowadays standard drain fittings are usually used.

Vents must rise at least 6 inches above a fixture's flood level—for instance, the top of a sink bowl or bathtub. (In some cases, the overflow hole is considered the flood level, since water cannot rise above it.)

A **loop vent**, right, connects to the drain at or near the trap and rises above the flood level before descending and perhaps running horizontally to join a vent pipe. In another revent alternative, right, the vent pipe is attached not adjacent to the trap, but somewhere along the length of a horizontal drain line.

Back venting refers to running a vent pipe up for a distance before joining to an existing vent at a point above all the house's plumbing fixtures. You can back vent inside a wall using Wye or tee fittings, but it is often easier to make the connections inside the attic.

The bathroom setup shown, facing page, shows a simple but common arrangement. A true vent, which is the upper portion of a main stack, is directly connected to a toilet. The sink is connected via a revent pipe. The tub is wet-vented using a large-diameter pipe.

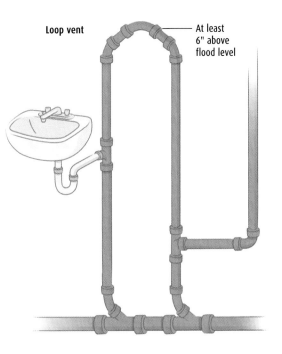

Loop vent

At least 6" above flood level

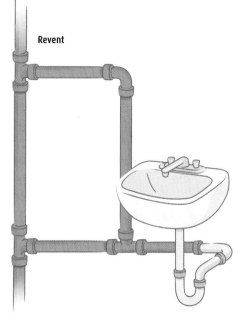

Revent

Common vent

Connecting PVC pipe

PROJECT DETAILS

SKILLS: Cutting pipe and connecting plumbing fittings
PROJECT: Connecting PVC pipe

TIME TO COMPLETE

EXPERIENCED: 10 min.
HANDY: 20 min.
NOVICE: 25 min.

STUFF YOU'LL NEED

TOOLS: Tubing cutter, hacksaw or miter saw and box, deburring tool or emery cloth, torpedo level, utility knife
MATERIALS: PVC pipe and fittings, primer, cement, rags

Use rigid PVC pipe for drain, waste, and vent systems. Check local codes to find the required pipe size. When in doubt about the correct size, use the next-largest sized pipe if practical.
■ Use 1¼-, 1½-, and 2-inch ID PVC for sink drains lavatories and tubs.

■ Use 2-inch ID pipe for showers.
■ Use 3- or 4-inch ID for toilets.
■ Drain lines and vent stacks can use 1½-, 2-, or 3-inch ID.
In some locales, ABS is preferred over PVC (see page 186).

DRY-FIT ALL THE CONNECTIONS BEFORE THE FINAL ASSEMBLY
Dry-fit the connections before applying primer and cement—once you've cemented the pipe, it can't be changed. Check the fall with a torpedo level. There should be a ¼-inch fall for each lineal foot of run.

1 **USE THE RIGHT PRIMER AND CEMENT FOR THE JOB**
The right primer and cement guarantee good connections. The right size dauber is important as well. Daubers should be half the diameter of the pipe to be joined to reduce application time.

2 **CUT THE PVC SQUARE**
A straight cut is necessary for a good connection. There are PVC tubing cutters specifically for small-diameter pipes. Cut large-diameter pipes with a miter saw, hacksaw, or plastic pipe saw.

3 **DEBURR THE CUT**

After each cut, deburr the pipe with a knife, emery cloth, or rag to ensure that it seats snugly into the fitting.

4 **APPLY PRIMER TO THE CONNECTIONS**

The primer softens the ends, preparing them for application of the cement.

5 **COAT THE PIPE AND FITTING WITH CEMENT**

Apply an even coat of cement to the surfaces. Apply a thin coat; too much cement can weaken the pipe and destroy the fitting.

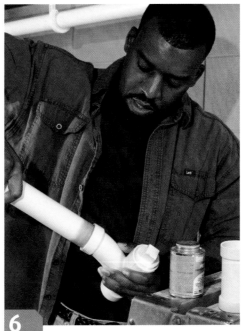

6 **WORK QUICKLY TO CONNECT THE PIECES**

Insert the pipe into the fitting with a quick push and a quarter-turn to seat. Hold the connection for 10 seconds to prevent the heat produced by the cement from pushing the connection apart. The cement melts the surfaces and forms a secure bond. Wipe away excess cement, which can weaken the joint, with a rag.

WORK SMARTER

TIPS FOR CONNECTING RIGID PLASTIC PIPE

- Use the correct primers and cements for the pipe you're installing. CPVC, PVC, and ABS are not interchangeable without transition fittings.
- Cure time depends on the cement used, the size and tolerance of the pipe and fitting, and the air temperature. You will weaken the bond by trying to speed or retard the cure.
- Keep the lid on cements and primers when not in use.
- Stir or shake cement before using.
- Use a ¼-inch dauber on small-diameter pipes, 1½-inch dauber on up through a 3-inch pipe, and a natural-bristle brush, swab, or roller one-half the pipe diameter on pipes 4 inches and up. Do not allow daubers to dry out.
- DO NOT mix primer with cement. Do not use thickened or lumpy cement. Syrup or honey is the right consistency.
- Do not handle joints until they are fully cured.
- All colored cements and primers will leave a permanent stain.

THE DRAIN-WASTE-VENT SYSTEM

Replacing and repairing cast-iron pipe

Cast iron was the mainstay of drain and vent systems until the introduction of ABS and PVC. The mechanics of repair are not difficult to master, but cast-iron pipe is awkward, heavy, and difficult to cut. You will need a reciprocating saw, or you can rent a special cast-iron snap cutter, which is more efficient. Sections of damaged pipe are commonly replaced with ABS or PVC, which is lighter and easier to handle than cast iron.

Support the pipe

It is extremely important to support the pipe while you are making the repair. Riser clamps must be attached above and below the damaged section. These clamps must rest securely on wooden frames on the floor and be framed or chained to the ceiling joists above.

⊘ **SAFETY ALERT**

BEFORE YOU BEGIN, CLEAN THE DRAIN LINE
Flush the toilets and run some water through the fixtures to clean out the drain. Alert your family not to use house fixtures like toilets or sinks while you are making this repair. Waste in the lines is a potential biohazard. Wash your hands and change clothes when you're finished.

1 **SHUT OFF THE WATER MAIN AND MARK THE PIPE**
Use chalk to mark at least 6 inches above and below the damaged section. Build a support frame of 2×4s as shown in step 2 and install riser clamps above and below the damaged section to support the pipe.

2 **CUT OUT THE DAMAGED PIPE**
Wrap the chain of the cast-iron cutter around the pipe. Align the cutting wheels with the chalk line. Tighten the chain and cut. After both ends have been cut, remove the section.

3 CUT THE REPLACEMENT PIPE

Measure and mark out the length of the replacement PVC pipe and cut a section 1 inch shorter than the span to be replaced.

4 PLACE THE COUPLING BAND

Slip a banded coupling with a neoprene sleeve over each end of the cast-iron pipe. Make sure the cast iron is seated tightly against the rubber separator ring molded into the sleeve.

5 FOLD BACK THE SLEEVE

Expose the ends of the cast iron by folding back the neoprene sleeve on both sections.

6 POSITION THE NEW SECTION OF PIPE

Align the PVC pipe with the cast-iron pipe. Roll the neoprene sleeves over the plastic pipe.

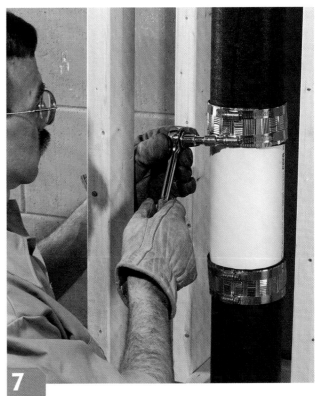

7 SLIDE THE BANDS OVER THE SLEEVES

Once in place, tighten the bands with either a screwdriver or a socket and ratchet wrench until snug. Remove the riser supports when the pipe is secured in place.

Connecting ABS pipe

PROJECT DETAILS

SKILLS: Cutting pipe and connecting plumbing fittings
PROJECT: Connecting ABS pipe

TIME TO COMPLETE

EXPERIENCED: 10 min.
HANDY: 20 min.
NOVICE: 25 min.

STUFF YOU'LL NEED

TOOLS: Tubing cutter, hacksaw or miter saw and box, deburring tool
MATERIALS: ABS pipe and fittings, cleaner, cement, dauber, rags

CLOSER LOOK

LOOKS CAN BE DECEIVING

It's easy to assume all plastic pipe is the same, but that kind of thinking can get you in a lot of trouble. Each type is a different composition of materials and requires its own blend of cleaners and cements to make a proper bond. If you're in a situation where you have to join PVC and ABS, you'll need a special transition fitting to make the hookup.

WORK SMARTER

USE THE RIGHT DAUBER

Using the right size dauber is the key to successful connecting. Because the cement dries very quickly, speed is of the essence. You should use a dauber that's no less than half the diameter of the pipes and fittings so you can minimize the time it takes to apply the cement and make the joint.

The first rigid plastic pipe approved for use in drain, waste, and vent systems was ABS. It is easy to cut, lightweight, and very rigid. However, it becomes brittle over time and therefore is susceptible to cracking and breaking. Before purchasing ABS pipe, check your local plumbing codes. Some communities don't allow ABS to be used.

1 CHOOSE THE RIGHT SOLVENTS AND DAUBER
Read the label to make sure the solvents are for use with ABS pipe. The dauber should be half the diameter of the pipe being joined to reduce the time for application.

2 USE THE RIGHT CUTTING TOOL FOR THE JOB
Tubing cutters are perfect for cutting small-diameter pipe. Cut larger pipe with a hacksaw, abrasive disk, or miter saw. Be sure to make straight cuts—they allow for proper seating into the fitting.

3 DEBURR THE CUT PIPE
Use a deburring tool to remove burrs and shavings. If you don't have a deburring tool, a knife or emery cloth will work. Dry-fit the pipe and fittings. Make sure the proper fall of ¼ inch per lineal foot run is made to allow proper drain flow. A fitting that is glued crooked can throw off a whole run. Discover potential problems by dry-fitting.

4 APPLY THE SOLVENTS TO THE FITTING AND BASE
Apply the cleaner to the pipe surface to remove ink, oils, grease, and dirt. Allow the cleaner to dry. Coat the surfaces with ABS cement. Don't puddle the cement on—too much cement can weaken the pipe wall. Push the connections together with a twisting motion until properly seated.

5 HOLD THE CONNECTION FOR 30 SECONDS
The solvent produces heat that may cause the connection to push apart. The cement melts the ABS pipe to fuse the connection together. Wipe away excess cement with a rag to prevent weakening of the ABS pipe walls.

Tubs and showers

Chapter 11 highlights

 emoving or installing a bathtub is a big job. It requires plumbing, carpentry, drywalling, electrical, and sometimes, tiling skills. Most bathrooms have limited space, so you'll probably have to remove other fixtures, such as the toilet and lavatory sink, to give yourself enough room to work. You may want to consider hiring professionals to do some or all of the work.

Plan for removal

You've heard about the guy who built a boat in his basement? Well, before you take out the old tub, know how you're going to get it out the door, down the hall, down the stairs, and out into the yard. Measure to make sure it will fit through doors and hallways. Call your local waste removal service to arrange for its disposal. Have friends help carry it out—a bathtub is too heavy and awkward for one person to handle. However a cast-iron tub can be broken apart with a sledgehammer into manageable pieces.

Tub facts

Tub material determines the difficulty of installation. Acrylic, steel, and fiberglass tubs range from 60 to 120 pounds and some need to be installed on a bed of mortar. Cast-iron tubs don't need mortar, but they can weigh more than 300 pounds, so make sure the floor will support the weight.

 REAL WORLD

NEEDED: UMBRELLAS IN THE BASEMENT

It's important to thoroughly check a new installation for leaks. Experience has shown that an inspection by a professional may prevent a new installation from having to be redone, or to prevent any damage caused by a leak. A comprehensive inspection should include checking the supply risers, faucets, and P-trap; running water through the system; and ensuring that everything is sealed properly.

COMMON MISTAKES DO-IT-YOURSELFERS MAKE

- Ignoring or violating local code restrictions.
- Using pipes that are too small for the job.
- Connecting copper to galvanized pipe without a brass or dielectric fitting between them.
- Not using pipe tape or compound at threaded joints.
- Not leveling the fixture controls.
- Not installing access and shutoff valves.
- Not aligning tubing into compression fittings or stop valves.

GOOD IDEA

THE PERFECT BEAD

To get a "perfect bead" when using silicone caulk around a shower, smooth the caulk line with a small spoon dipped in soapy water.

Bathtub types

The National Kitchen and Bath Association (NKBA) categorizes bathtubs according to installation type: recessed, corner, freestanding, and platform or drop-in.

Recessed tubs have a finished front with unfinished sides that are concealed by the surrounding alcove walls.

Corner installations have three finished sides facing outward and the two unfinished sides concealed by the adjoining walls.

Claw-foot tubs are freestanding and can be placed anywhere that space allows.

Drop-in tubs are installed in a prebuilt platform and offer many design options by coordinating the color of the tub with the material of the platform structure.

Material choices

Bathtubs constructed of **acrylic**, **fiberglass**, and **plastic composites** are durable, attractive, and a good alternative to traditional cast-iron construction. They weigh less, come in a range of colors, and have a nonporous surface that's easy to clean. Bathtubs made of acrylic, fiberglass, and plastic materials are easily molded into a variety of shapes and sport features such as foot and back supports and headrests.

Cast iron is strong and durable and offers contemporary as well as traditional designs (such as the claw-foot style). Bathtubs are also made of **enameled steel** and **cultured marble** which are made with a wide range of metal trim and colors. It's not unusual for the same model tub to be available in more than 15 colors. White is usually the least expensive.

Needed skills

Successful bathtub and shower installations require careful planning, adequate time to do the job right, and a combination of plumbing and carpentry skills. If you want to install a light and vent fan, you will also need to do some electrical work.

Special features

Some manufacturers offer special surfaces designed to limit bacterial growth. **Antibacterial surfaces** can be especially in demand in homes with small children.

Whirlpool tubs provide basic bathing, but they also feature a motorized pump that draws water from the bathtub, mixes it with air, and injects it back into the bathtub through strategically placed jets to massage and relax tense muscles after a hard day of plumbing.

The big picture: Function and design

Think about the design of the entire bathroom before you begin working. If you have the space, you may want to install a separate tub and shower. Tubs, showers, and tub/shower combinations come in a variety of shapes and sizes. Check out the options and consult with the experts at your local home center before finalizing your bathroom design. You may find that there are options for shapes and sizes that will provide better use of space and allow for some additional amenities.

Check local codes

Check local codes before beginning any shower or tub installation. You may need to have an inspector check your work at certain points in the project.

Planning and prep

Proper preparation is key for the successful installation of any shower enclosure. Before beginning, prepare the walls.

- Wipe the wall surfaces with a damp cloth to remove soap scum and debris.
- All surfaces must be square, level, smooth, and dry before installing enclosure panels.
- Plaster can pose problems because of rough or uneven textures. Prepare a plaster surface for adhesives by sanding the plaster smooth. Use a rotary sander and medium-grit paper.
- You can install an enclosure over old ceramic tile, but remove any loose tiles first. Remove plastic tiles or old wallpaper.
- Seal any wall surface with two coats of primer or all-purpose enamel paint. This provides a better surface for the adhesive, allowing a stronger bond.

Allow for expansion

Tub and shower enclosures expand and contract slightly. Follow the manufacturer's instructions. Allow an extra ⅛-inch space for expansion for every 5 feet of enclosure length. Allow 1/16 to ⅛ inch of space at the bottom, between the panels and the base.

The NKBA (National Kitchen and Bath Association) Guidelines for Shower Design

- Make sure the interior dimensions of an enclosed shower include at least 34×34 inches of usable space. Measure from wall to wall. Grab bars, controls, and movable and folding seats don't reduce the measurement; but built-in seats do. You can settle for 32×32 inches, but it will make the shower uncomfortable for some users.
- Design shower doors so they open into the bathroom—not into the stall—to avoid crowding the space in the shower.
- To reduce the risk of falls, avoid installing steps for climbing into the shower.
- Install a pressure-balancing/temperature regulator or a temperature-limiting device for the showerhead to prevent scalding.

- Design the shower so you can reach the controls from inside and outside the stall. Put the controls 38 to 48 inches above the floor, and above the grab bar if there is one. Locate the controls between the showerhead and the stall door. You can install a hand-held showerhead instead of a fixed one. Place a hand-held model no higher than 48 inches above the floor in its lowest position.
- Install only laminated safety glass with a plastic interlayer, tempered glass, or approved plastic for any clear face of a shower enclosure or partition that reaches to within 18 inches of the floor.

Removing an old bathtub

PROJECT DETAILS

SKILLS: Carpentry and disconnecting plumbing fixtures
PROJECT: Removing an old bathtub

TIME TO COMPLETE

EXPERIENCED: 3 hrs.
HANDY: 5 hrs.
NOVICE: 8 hrs.

STUFF YOU'LL NEED

TOOLS: Crowbar, pry bar, keyhole saw, screwdriver, pliers, shower stem socket set, gloves, safety glasses
MATERIALS: 1×4 slides

Make sure you have plenty of room to work before you tackle tub removal. You will need a clear space at least 3 feet deep when pulling the tub straight out from the wall. You need to be able to work around the tub when it's away from the wall. It's a good idea to remove other plumbing fixtures, such as the sink or vanity and toilet.

Map your route

Measure the width of all door openings and the hallway along the path for removing the tub. Not only is this important for removing the old tub, but it's essential for bringing in the new one. There's nothing worse than having torn up your bathroom to remove the old tub and discovering that the new one will not fit through the hall or doorways.

The order of battle

■ Turn off the water at the main water shutoff. Drain the water supply lines by opening a faucet below the tub level.
■ Remove the faucet handles, spout, and drain.
■ Cut away at least 6 inches of drywall above the tub on all sides. Remove the screws or nails holding the tub flange to the studs. If you find a galvanized strip along the tub flange, use a flat bar or pry bar to remove it.
■ Lift up on the front edge of the tub with a pry bar and slide a pair of 1×4s beneath the tub.
■ Pull the tub away from the wall using the 1×4s as a skid. You'll need help carrying the tub, especially if it's cast iron. If you're not saving it or reusing it, cover the tub with a tarp and break it into pieces with a sledgehammer. Fiberglass and polymer tubs can be cut into pieces with a reciprocating saw.

Give yourself plenty of room to work when you're removing a tub. Cut away at least six inches of drywall above the tub.

Running a drain line

PROJECT DETAILS

SKILLS: Working with plastic drain-pipe, understanding venting, running pipes through walls and floors
PROJECT: Running new drain and vent lines for a new plumbing fixture

TIME TO COMPLETE

EXPERIENCED: Half a day
HANDY: One day
NOVICE: Two days

STUFF YOU'LL NEED

TOOLS: PVC saw, level, reciprocating saw, drill
MATERIALS: Drain and vent pipe with fittings, primer and cement, pipe straps, screws

Installing drain lines for a new bathroom is a complicated project that is probably best left to the pros. However if you have good plumbing skills and a good relationship with your plumbing inspector, you may attempt it. It's a good idea to at least get the advice of a plumber before proceeding.

Drain and vent pipes must be run precisely, so water drains well and the vents work. It also takes careful planning to design paths for the pipes that minimize damage to your home's framing. After all your planning, however, you may find that you need to modify your plans. As much as possible, dry-fit all the pieces together and make sure the assembly works before you start gluing.

When running horizontal drainpipes in a floor, calculate the altitude, which is the amount of vertical space you will need. Take into account the thickness of the pipes, plus the distance it needs to fall in order to maintain a slope of at least ¼ inch per foot. Whenever possible, avoid running pipes across floor joists.

Cut away any drywall or plaster on the walls where the pipes will run. It usually saves time in the long run to remove entire wall sections rather than cutting narrow sections for the pipes to run through.

The steps shown on these pages address some of the most common ways to run pipes. You will probably run into obstacles and circumstances that call for different—even ingenious—solutions. Again consult a plumber and your inspector to learn how to deal with your particular design problems.

Connecting a toilet drain

1

CONNECT A CLOSET BEND

A closet bend typically is 4 inches in diameter and reduces to fit a 3-inch pipe that travels to a fitting in the wall. Be sure the closet bend is centered at the right distance—usually 12 inches—from what will be the wall's finished surface. (If you will install ½-inch drywall, the bend should be centered 12½ inches from the framing.) A low-heel vent fitting is often the best way to make the connections in the wall. Run the 3-inch pipe at a slope into the fitting. Hold the pipes firmly in place using pipe straps and screws.

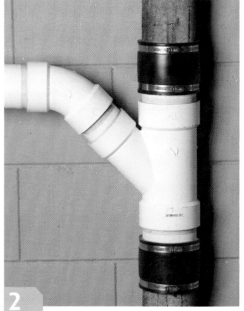

2

CONNECTIONS TO THE DRAIN LINE

Run 3-inch drain pipe to a nearby stack, connect it to a 45-degree elbow, and then to a Y fitting. Hold the assembly in place, check that the pipe slopes correctly, and measure for cutting the stack. Support the stack while you cut it. (If you are working with cast iron, see pages 184–185). Attach the Y-fitting with no-hub connectors. Once all the parts are dry-assembled and checked for slope, disassemble, apply primer, and glue them in order.

Connecting a sink drain

1

DRILL HOLES IN STUDS

Dry-assemble the parts for the drain and vent lines and hold them temporarily in place against the studs using pipe straps. Check that the drain line slopes at least ¼ inch per foot. Some inspectors want the vent line to slope in the opposite direction, so condensation water can trickle back into the drain. Mark the studs for holes. Because pipes cannot bend very much and space may be limited, you may need to cut one or more notches instead of holes in order to get the pipes through.

2

CUT THE STACK OR VENT PIPE

Where each of the drain and vent pipes will tie into an existing stack or vertical vent pipe, dry-fit a tee and two short lengths of pipe onto the pipe ends, and mark the existing pipe for cutting.

3

CONNECT WITH NO-HUB COUPLINGS

Slide a no-hub fitting onto either side of the existing pipe and slide or roll it up so you can slip in the new pipes. Slip the fittings back down so they are centered over the two pipes and tighten the nuts.

WORK SMARTER

Connecting several drains

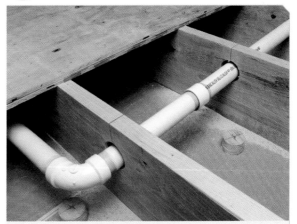

When installing fixtures for a new bathroom, you will want to assemble all the drains at the same time. In the arrangement shown, the tub and sink drains are connected to a horizontal pipe that runs to the drainpipe for the toilet. A grouping like this is much easier to assemble if you are working in a basement below. If not, you may choose to enclose the pipes by framing around them and creating a soffit.

If you must run drainpipe across joists, work very carefully. If joists are 16 inches apart, each succeeding hole should be about ⅜ inch lower than the preceding one, to maintain pipe slope of ¼ inch per foot. Drill holes that are about ¼ inch larger than the outside diameter of the pipe. To strengthen a joist, install strips of ¾-inch plywood on either side.

Installing a supply control riser and tub drain

PROJECT DETAILS

SKILLS: Carpentry skills and connecting plumbing fixtures
PROJECT: Installing supply risers and a bathtub drain

TIME TO COMPLETE

EXPERIENCED: 6 hrs.
HANDY: 8 hrs.
NOVICE: 12 hrs.

STUFF YOU'LL NEED

TOOLS: Propane torch and striker, tubing cutter, soldering kit, fiberglass flame barrier, hammer, electric drill, spade bits, screwdriver, saber saw, PVC cutter, tape measure, carpenter's level, pencil, gloves, safety glasses
MATERIALS: Copper supply pipe, copper fittings, integral stops, copper tube straps, faucet assembly, shower tee, solder, flux, PVC drainpipe, PVC fittings, PVC P-trap, tub overflow and drain assembly, PVC primer and adhesive, galvanized nails, Teflon tape, 2×4 blocking, silicone caulk

Sketch an installation plan of the layout for your supply control riser so you can break the process into manageable phases. (Use the illustration below as a guide.) Use the drawing to make up a tool and materials list. You may find it easier to install the system in the bathroom and then connect the supply lines and the drain downstairs.

Replacing an old system

If you're replacing older galvanized pipe with copper, and the interior wall structure isn't water damaged or otherwise deteriorated, the riser holes and the blocking will most likely be in place.

New construction

For a new installation, determine where you want the tub, then where you'll tap into the water supply and drainage systems. Next measure and sketch out both runs. If you're involved in new construction, you'll have to drill the riser holes and install blocking. If a stud is in the way of the faucet, you'll have to relocate it.

Adhere strictly to local codes and, if an inspection is required, make sure the inspector signs off before you close up the walls.

Supply control riser

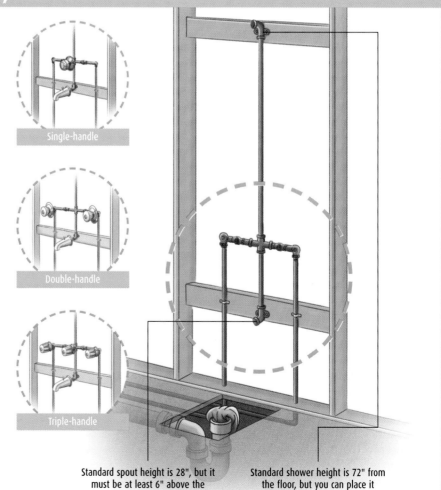

Single-handle

Double-handle

Triple-handle

Standard spout height is 28", but it must be at least 6" above the finished top of the tub.

Standard shower height is 72" from the floor, but you can place it higher if you prefer.

1 DRILL HOLES FOR THE RISERS

Drill riser holes through the stud wall into the basement. The diameter of the holes should be at least 1/4 inch larger than the diameter of the riser, so you'll have some flexibility when you're hooking up the supply lines. The type of faucet you're installing will determine the spread and placement of the riser holes.

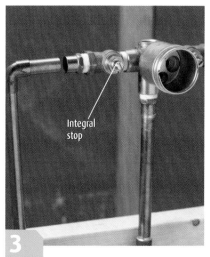

2 INSTALL THE BLOCKING

Blocking for a tub spout should be centered 4 inches above the top of the tub. Faucets installed more than 6 inches above the spout need separate blocking. The blocking should be level, at the correct depth inside the wall, and toenailed firmly to the studs. Install blocking at the height you've chosen for the showerhead.

Integral stop

3 CUT THE RISER ASSEMBLY

Cut the pipe for the supply risers, integral stops, and tub spout. Fit the adapters onto the faucet assembly using Teflon tape. Attach the pipe and fitting for the tub spout. Measure and cut the pipe for the supply and shower risers.

If local code requires an inspection, make sure you do it before you close up the walls around the risers and faucet.

4 ASSEMBLE THE PIECES

Make sure the faucet controls are centered and level and the stops fit. Do a dry-assembly as you go to make sure everything fits. Make any necessary adjustments and solder pieces into place.

5 SECURE THE SPOUT TO THE BLOCKING

After securing the spout to the blocking, connect all the pipes and fittings. (See pages 166–168 for soldering copper pipe and pages 169–170 for connecting CPVC.) Attach a drop-ear elbow for the spout.

6 SECURE THE SHOWER RISER

Screw a drop-ear elbow for the showerhead into its blocking.

Dummy nipple

7

SECURE THE RISERS TO THE BLOCKING

Screw the risers to the riser blocking and install a dummy nipple in the tub spout to protect the threads and serve as a guide.

CUT AN ACCESS HOLE INTO THE SUBFLOOR FOR THE DRAIN

Measure and mark an opening in the floor 4 to 9 inches wide and 12 inches from the center of the end wall. Drill out the corners and cut out the opening with a saber saw.

Options for proceeding

At some point you've got to test the system for leaks, and an inspection may be necessary before you install and finish the walls. After you've cut the access hole for the drain, you have a couple of options:

A You can install the tub and then hook it up to the drain and run the supply to the risers. (See "Installing a Tub on a Subfloor," pages 195–198.)

B If you're not ready to install the tub at this point, you can go below to run and connect the supply lines to the risers and run the drain line to the access hole (see below). Once the supply lines are hooked to the mains, test the system. Temporarily attach the faucet and spout and run water through the pipes to test for leaks at all the joints. Once you're satisfied the system is sound, finish the installation or schedule an inspection.

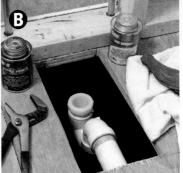

A

B

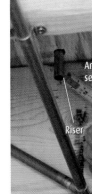

8

Anchor pipes securely to floor joists

Riser

Supply

DOUBLE-CHECK THE MEASUREMENTS FROM THE PLAN

Cut pipe lengths. Test-fit each supply line. Mark adjustments on the piping. Take the runs apart and make the changes. Anchor the pipes securely to the joists.

9

Secure pipes as you go

SOLDER THE PIPE AND FITTINGS

Secure each run with hangers to prevent stress on the fittings and reduce line vibration. Run the hot water supply to the right side of the riser and cold water to the left.

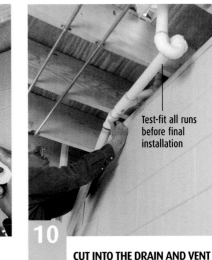

10

Test-fit all runs before final installation

CUT INTO THE DRAIN AND VENT STACK SYSTEM AND RUN PIPES TO THE DRAIN

(See chapter 10, "The Drain-Waste-Vent System".) Cut the runs and test-fit all the pieces before you glue them. Mark each connection with a black mark for easy reassembly. For horizontal runs, slope the drain and vent pipes ¼ inch per foot. When satisfied with the setup, disassemble the pipes and cement them in place.

11

TUBS AND SHOWERS

Installing a tub on a subfloor

I nstalling a tub isn't rocket science, but it does require solid plumbing, carpentry, and sometimes, tiling skills. Before installing a tub, review everything that affects the project. Make sure you've qualified yourself for the job and are comfortable attempting it. Rather than have a contractor take over a halfway-completed project, it's better to consider hiring one before you begin. This is also one job where it's great to have a helper to hold and heft.

Cover the tub with a protective liner, or place a blanket or piece of old carpet in the bottom of the tub to protect it while you are working. Dropped tools can easily crack or chip the finish.

Bathtubs are designated either left-handed or right-handed. If you're facing the tub and the drain is on the left side, it's a left-handed model.

WORK SMARTER

PLAN AHEAD

Install an access panel behind the faucets and supply pipes so you won't have to remove the wall to work on them. Include shutoff valves or integral stops on the supply plumbing run. They isolate the plumbing from the rest of the house. **Check local codes regulating installation of scald guards.** They prevent someone from being scalded in the shower when cold water pressure changes as a toilet is flushed. Bathtubs are heavy. Have someone help with the installation. Measure the width of doors and passages. Make sure you not only can get the old tub out, but that the new one also fits into the bathroom.

1

FRAME THE WALLS AND RUN THE SUPPLY CONTROL RISER

Frame the walls so the alcove opening is just large enough to slide the tub into place. Leave a gap of ⅛ inch or less at the head and foot of the tub. Install plumbing for the risers, faucet, and showerhead (see pages 192–194).

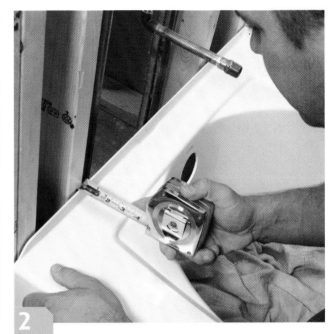

2

TEST-FIT THE TUB

After you've run the supply and cut the access hole, slide the tub into the alcove for a test fit.

3

CHECK FOR LEVEL

Lay a carpenter's level on the tub to check for level. Shim the tub to level it. Don't use wood shims for a tub because they will rot when exposed to moisture. Composite or plastic shims work well. Once level, mark the top of the nailing flange at each stud.

4

DETERMINE THE LEDGER BOARD MOUNTING HEIGHT

Ledger boards are required for fiberglass and polymer/acrylic tubs. Measure the distance from the top of the nailing flange to the underside of the tub rim inset. Subtract that figure—about 1 inch—from the marks on the wall studs and mark the ledger board mounting height.

11

TUBS AND SHOWERS

5 CONNECT THE P-TRAP

Install the drainpipe and P-trap if they have not already been roughed in (see pages 188 and 190–194). Cut an access hole into the subfloor. Make it 4 to 9 inches wide and extending 12 inches from the center of the end wall. Connect the 1½-inch P-trap below the floor level so the slip nut fitting is centered directly under the overflow and drainpipe on the tub.

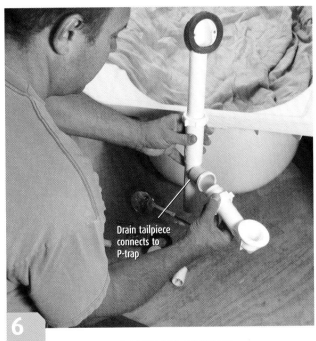

6 DRY-FIT THE TUB DRAIN AND OVERFLOW

Following the manufacturer's instructions, assemble the drain system so you can measure and trim the drain tailpiece to connect with the P-trap. (See the "Tub Drain Assembly" sidebar, page 198.)

Drain tailpiece connects to P-trap

 BUYER'S GUIDE

Drain tailpiece

7 TRIM THE DRAINPIPE

The tub drainpipe will slide into the pressure fitting on the P-trap. It may be necessary to trim the pipe so it fits smoothly. Check the manufacturer's instructions for installation.

11

TUBS AND SHOWERS

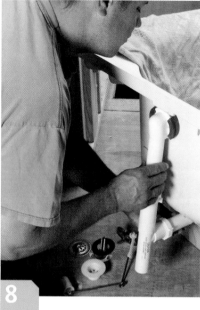

8

CONNECT THE OVERFLOW AND DRAIN TO THE TUB

Connect the overflow and drain to the tub. Plan how you will slip the overflow into the trap (step 10).

9

INSTALL LEDGER BOARDS

Cut the ledger boards to fit the alcove. Then use wood screws or galvanized nails to attach them to the studs following the marks you made in step 4. Install the boards in sections, if necessary, to make room for any structural braces at the ends of the tub. Double-check for level.

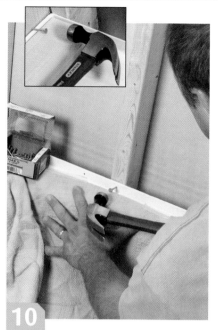

10

SET THE TUB INTO PLACE

Seat the tub on the ledgers. The tub must sit firmly on the ledger strips, and the drain must fit smoothly into the P-trap. Nail through the predrilled holes using galvanized nails. (If there are no holes, drive the nails so the nailheads anchor the tub to the studs; see above inset.) Protect the tub with cardboard placed underneath a towel or rag.

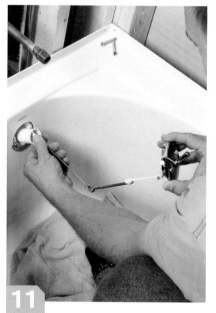

11

INSERT THE DRAIN PLUG LINKAGE

Install the drain linkage through the overflow opening. Attach the overflow cover plate to the mounting flange with screws. Test the system for leaks and schedule an inspection, if necessary, before you finish the walls and tile.

12

CONNECT THE FAUCET HANDLES AND TUB SPOUT

Use tub-and-tile caulk to seal around the faucet handles and tub spout. Apply a bead of caulk around the edge of the tub. Turn the water on and check for leaks.

Tub drain assembly

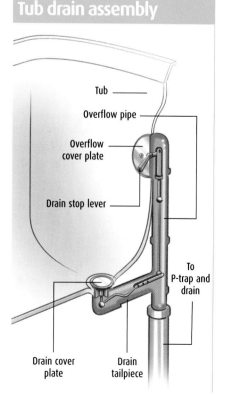

Tub

Overflow pipe

Overflow cover plate

Drain stop lever

To P-trap and drain

Drain cover plate

Drain tailpiece

Installing a tub on a slab

WORK SMARTER

WILL IT FIT?

Measure the doorways in the house before purchasing a tub so you will know you can get it into the bathroom.

NOTE: Bathtubs are heavy and awkward. Have someone help you with the installation.

S lab installations present unique problems. You don't have access from beneath, which limits where you can place the tub. The drain lines should be installed and roughed in before the slab is poured. If not, cut the slab to allow installation of the drain line— a messy and difficult job for the average do-it-yourselfer. Consider hiring a professional contractor if you need to install the drain line.

Check local codes. You may have to install scald guards. They prevent a person from being scalded in the shower when a toilet is flushed anywhere in the house.

1

FRAME THE AREA FOR THE TUB

Using the measurements of the tub and the manufacturer's recommendations, frame the enclosure. Leave enough space to slide the tub into place and still maintain ⅛ inch of clearance at the head and foot of the tub. Test-fit the tub by sliding it into the alcove.

2

INSTALL THE SUPPLY PIPES

Mount the riser piping to a 2×4-inch crossbrace mounted between the studs. Attach the antiscald faucet body assembly and showerhead to the water supply pipes (pages 192–194). Install shutoff valves on the hot and cold water supply lines. In the installation above, the escutcheon plate will allow access to integral shutoffs. If that's not the case, install regular shutoffs on the risers and put in an access panel behind the faucets so you can reach the shutoffs for repairs.

3

LEVEL THE TUB

Slide the tub into place and use a carpenter's level to make sure it's level. Shim with plastic or metal shims if necessary. Never use wood shims; they will rot in moist environments. Use a carpenter's level to mark the top of the nailing flange at each stud. Slide the tub back out.

4

MEASURE THE FLANGE

Use a tape measure to find the distance from the top of the nailing flange to the underside of the tub rim. Subtract the measurement from the marks on the wall studs to determine the mounting height of the ledger board, which is required for fiberglass or polymer/acrylic tubs.

5

INSTALL THE LEDGER BOARD

Measure the length for each ledger board. Cut the strips and attach them to the wall studs just below the mark for the underside of the tub rim. You may need to install the ledger board in sections if you need to make room for any structural braces at the ends of the tub. Check the boards for level.

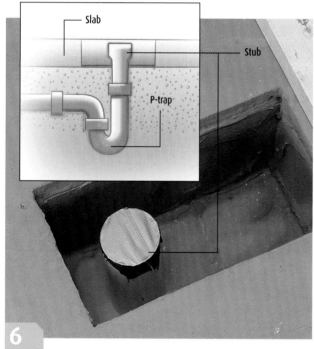

Slab — Stub — P-trap

6

ANATOMY OF THE STUB

The P-trap for the drain is buried underneath the slab. All you will see is the stub rising out of tar or concrete, which helps keep insects and vermin from coming up from underneath the slab. Running the drain line beneath the slab and running the vent line is usually a job for a professional. The drain stub is wrapped in duct tape to keep debris out of the line—don't remove it until you're ready to install the tub. The illustration shows how the drain line gets to the pit.

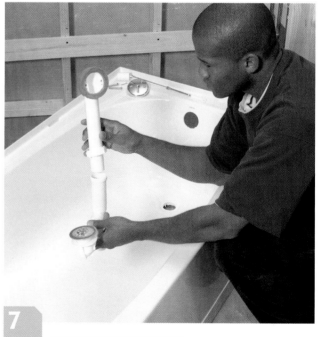

7

CONNECT THE OVERFLOW PIPE

Install the slip nut fitting centered under the overflow pipe of the tub. Adjust the height of the overflow unit to fit the drain and the overflow opening of the tub. Follow the manufacturer's instructions for installing any washers and gaskets for the overflow.

11

TUBS AND SHOWERS

Installing a tub and shower surround

PROJECT DETAILS

SKILLS: Using cutting tools, applying adhesive, and installing panels
PROJECT: Installing a tub and shower surround

TIME TO COMPLETE

EXPERIENCED: 3 hrs.
HANDY: 5 hrs.
NOVICE: 8 hrs.

STUFF YOU'LL NEED

TOOLS: Tape measure, pipe wrench, screwdriver or hex wrench set, bucket, sponge, hole saw, utility knife, carpenter's pencil, screwdriver, caulking gun
MATERIALS: Tub enclosure, detergent cleaner, cardboard for template, double-stick tape, tub surround adhesive, rags, silicone caulk, expanding foam

BUYER'S GUIDE

PROVIDING VENTILATION FOR THE BATHROOM

A new shower surround will often cover a window, which is the primary source of ventilation for the bathroom. If that's the case, you'll need to install a vent fan or make a cutout in the surround to allow access to the window. Kits are available with all the materials you'll need to do the framing job, or you can trim it out with a primed, painted, and sealed wooden frame.

S hower surrounds can be installed directly over securely fastened ceramic tile. Loose ceramic tiles—and any plastic tiles—must be removed and the walls sanded smooth before installation.

Dealing with windows

In many cases, the surround will cover a window in the bathroom that is the primary source of ventilation. If that's the case, you'll need to install a vent fan or make a cutout in the surround so you have access to the window. (See "Providing Ventilation for the Bathroom," page 202, for more information.)

Pick your features

When selecting a surround, consider features such as built-in soap and shampoo caddies and towel bars that provide space for bathroom items.

1 PREPARE THE ENCLOSURE

Turn off the hot and cold water valves or shut off the main water supply. Remove the faucet, escutcheons, filler spout, and any fittings mounted to the wall, such as towel bars and soap dishes. Remove soap film and dirt from the wall surface with a detergent cleaner. Wipe dry. Depending on the condition of the surface, it's often a good idea to prep it with a stain-blocking primer to create a good bonding surface with the tub surround adhesive. (See step 1, page 205.) Allow the surface to dry completely before installing the tub surround.

2 SELECT A CORNER PANEL

It doesn't matter which corner you start in. Select a corner panel and test-fit it. Remove the panel and lay it on the floor with the surface that goes next to the wall facing up. Apply a pressure-sensitive, double-sided, 1-inch tape along the vertical edge of the panel.

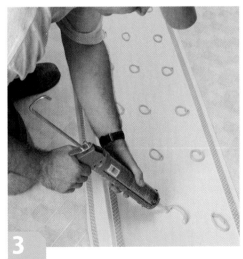

3 APPLY ADHESIVE TO THE PANEL

Use a caulking gun to apply the adhesive. Apply dots of the adhesive at intervals of no more than 12 inches along the vertical length of the panel. Rows of adhesive near the edge should be set back from the edge by 3 inches.

4 INSTALL THE FIRST CORNER PANEL

Position the panel. Press it firmly onto the wall, then pull it back about 6 inches for a few minutes (or per the manufacturer's instructions) to let the adhesive set up. This will provide a permanent bond. Push the panel back in place. Apply pressure with your hands, up and down and side to side, making firm contact with the wall. Repeat this procedure in the opposite corner.

5 MEASURE THE OUTLETS

Create a template to cut the openings into one end panel for the faucet and spout piping. Use a tape measure to determine the height from the bottom of the panel and the distance of each fitting from the inside edge of the panel. Make the template from a piece of cardboard. Cut the openings into the cardboard.

6 TEST-FIT THE TEMPLATE

Lay the cardboard template against the wall and make sure the template openings line up with the pipe outlets. If they don't, remeasure them and make a new template.

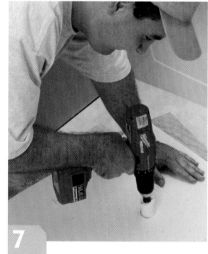

7 CUT THE OPENINGS IN THE PANEL

Mark the positions of the openings on the panel by laying the template over the back of the panel—drill from the back of the panel to minimize chipping. Place a piece of scrap wood beneath the panel under the markings for the openings to produce a cleaner edge to the hole. Test-fit a final time before cutting to make sure the markings line up with the openings. Use a hole saw to cut the openings.

Fill crevices with expanding foam to make the panel more rigid.

8 APPLY PRESSURE TAPE AND ADHESIVE

You can fill the crevices in the panel with expanding foam to make them more rigid. Apply carefully; too much foam can expand and crack the panel. Position the panel onto the wall. Apply pressure by hand—side to side—to mount. Install the remaining panels.

9 SEAL WITH A BEAD OF CAULK

Use a caulking gun to apply a quality tub and tile sealant. Seal along the outside edges of the panel and around the fixtures. To get a "perfect bead," use a small spoon dipped in soapy water to smooth the caulk line. Do not use for at least 24 hours or follow the manufacturer's instructions.

11

TUBS AND SHOWERS

Installing a shower base

PROJECT DETAILS

SKILLS: Assembling and hooking up a drain and installing control riser, pan, and enclosure
PROJECT: Installing a fiberglass shower base and enclosure

TIME TO COMPLETE

EXPERIENCED: 2 days
HANDY: 3 days
NOVICE: 5 days

STUFF YOU'LL NEED

TOOLS: Tape measure, PVC tubing cutters, carpenter's level, screwdriver, power drill and bits, hammer, caulking gun, propane torch, spark lighter, 4-in-1 tool, hole saw
MATERIALS: Shower base, drain assembly, shower enclosure, copper pipe, copper fittings, shower fixtures, rags, PVC primer, PVC cement, galvanized nails, silicone caulk, panel adhesive, faucet and spout fittings, lead-free flux, lead-free solder, emery cloth, pipe joint compound, 2×4 for blocking

T he first step in making a shower in the basement is installing a shower base. The base fits over a drain flange which is roughed into the slab. Choose the base before you have the drainpipes installed to make sure it will fit. Allow space for the studs and framing as well as for the enclosure or tile that will finish the job. Shower bases and enclosures come in many colors and shapes.

Position is everything

The most critical part of the job is getting the drain positioned properly in the slab. Unless you've had some experience, this is usually a job better left to a professional.

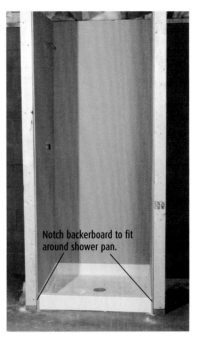

Notch backerboard to fit around shower pan.

CLOSER LOOK

Drain flange

To install a shower base, you will need a drain flange, drain screen, PVC pipe primer and cement, and a shower pan.

Some bases require a stand, underlayment, or a coat of thinset; some are freestanding. Follow the manufacturer's instructions for installation.

1 **DECIDE ON A SHOWER BASE AND ROUGH-IN THE DRAIN**
Choose a shower base, then have the drain roughed in to meet that dimension. Make sure there is enough room between the pan and the wall to allow for studs and framing. Check to make sure the floor is level. If not, you will have to level the area where the base will rest.

11

TUBS AND SHOWERS

2

TEST-FIT THE SHOWER PAN

Verify that the shower base will fit and that the drain will be under the opening in the shower base. Be sure the floor is level and clean.

3

ATTACH THE FLANGE TO THE DRAINPIPE

Test-fit to make sure the flange will be flush with the surface of the shower base. Add an extension to the drainpipe if necessary. Apply primer and cement to the flange and the drainpipe, then attach.

4

ADJUST THE TOP OF THE FLANGE SO IT'S FLUSH WITH THE FLOOR SURFACE

Allow the cement to dry according to the cement manufacturer's directions. Attach the gaskets and set the base in place.

5

CAULK AND SEAT THE DRAIN BODY

Caulk the drain flange with silicone. Line up the holes in the drain body with the screw holes in the flange body. Press the drain body firmly into place and attach the drain screen with the screws that came with the assembly.

Cement backerboard hangs ⅜" above lip of shower pan.

6

PREDRILL HOLES INTO THE SHOWER BASE RIM

Check the base for level. Mark the rim at the center of each wall stud. Predrill a pilot hole for the galvanized nails that hold the base to the stud walls. Use rustproof galvanized nails and shim as necessary to keep the shower base square. The cement backerboard will hang ⅜ inch above the shower pan so you can caulk.

Notch backerboard to fit around shower pan.

7

INSTALL THE SHOWER RISER AND THE ENCLOSURE

Install the shower riser. Test for leaks and get an inspection, if necessary, before you install the enclosure. Apply cement backerboard to the stud walls, tape, and fill as necessary. Prime and install a plastic enclosure or tile the walls.

11

TUBS AND SHOWERS

Installing a shower enclosure

Preformed enclosures are easier and faster to install than tiling a shower surround. Between prepping, painting, and mounting the enclosure, you can expect to spend a weekend completing this project. You might have to make a cutout to gain access to a window for ventilation. (See "Providing Ventilation for the Bathroom," page 202, for more information.)

Big enough to fit

Before selecting a new enclosure, measure the existing space and purchase the largest enclosure that will fit. If possible, avoid shower surrounds smaller than 34×34 inches—people need to turn around comfortably.

1 **PREPARE THE WALLS FOR THE PANELS**
Waterproof drywall or marine plywood are the best subsurfaces for a shower enclosure. If you're installing in an existing shower area, shut off the water supply and remove all fixtures. Clean the surface with denatured alcohol to ensure a good bond for the enclosure panels. Prime or water-seal raw plaster, wallboard, or spackling before you install the panels.

2 **TEST-FIT THE ENCLOSURE**
Use the cardboard shipping carton to make a template. Mark the front of the template so you know which side is which. Draw a vertical line from the base corner of the shower to an inch below the ceiling. Measure the center of the showerhead pipe and faucet valve stems from the top of the mounting surface along the vertical line. Transfer these measurements to the template. Cut holes in the cardboard large enough to fit over the fittings. Place the template on the wall and over the fittings. Align the front edge with the vertical line. Line up the holes to check the fit. Mark again as necessary.

3 CUT THE PANEL OPENINGS

Lay the template over the end panel with the exposed surfaces facing down. Mark the holes using the template. Drill the holes in the panel using a carbide hole saw. Make the holes large enough to allow clearance for the pipe but small enough so the escutcheon completely covers the hole. To avoid chipping the surface while drilling, drill from the back side of the panel. Test-fit the panel against the wall and check for accuracy by lining up the edge with the marked vertical line.

4 APPLY ADHESIVE TO THE PANEL

Use a caulking gun to apply adhesive to each corner of the panel. Apply adhesive following the manufacturer's instructions. Carefully position the panel and press it firmly onto the wall, then pull it back about 6 inches for a few minutes (or per the manufacturer's instructions) to let the adhesive set up. This will provide a permanent bond. Push the panel back in place and apply pressure with your hands, up and down and side to side, making sure that all areas of the panel are in firm contact with the wall.

5 CONTINUE TO APPLY ADHESIVE TO THE WALL FOR EACH PANEL SECTION

Place a line of adhesive an inch below the top of the panel and in 1½-inch-diameter dots at 12-inch intervals, 3 inches from the side edges of the panel.

📖 WORK SMARTER

USE THE RIGHT ADHESIVE!

Check the manufacturer's instructions to make sure you use the recommended kind of cement for the panels. Some adhesives are too "hot" and will melt into the panel, showing through on the finished side of the enclosure.

6 INSTALL THE REMAINING PANELS

Use a carpenter's level to line up the top of each panel and make sure it's level. Seal each panel (see step 4 above) to the wall by applying hand pressure over the surface, up and down and side to side, to ensure maximum contact. Remove excess adhesive. Don't use the shower for 24 hours. Install the fixtures after the adhesive has dried.

Installing a shower pan liner

A shower floor requires a three-layer mortar bed to support the tiles. The first is sand mix—a mixture of portland cement and sand that forms a strong substructure. The second layer is a plastic liner. The third layer is regular mortar that goes on top of the liner. Together the three layers provide a dense, watertight surface that won't flex. The bed is covered by a layer of thinset and finally, the tile.

The liner—a flexible 40-mil sheet of CPE plastic—keeps the water from soaking through the tile and mortar into the subfloor. When you buy the drain fitting for the shower stall, make sure you get one called a tile shower drain, which is designed to make the whole system watertight.

Choose the correct tile. Floor tiles can be applied to a wall, but wall tiles are too thin to use on the floor.

1

BUILD THE SHOWER ENCLOSURE

Frame in the shower walls with 2×4 studs. Frame the curb with three pressure-treated 2×4s on edge. End nail 2×6 pressure-treated blocking between the studs so you can staple or nail the shower pan liner into place.

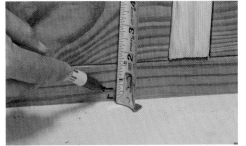

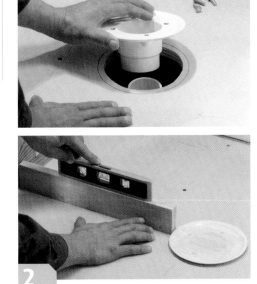

2

INSTALL THE DRAIN BASE

Cut a hole in the floor and install the lower piece of the drain, called the drain base. Temporarily tape the opening shut.

PREPARE FOR THE FIRST MORTAR BASE

Mark the level position of the floor at the drain to the walls and curb to account for any irregularities on the floor's surface. Make marks every foot along the curb and walls.

3

MAKE GUIDE MARKS AROUND THE BASE

Measure ¼ inch above the original mark for every foot between the drain and the wall and make marks around the walls and curb to act as guides for the mortar base.

MAKE MORTAR

Mix the mortar mix with enough water to make a crumbly mixture that just holds together.

4

FORM THE BED
Lay a sand mix bed between the drain and the marks on the wall to create the slope of the shower.

SCREED AND FINISH THE BED
Screed the bed with a piece of wood so it slopes from the line on the wall to the floor at the drain base but not over it. Finish with a steel trowel to create a smooth surface. Let the bed cure per manufacturer's instructions.

CLOSER LOOK

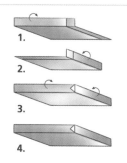

1.
2.
3.
4.

TO MAKE A HOSPITAL CORNER:
1. Fold and crease one flap.
2. Fold and crease the second flap.
3. Join both flaps at the corner and pinch them together to form a triangle.
4. Press the triangle to one side, then staple in place.

TO SEAM A CPE SHOWER PAN MEMBRANE:
1. Remove dust, oil, and grease as recommended by the manufacturer.
2. Coat both the mating surfaces with the recommended cleaner/primer. Let dry.
3. Coat mating surfaces with solvent.
4. After 1 minute, line up surfaces and roll together.
5. Wait 5 minutes, then try to separate. If the seam opens, pull apart; repeat steps 3 through 5 until the seam holds.

5

PREPARE THE PAN LINER
Cut the 40-mil CPE pan liner to size, seaming as necessary. Extend the liner 2 inches above finished height of curb on the sidewalls and long enough to go over the curb and about halfway back down to the floor.

CAULK DRAIN BASE
Apply a bead of silicone caulk around the face of the drain base. Screw the drain bolts part way in.

6

PUT THE LINER IN PLACE
Cut a small X over each bolt head so the liner will slip over it. Push the liner into the caulk. Flatten the liner with your hands, working from the drain toward the walls to smooth out the air bubbles.

FOLD AND STAPLE
Make hospital corners and staple the liner to the wall ½ inch below the edge of the liner.

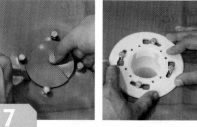

7

FINISH PAN LINER
On outside corners or curbs, cut along the corner to allow the material to make the bend. Cut out the excess. Glue on a patch made by the manufacturer that's shaped to fit corners and curbs.

CUT OUT THE DRAIN HOLE
Put the clamping ring over the bolts and tighten. Allow the liner to cure overnight before applying the mortar bed.

8 TEST FOR LEAKS

Plug the drain with a test plug, available in the plumbing department. Fill the pan to the top of the curb. Check for leaks after 4 hours. Patch as needed.

INSTALL WALL LINER

Staple 4-mil poly to the walls, letting it overlap the liner by 2 inches. Staple it to the studs just above the top of the liner, but don't staple through the liner.

9 INSTALL ½-INCH BACKERBOARD ON THE WALLS AND CURB

Leave 1 inch between the bottom edge of the wall and the liner. Don't drive any screws through the shower pan liner. Install backerboard on both sides of the curb before you install the top of the curb. The curb panels need to be screwed in, but use no more than three screws on each.

TRANSFER THE FLANGE HEIGHT TO THE WALL AND MARK FOR THE PITCH TO THE DRAIN

Use a level and a straight board to transfer the height of the drain flange to the wall. Add ¼ inch per foot for the slope to the drain and make a mark. Use your level to extend the mark around the entire enclosure as a guide for the mortar bed.

10 PREPARE DRAIN FOR MORTAR

Mark the walls, curb, and drain barrel 1½ inches above the liner. Cover the weep holes around the drain with pea gravel to keep the mortar from them. You will cover the gravel with the final mortar bed.

PLACE MORTAR

Fill the pan with mortar to the level of the marks you made in step 9. Cover the pea gravel, being careful not to plug the weep holes. Screed a slope to the drain following the marks.

11 FINISH THE BASE

Finish with a steel trowel, creating a smooth plane between the floor and the drain. Let the mortar cure for 24 hours.

TILE THE WALLS AND CURB

Most professionals tile the walls first to avoid damaging the floor tile. Protect the shower floor with cardboard. Use a notched trowel to apply latex modified thinset and set the wall tiles.

12 SET TILE

Set the floor tile in thinset, cutting the tile to fit around the drain. Let the mortar cure, as directed on the bag, and then apply grout first to the wall and then to the floor. Follow manufacturer's instructions for grout drying time and proper cleaning methods.

WORK SMARTER

THE ORDER OF WORK IS EVERYTHING!

Following the order of work in big projects is the key to success. When you're installing a tile shower with a shower pan lining, this is how it should go:

1. Frame out the enclosure, install the supply and set the drain. Apply the mortar bed and liner. Test.
2. Install the poly barrier and hang the backerboard.
3. Tile the shower walls.
4. Install the tile floor.
5. Let it all dry. Take a shower.

Outdoor systems

Chapter 12 highlights

211 INSTALLING A HOSE BIB

213 INSTALLING AN IRRIGATION SYSTEM

219 INSTALLING A DRIP IRRIGATION SYSTEM

T he earth may be three-quarters water, but it still seems the wet stuff is never exactly where you want it. If you're tired of dragging a hose and sprinkler around to water the far corners of the yard or mopping up standing water from seepage in the basement, it may be time to consider some outdoor plumbing solutions.

Hose bibs installed in more convenient locations will make general watering easier. A more efficient solution is to install underground irrigation or perhaps a drip irrigation system. Indoors or out, the same plumbing techniques apply—good planning, proper tool use, and following code.

Installing a hose bib

PROJECT DETAILS

SKILLS: Connecting plumbing fittings, drilling holes
PROJECT: Installing a hose bib

TIME TO COMPLETE

EXPERIENCED: 45 min.
HANDY: 1 hr.
NOVICE: 1.5 hrs.

STUFF YOU'LL NEED

TOOLS: Hole saw, tubing cutter, 4-in-1 tool, propane torch, spark striker, adjustable wrench, pipe wrench, caulking gun, screwdriver or power screwdriver
MATERIALS: Hose bib, wood screws, copper pipe and fittings, threaded adapter fitting, union fitting , lead-free flux, lead-free solder, rags, silicone sealant

ong runs of watering hose get heavy when you're dragging them around the yard on a hot summer day. You can shorten the length of the hose by installing hose bibs in more convenient exterior locations. You'll have to tap into a water line and solder some copper pipe to connect the bib.

Bib options

You can buy plain hose bibs, anti-siphon hose bibs that prevent wastewater from backflowing into the house water supply, "frost-free" hose bibs that won't freeze during the winter, and anti-siphon attachments that thread onto the spout of a standard hose bib valve.

1 DRILL A HOLE FOR THE PIPE
From the inside, drill a locator hole to the outside. Outside, use a hole saw or spade bit about ⅛ inch larger than the outside diameter of the hose bib's pipe to drill a hole in the exterior wall.

2 ATTACH THE HOSE BIB
Slide the hose bib shaft through the hole. Attach the hose bib's flanges to the exterior wall with two screws. Local codes may require use of a frost-free bib that extends into the house. See page 212.

3 CUT INTO THE LINE
Shut off the water. Cut into a nearby water supply line with a tubing cutter. (To cut into a galvanized line, see pages 173-174.)

12

OUTDOOR SYSTEMS

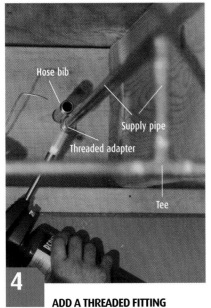

4 ADD A THREADED FITTING

Solder tee into the line you cut into, supply pipe to reach the hose bib, and a threaded adapter fitting to connect the pipe to the hose bib using a union.

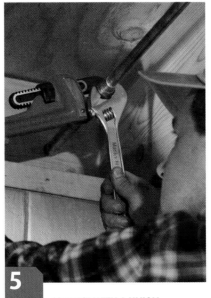

5 CONNECT WITH A UNION

You may choose to install a shutoff valve here. Cut pipes to fit and solder on a union fitting. Use an adjustable wrench to hold the adapter fitting and a pipe wrench to tighten the union nut.

6 CAULK THE FLANGE

Turn on the water and check for leaks. Turn on the hose bib to test it. Apply caulk around the outside of the hose bib's flange.

Up to code

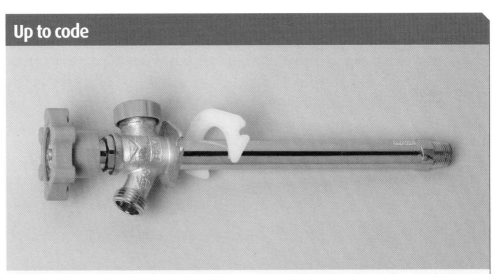

A frost-free hose bib has a long stem that actually shuts off water inside rather than outside. That means you don't have to remember to shut off the water every fall. It also comes with a threaded pipe end, eliminating the need for installing a threaded adapter (step 4, above). And it's required by some local codes.

It's also a good idea—and perhaps required by your codes—to install a shutoff valve just inside the house, to control the hose bib only. This will allow you to keep neighbor kids from turning on your hose.

12

OUTDOOR SYSTEMS

Installing an irrigation system

Manufacturers have simplified the installation of underground irrigation systems to the point that all you need are a good plan that meets local code requirements, basic plumbing skills, and a little elbow grease. Whether you are adding on to an existing system or starting from scratch, there are many options for installation. This project is designed to be hooked up to a city water supply using PVC pipe, but systems can also draw service from private wells and lakes and, depending on local codes, some installations will use Poly pipe and fittings for the service.

Consult your home center to get help with the layout and for recommendations for a system that will work for you. Some sprinkler manufacturers will send you detailed plans and a list of materials if you fill in their form and mail it to them.

Some areas require the use of "reclaimed" water for irrigation systems. It is not potable and requires specially coded pipes and fittings.

Homeowners install irrigation systems to get lush, green lawns.

1 **CHECK THE WATER PRESSURE AND THE SIZE OF THE WATER METER**
Screw a pressure gauge onto an outside faucet. Turn off all inside and outside faucets. Fully open the valve with the pressure gauge. Read the gauge in pounds-per-square-inch (PSI) units of measure and record it.

2 **DETERMINE THE WATER CAPACITY**
Place a 5-gallon bucket near an outside faucet. Turn off all faucets inside and outside. Turn on the faucet and use a stopwatch to determine how long it takes to fill the bucket. Calculate the capacity. Divide the number of gallons (5) by the number of seconds needed to fill the bucket, then divide the result by 60 seconds. Round down to the nearest whole number to calculate the gallons per minute (GPM).

12

OUTDOOR SYSTEMS

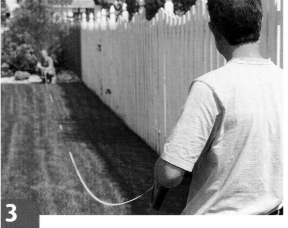

3

MEASURE THE PROPERTY

Find a fixed starting point such as a corner of a fence or house so you can tie all the measurements together. First measure the size of the lot and record it. Outline the house, garage, and any structures on the property. Locate walks, drives, slabs, decks, and surface areas. Record tree and shrub locations. Identify areas of groundcover, grass, flowerbeds, and landscaping. Note the location of the water meter.

4

SKETCH OUT THE PROPERTY

Use graph paper and set a scale of one square for 1 foot or one square for 10 feet. Show all structures. Locate the manifold position. Place sprinkler heads along the perimeter and work toward the center. Don't mix sprinkler sizes within zones. When placing stationary heads, use one-fourth sprays in the corners, one-half sprays along the edges, and full sprays for interior areas. Avoid setting sprinklers that spray the side of the house, walls, fences, drives, sidewalks, and into the street.

5

DETERMINE COVERAGE

Use a compass to draw the areas of coverage for each sprinkler head. Overlap areas to compensate for wind and pressure fluctuations. Unless you have a very small yard or unlimited water pressure, break up the system into zones. A zone is a group of similar-type sprinklers such as standard impact that operate together and are supplied by one common valve. (See "Select the Right Sprinkler," page 217.) Don't mix different types of sprinklers in the same zone. A zone's capacity must not exceed that of the water supply system. Record the GPM usage of each sprinkler head. The total is the GPM for each zone. If the total flow exceeds the water capacity, split the zone. Zones are also split based on area of coverage, slope, sun, and shade. The number of zones equals the number of manifold valves required.

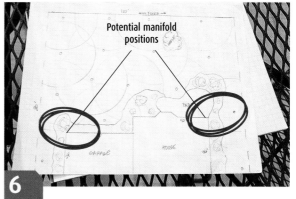

Potential manifold positions

6

GROUP THE MANIFOLD VALVES

Separate valve locations or manifolds will be needed to cover all the zones on a large property. The actual number of valves should be equal to or less than the number of zones available on the automatic timer. Locate the valves as close to the water supply as possible.

Lay out the pipe runs with different kinds of lines to represent different runs—a heavy dashed line for the main line and a short dashed line for the branch lines. Branch line connections should be at right angles to the main line. Plan straight runs and avoid turns that will cause a loss of pressure. Once you're satisfied with the layout, it's time to tap into the main for the irrigation system supply and to install the valve manifold. (See "Supply and Manifold" on page 216.)

12

OUTDOOR SYSTEMS

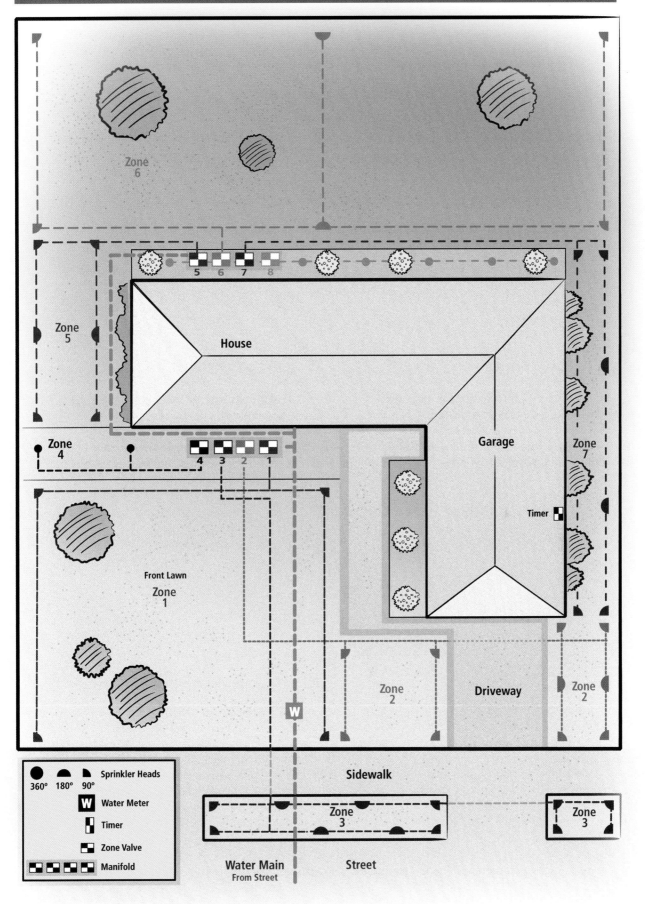

Zone 6

5 6 7 8

Zone 5

House

Zone 4

4 3 2 1

Garage

Zone 7

Timer

Front Lawn
Zone 1

Zone 2

Driveway

Zone 2

W

Sidewalk

Sprinkler Heads
360° 180° 90°

W Water Meter

Timer

Zone Valve

Manifold

Zone 3

Zone 3

Water Main
From Street

Street

12

OUTDOOR SYSTEMS

Supply and manifold

Requirements for proper installation of an irrigation system vary around the country according to climate conditions, water sources, and local codes. Common to every area, however, is tapping into the water supply correctly and grouping the approved system of control valves into a manifold or series of manifolds to create centrally located controls for the system.

Before you tap into the supply system and start digging trenches, you need to know the source of the supply and its operating pressure. Installing the right manifold system depends on the climate in your area (frost zone or frost free), the construction of your home (basement or slab), and local code requirements for operation. To help you get the right answers, check local codes and get installation advice directly from the manufacturer or from your local home center. The following is an overview of the different options and some of the choices you will have to make.

TAPPING THE WATER SUPPLY SYSTEM

The water for your irrigation system can come from several sources—potable water from the municipal system, reclaimed (nonpotable) water from the municipal system, water from a private well, or water from a lake. If your water comes from the municipality, you will need to make sure you have enough pressure to run the system. If your water comes from a well or a lake, a separate or more powerful pump may need to be installed to provide the proper operating pressure.

In colder climates, the supply pipes will be buried below the frost line, and you will probably tap into the system from your basement. In warmer climates where slab construction is more common and the water meter is buried outside in the yard, the tap will be located in the main supply after the meter and before it enters the house.

In either case, you will break into the line and install a soldered or compression tee, a shutoff valve for the irrigation system, and a drain cap so you can flush or drain the system. You will run the supply line from the main to the position you've chosen for the manifold, which will contain the valves that operate the watering zones.

INSTALLING THE MANIFOLDS

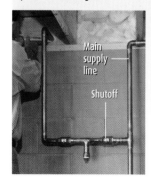

Main supply line

Shutoff

The location you choose for the manifold should be easily accessible for maintenance and placed where you're not likely to get a shower while you're adjusting the system. A large system may actually require several manifold locations to provide the most efficient operation. There are two basic options for installing the manifold—above ground (inside or outside), or below

ground in a manifold box. Local codes will also help determine the above or below question, as well as the kind of manifold valves you should install. Wiring for an automated system will run back to the timer location in the same trench as the manifold supply line. Check with local codes and the timer manufacturer to determine the correct type of wire and method of installation.

VALVE BASICS

There are basically three types of valves designed for use in irrigation systems. Some valves offer either electronic or manual operation or both. Which ones can be used in your area will probably be defined by local code. Electric valves are operated by a solenoid.

- **In-Line Valves.** In-line valves are usually installed below ground level in a square or in a round box to allow access for maintenance and inspection.
- **Piston Valves.** A piston opens and closes the valve. These are installed below ground. Piston valves are not recommended for use with pumps, wells, or where dirty water is a factor.
- **Anti-Siphon Valves.** Anti-siphon valves are installed above ground 8 to 12 inches above the highest sprinkler head in a location where water can flow away from the valve. This allows the system to drain if there is a loss of pressure from the main supply line and prevents wastewater from flowing back into the system. Used where codes do not require a pressure vacuum valve.

Local codes often require the installation of a device called a pressure vacuum breaker or backflow preventer, which prevents contaminated water from flowing back into the potable supply system. A pressure vacuum breaker is installed in-line a minimum of 12 inches above the head of the highest sprinkler head.

INTO THE TRENCHES

Once you've tapped the supply and installed the manifolds, you're ready to lay out the sprinkler system.

In-line sprinkler valve

Anti-siphon sprinkler valve

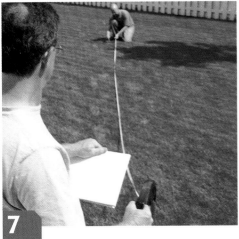

7

MARK THE TRENCH LINES

Measure and mark the lines with flour or spray paint to make them easy to follow. Flag the sprinkler and valve locations. Pull up the sod, set aside, and dig the trenches 8 to 12 inches deep or below the frost line—the depth should allow a ⅛-inch-per-foot slope in the lines for draining. Place removed soil on one side of the trench and sod on the other so it will be easier to backfill the trenches and to replace the sod.

8

TEST-FIT THE LINES

Start from the valve set and move outward, cutting, fitting, and laying the connecting pipe along the bottom of the trench. Place tees and elbows as needed. (Depending on local codes, the pipe will be PVC or Poly.) If you want to drain the system in the winter, install drain valves at the ends of lines and set a valve box to allow access to the valve. Maintain a ⅛-inch-per-foot slope toward the drain.

WORK SMARTER

SAVE YOUR BACK
Trenchers are easier and faster than using a shovel and are available at your local rental center. Review operating and safety information with the salesperson. Don't use a trencher to dig through groundcover, in flowerbeds, on steep slopes, or near buildings.

Up to code

Pipes and fittings for irrigation systems are defined by local codes. Depending on your area, you will probably use PVC or Poly pipe and fittings.

BUYER'S GUIDE

SELECT THE RIGHT SPRINKLER
No matter which type of sprinkler head you choose, it must cover the area adequately, sprinkling water only where you want it. Ranges of coverage vary from full 360-degree circles to custom settings for tighter areas, such as side yards and sidewalks. Throws vary from very short to as much as 45 feet. Heads are usually purchased with a fixed or adjustable spraying radius.

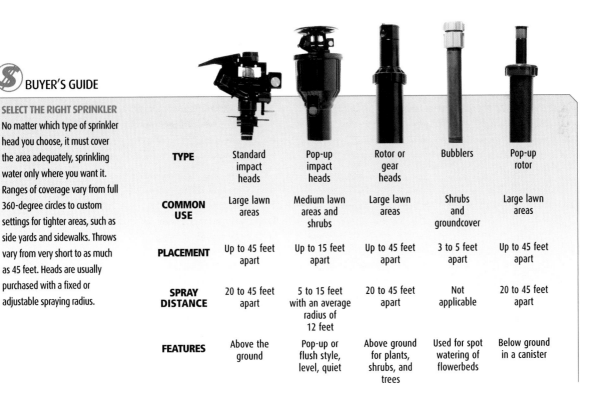

TYPE	Standard impact heads	Pop-up impact heads	Rotor or gear heads	Bubblers	Pop-up rotor
COMMON USE	Large lawn areas	Medium lawn areas and shrubs	Large lawn areas	Shrubs and groundcover	Large lawn areas
PLACEMENT	Up to 45 feet apart	Up to 15 feet apart	Up to 45 feet apart	3 to 5 feet apart	Up to 45 feet apart
SPRAY DISTANCE	20 to 45 feet apart	5 to 15 feet with an average radius of 12 feet	20 to 45 feet apart	Not applicable	20 to 45 feet apart
FEATURES	Above the ground	Pop-up or flush style, level, quiet	Above ground for plants, shrubs, and trees	Used for spot watering of flowerbeds	Below ground in a canister

9 MAKE THE FITTINGS

If you are running PVC, apply the proper primer and cement. Connect the pieces and hold until they are set. Wipe excess cement away with a rag. After the connections are set, place the runs in the trench.

10 SET THE SPRINKLER HEIGHT

Block the elbow into place. Position the sprinkler body in the trench so the top of the sprinkler is at the proper height per manufacturer's instructions. Cut an extension of PVC with a threaded end or attach a flexible extension (part of the manufacturer's system) to receive the sprinkler body, wrap the threads with Teflon tape, and install.

Sprinkler head

In-line water supply

11 SET THE SPRINKLER HEADS

Install sprinkler heads one zone at a time per your layout. Turn on the water and flush the lines per the manufacturer's instructions one zone at a time until the water runs clear. Check for leaks and repair as necessary. Have materials to make repairs on hand when you test the system.

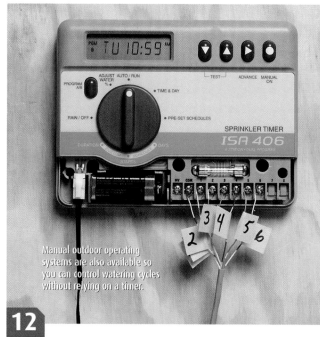

Manual outdoor operating systems are also available so you can control watering cycles without relying on a timer.

12 CONNECT THE TIMER

Put the timer where it's convenient to use, such as in the garage or the basement. If you have to locate it outside, plan on building a cabinet to protect the timer from the elements. Make sure adequate power is available—timers require a standard AC outlet. Follow the manufacturer's instructions for hooking it up. When the installation is complete, try the system out. Slowly turn on the sprinkler system. Turn on one zone at a time. Adjust the screws on the sprinkler heads to fine-tune the spray patterns. Backfill the trenches and replace the sod. Program the timer.

💲 BUYER'S GUIDE

SELECT THE RIGHT SIZE TIMER FOR YOUR SYSTEM

Timers control valve and sprinkler operation. Many automatic timers are available with a wide selection of features—multiple zones, multiple programs, seasonal adjustment for water conservation, rain delay, and battery backup. Select a timer that has a station for every zone on the system. You might want to buy a timer with extra stations in case you expand.

The two types of timers are mechanical and digital.

Rain switches save water by shutting down the system during storms, which also prevents overwatering the lawn. **Check with your local building codes—a rain switch may be required.**

Timers can be installed indoors or outdoors. If you locate it outdoors, protect the timer from the elements with an outdoor cabinet.

Installing a drip irrigation system

Drip irrigation systems conserve water by providing low-flow irrigation to flowerbeds, vegetable gardens, and landscaped areas. They can go anywhere, in fact, where plants with similar watering requirements are grouped together. They suit themselves to oddly shaped areas and work effectively in windy locations where a regular sprinkler system would cause loss of water through evaporation.

They can run effectively off a standard hose bib, as part of a more extensive irrigation system, or attached to an existing sprinkler line. The systems can be attached to a timer or operate separately from the timer.

WORK SMARTER

KNOW THE CODE
A backflow preventer which stops wastewater from coming back into your supply system is required by many city and municipal codes. It can usually be purchased as part of the kit.

LAY OUT THE DRIP LINES
Sketch a layout of the pipe run before you do the actual installation so you can get the most benefit from the system. Once the system is installed, turn it on, take a tour of the run, and check for leaks.

DRIP IRRIGATION SYSTEMS
Drip systems can be as simple as a perforated hose hooked to a hose bib, or they can come in kits complete with fittings and pipe so you can customize the installation. The kits provide all the parts necessary for installation, and the systems are easy to set up and operate.

Jim Dionian
Seminole, FL

Roisin Marascio
Toronto, Ontario

Joseph M. Czyzewski
Lawnside, NJ

Lisa Shelton
Sicklerville, NJ

James D. Shoemaker
Orlando, FL

Jeff Roeser
Grand Chute, WI

Frank Delguercio
Deptford, NJ

Lawrence Edwards
Albuquerque, NM

Pat Houlahan
Toronto, Ontario

Liz Sprague
Toronto, Ontario

Paul Gurien
Broomfield, CO

Thomas C. Dolgos
Sicklerville, NJ

Many thanks to
the employees of
The Home Depot®, whose
"wisdom of the aisles"
has made Plumbing 1-2-3®
the most useful
book of its kind.

Brian D. Askin
West Berlin, NJ

Anthony N. Marroletti
Sicklerville, NJ

Mathew Martini
Lakewood, CO

Ernie Harris III
Orlando, FL

Michael S. Foster
Castle Rock, CO

Jeff Kern
South Plainfield, NJ

Anne Reissing
Atlanta, GA

Karen Krabbenhoft
Aurora, CO

Nathan D. Ehrlich
Atlanta, GA

Keith Stroud
Orlando, FL

Sam Lynn
Grand Chute, WI

Arthur Schwarz
Arvada, CO

Tom Sattler
Atlanta, GA

Deborah Reeves
Largo, FL

James F. Mintell
Daytona Beach, FL

Toolbox essentials: nuts-and-bolts books for do-it-yourself success.

Save money, get great results, and take the guesswork out of home improvement projects with a growing library of step-by-step books from the experts at The Home Depot®.

Packed with lots of projects and practical tips, these books help you design, remodel, decorate, and repair your home or garden. Easy-to-follow, step-by-step instructions and colorful photographs ensure success. Projects even estimate time, skills, materials needed, and tools required.

Look for the books that help you say "I can do that!" at The Home Depot®, www.meredithbooks.com, or wherever quality books are sold.